NORTHERN AND PROUD

THE BIOGRAPHY OF
BOB STOKOE

NORTHERN AND PROUD

THE BIOGRAPHY OF BOB STOKOE

PAUL HARRISON

KNOW THE SCORE BOOKS SPORTS PUBLICATIONS

CULT HEROES	Author	ISBN
CARLISLE UNITED	Paul Harrison	978-1-905449-09-7
CELTIC	David Potter	978-1-905449-08-8
CHELSEA	Leo Moynihan	1-905449-00-3
MANCHESTER CITY	David Clayton	978-1-905449-05-7
NEWCASTLE	Dylan Younger	1-905449-03-8
NOTTINGHAM FOREST	David McVay	978-1-905449-06-4
RANGERS	Paul Smith	978-1-905449-07-1
SOUTHAMPTON	Jeremy Wilson	1-905449-01-1
WEST BROM	Simon Wright	1-905449-02-X

MATCH OF MY LIFE	Editor	ISBN
DERBY COUNTY	Nick Johnson	978-1-905449-68-2
ENGLAND WORLD CUP	Massarella & Moynihan	1-905449-52-6
EUROPEAN CUP FINALS	Ben Lyttleton	1-905449-57-7
FA CUP FINALS 1953-1969	David Saffer	978-1-905449-53-8
FULHAM	Michael Heatley	1-905449-51-8
LEEDS	David Saffer	1-905449-54-2
LIVERPOOL	Leo Moynihan	1-905449-50-X
MANCHESTER UNITED	Ivan Ponting	978-1-905449-59-0
SHEFFIELD UNITED	Nick Johnson	1-905449-62-3
STOKE CITY	Simon Lowe	978-1-905449-55-2
SUNDERLAND	Rob Mason	1-905449-60-7
SPURS	Allen & Massarella	978-1-905449-58-3
WOLVES	Simon Lowe	1-905449-56-9

GENERAL FOOTBALL	Author	ISBN
2006 WORLD CUP DIARY	Harry Harris	1-905449-90-9
BEHIND THE BACK PAGE	Christopher Davies	978-1-84818-506-7
BOOK OF FOOTBALL OBITUARIES	Ivan Ponting	978-1-905449-82-2
BURKSEY	Peter Morfoot	1-905449-49-6
HOLD THE BACK PAGE	Harry Harris	1-905449-91-7
MY PREMIERSHIP DIARY	Marcus Hahnemann	978-1-905449-33-0
OUTCASTS	Steve Menary	978-1-905449-31-6
The Lands That FIFA Forgot		
PARISH TO PLANET	Eric Midwinter	978-1-905449-30-9
A History of Football		
TACKLES LIKE A FERRET	Paul Parker	1-905449-47-X
(England Cover)		
TACKLES LIKE A FERRET	Paul Parker	1-905449-46-1
(Manchester United Cover)		
THE DOOG	Harrison & Gordos	978-1-84818-502-9
THE RVALS GAME	Douglas Beattie	978-1-905449-79-8

RUGBY LEAGUE	Author	ISBN
MOML LEEDS RHINOS	Caplan & Saffer	978-1-905449-69-9
MOML WIGAN WARRIORS	David Kuzio	978-1-905449-66-8

CRICKET	Author	ISBN
ASHES TO DUST	Graham Cookson	978-1-905449-19-4
CRASH! BANG! WALLOP!	Martyn Hindley	978-1-905449-88-0
GROVEL!	David Tossell	978-1-905449-43-9
MOML: THE ASHES	Pilger & Wightman	1-905449-63-1
MY TURN TO SPIN	Shaun Udal	978-1-905449-42-2
WASTED?	Paul Smith	978-1-905449-45-3

FORTHCOMING PUBLICATIONS IN 2008

MATCH OF MY LIFE	Editor	ISBN
BRIGHTON	Paul Camillin	978-1-84818-000-0
IPSWICH TOWN	Mel Henderson	978-1-84818-001-7

GENERAL FOOTBALL	Author	ISBN
FORGIVE US OUR PRESS PASSES	Football Writers' Association	978-1-84818-507-4
JUST ONE OF SEVEN	Denis Smith	978-1-84818-504-3
MAN & BABE	Wilf McGuinness	978-1-84818-503-6
MANCHESTER UNITED: Player by Player	Ivan Ponting	978-1-84818-500-1
PALLY	Gary Pallister	978-1-84818-500-5
PLEASE MAY I HAVE MY FOOTBALL BACK?	Eric Alexander	978-1-84818-508-1
TOTTENHAM HOTSPUR: Player by Player	Ivan Ponting	978-1-84818-501-8

Know The Score Books Limited
118 Alcester Road
Studley
Warwickshire
B80 7NT
01527 454482
info@knowthescorebooks.com
www.knowthescorebooks.com

A CIP catalogue record is available for this book from the British Library
ISBN: 978 1 84818 505 0

Printed and bound by Polska Print, Poland

Contents

Acknowledgements

*T*he idea for this book first came about through my passion for the what I believe is the world's greatest football team, Carlisle United AFC. In my lifetime I have been fortunate enough to witness and enjoy some of Carlisle's finest football moments. I have seen some wonderful players and met some of the greatest managers the game can offer, Bill Shankly and Allan Ashman to name but two.

There was the 1974/75 season, when Carlisle played their football in the old First Division and topped it for three games, then there were appearances in two Wembley finals and a further two at the Millennium Stadium. Granted, these were in the lesser-known cup competitions, but all finals are to be revered and honoured nevertheless.

I have seen and met some of the great footballers to have donned the legendary blue-and-white shirt, including Chris Balderstone, Stan Bowles, Peter Beardsley and Hugh McIlmoyle, not forgetting Bill Shankly, and Bob's pal Ivor Broadis, who both played for and managed us at one time or another. Then there were the trainers; well, there is just one of any note really, the great Dick Young. And, of course, one name continually crops up in the more modern (my era) history of Carlisle United, that of Bob Stokoe, who managed the club on three separate occasions during his career.

Of all the football people I have met, two have had a profound impact upon me as a human being: Dick Young and Bob Stokoe, both of whom loyally served Carlisle United. I was fortunate enough to meet both of them and got to know Bob extremely well through my writing and press activity. Bob was always his own man and never once tried to disguise from me his genuine mistrust of the press and media.

There can be no doubting that this book would not have been achieved without the support and motivation of the late, great man himself. He was an inspiration to me. Whenever I left his company he made sure I did so with positive memories and our often lengthy discussions would end with one of his hilarious and, more often than not, unrepeatable anecdotes. I'm not certain that Bob ever knew the positive impact he had on football in general, or on my own personal football writing. This book reflects that and is solely about his life in football.

In researching this book, I have been helped along the way by a great many people, providing anecdotes and information and thoughts. These include Sir Bobby Robson, the late Ronnie Simpson, Tommy Docherty, Hugh McIlmoyle, Ivor Broadis, the late Jack Watson, Andrew Jenkins and David Dent, to name but a few. The last two mentioned knew Bob from his time at Carlisle, with Andrew Jenkins employing him on three separate occasions.

My sincere appreciation also goes to John Halpin, the ex-Celtic, Carlisle and Rochdale player, who Bob believed at one time had the capability of becoming one of the greatest, most skilful footballers of his generation. Thanks also go to Theo Foley, who worked with Bob at Charlton Athletic; to football club staff at Blackpool FC, Rochdale FC and Sunderland AFC, who provided personal recollections and memories, as well as a wealth of facts and statistics regarding the great man's time with their respective clubs.

It is with some regret, however, that I want to state here that the only club not to participate, or provide any help whatsoever, was one of Bob's favourites, Bury AFC. Despite countless efforts to get them involved, I never received any response from their press office. That's a genuine shame and, one suspects, an opportunity lost to show some respect for one of their great managers.

My heartfelt appreciation goes to my own family, particularly Mandy for being there and backing me through what has been, at times, an emotional project.

It would be improper to omit the late Eric Wallace of Border Television for his enthusiasm. Eric often sat with me for many an hour, discussing recollections of his meetings and interviews with a man he always referred to as Mr Stokoe.

Also I want to thank the late Ian Porterfield, who was helpful in providing me with an insight into life as a player at Sunderland during Bob's tenure as boss and later for his honesty as the two "fell out" during his time as manager of Chelsea. I'd like to thank, too, the dozens of ex-players and football people who provided such candid comments about their own time in football and their opinions on certain situations.

To some involved in the game, Bob Stokoe could at times be something of an enigma. He was often classed as reclusive and deep thinking, yet inside him there existed a determination, a passion to succeed no matter where he travelled on his football journey. Personally I found him honest, open and full of integrity. There was a genuinely sensitive side to him, too, a side that cared passionately about his wife and family, a side that would nurture young and innocent footballers, helping them on their way and providing support and advice in matters both on and off the field.

However at times Bob didn't mince his words. Therefore take this as a warning that this book contains a few profanities scattered throughout its pages. It is not gratuitous bad language, but emotive narrative that displays the deep-rooted passion he held.

My appreciation goes to my publisher, Simon Lowe, who supported the idea from its very beginnings and Ivan Ponting who has crafted the 90,000 or so words I wrote into this wonderful book, a printed legacy of what Robert Stokoe achieved in the game and an effort to immortalise his name as one of the all-time greats.

Paul Harrison
August 2008

Foreword
by Jim Montgomery

*T*here's a statue of Bob Stokoe outside the Stadium of Light. It captures the iconic moment when Bob ran towards me at the final whistle of the 1973 FA Cup final. I'm sure that statue brings back memories for every supporter whenever they see it. For me, every time I go past the nine feet high edifice, complete with trilby hat, it brings the memories flooding back because that image is synonymous with Bob.

Bob Stokoe was great to play for. He was a manager that gave players the freedom to express themselves. He was a fierce competitor, which is something I knew about him long before he took over at Sunderland. Early in my career I'd played against him on the day in 1961 on which Brian Clough sustained the injury that ruined his playing career when Bob was playing for Bury. Whenever Bob played he badly wanted to win and it didn't matter if it was football, golf, badminton or squash. You name it Bob wanted to win at it.

Yet there were two sides to Bob Stokoe. When a game was taking place he was as competitive as they come, but away from sport he was a gentle and dedicated family man.

It was my pleasure to play for Bob. We had great times together and his contribution – not just to Sunderland but the other clubs he served as a player and manager – will never be forgotten.

Introduction

*S*unday the first of February 2004 is a day I shall never forget. I was engrossed and very busy working on a manuscript for a future book on Carlisle United. Writing is not the easiest occupation in the world, yet when the words begin to flow from mind to electronic page it can be among the most fulfilling form of employment I know. On that particular day, working from my study at my Essex home, I was desperately trying to keep within the tight schedules set by my diary. I was involved in meetings with publishers and agents, there were contractual talks with a football club for a season of marketing and communications work and, the highlight of my week, a further interview with Bob Stokoe, the ex-manager of several clubs including my own favoured team, Carlisle United, which had been arranged for the following Thursday.

I had first got to know Bob many years earlier, back in the 1980s. As the three-time manager of Carlisle, he was regarded as a god, an inspiration, a breath of fresh air. Without doubt supporters felt a sense of comfort and satisfaction that while first-team responsibilities were under his charge then things would be fine. Bob was that kind of person, someone you felt immediately at ease with when you were in his company. If you showed any sign of apprehension or nerves, he would instil a calming influence with his softly spoken north-eastern accent. Bob Stokoe was a man who captured your concentration and caused you to listen, especially when he talked football. The man knew the game and all its personalities and lesser known individuals, right from the top of the football pyramid through to the bottom of countless northern Sunday leagues. He knew the game inside out. We shouldn't be surprised by that; he was, after all, the tactical and motivational genius who pulled off one of the greatest shocks in football and FA Cup history, when at Wembley stadium in 1973 his Sunderland team outfought, outmatched and outmanoeuvred one of the biggest clubs in the land, Leeds United.

My own recollection of that marvellous feat was received through the adolescent eyes of a 13-year-old Carlisle United-daft and football-mad boy. The FA Cup final of that year meant a good deal to me as a Carlisle fan, as it entailed yet another ex-Carlisle United manager winning a major trophy at Wembley, Stokoe's predecessors in that vein being Bill Shankly with Liverpool and Allan Ashman with West Bromwich Albion. With that in mind it was an incredible personal experience for me, in 2000, to be spending time and putting together a football biography with the legendary Bob Stokoe at his behest. It was a privilege and indeed a great honour.

Returning to that fateful Sunday in 2004 – a day of rest by biblical guesstimates – the peace and tranquillity of my working environment was shattered by the sudden, shrill and annoying interruption of my telephone calling out to be answered. Instinctively I glanced at the time on my computer; it was three minutes after 12 noon. My concentration now broken, I dithered over whether to answer the call or to allow it to click into answer-phone mode. "Who on earth would call me on a Sunday?" I muttered to myself. Picking up the receiver I felt an unusual overwhelming feeling of insecurity sweep over me, I had no idea why. However, I was soon to get to the root of the reason.

"Hello," I said. The softly spoken, almost sympathetic voice with a north-eastern dialect spoke with an air of calm and serenity at the other end of the line. The caller quickly introduced herself as a nurse from University Hospital, Hartlepool. Immediately my mind began to machinate. Hundreds of thought patterns passed through my brain as I reasoned to myself: why would a nurse from Hartlepool be ringing me at home on a Sunday? For a few seconds I was bemused by the call. To be brutally honest, I believed it to be a wrong number so I wasn't listening with any intent to the rest of her introduction. I was on the verge of rudely interrupting her when she suddenly spoke my name, querying the accuracy of this information as she did so.

My heart sank and my stomach turned as the realisation dawned that sickening and unwanted news was about to be forced upon me. I confirmed that I was Paul Harrison. The tone of the nurse's voice now took on a more serious monotone delivery. It was one of those tones you dread to hear, as you just know the person is going to say something extremely serious. "Paul, I have been asked to ring you and I'm sorry to have to tell you that Mr Robert Stokoe has this morning passed away." "Robert who"? I queried. "Stokoe" came the instant response, "Bob Stokoe". Incoherently I murmured some insensible and brusque remark. For the first time in my life, words evaded me.

My entire body felt as though someone had poured one ton of liquid lead into my bones; everything felt depressingly heavy. The reality and gravity of the situation struck me like a fly hitting a 100 mph express train. My tired and saggy eyes stared blankly into space, I couldn't move a muscle. Oddly, I didn't know whether to thank the caller or not, so I took the easy option and said nothing, replacing the handset on to its receiver and standing perfectly still, unable to move my leaden legs and feet. Slowly I shifted my gaze towards a picture of the Carlisle United team circa 1983 that proudly adorns the wall of my study. My eyes focused on a figure that sat on the middle of the front row. It was the great man himself, Bob Stokoe, looking a picture of health and happily smiling away.

I'm not altogether certain how long I stood fixed in that position, but it was long enough to contemplate the loss of someone who I had regarded as a friend and a hero. I no longer felt the urge to write, preferring instead to sit in contemplation and in absolute silence. I felt an emptiness that I cannot describe. I know I was wonderfully lucky to have met and got to know one of my genuine football heroes. Few people achieve such a privilege, yet that didn't ease the shock of his untimely exit from this world. As the rest of that wintry day played out into a bland yet depressing drama, the clouds of doom, gloom and despondency slowly began to recede as I recalled some of the better times I had spent with Bob, the countless football anecdotes he shared with me, the promotion he celebrated at Carlisle, the satisfaction he felt at being asked back to the club for a second, then a third time. It was as though Bob himself was reaching out to put a smile back on my face, reminding me of the more joyous occasions I shared with him.

Subconsciously I checked Carlisle United's next fixture as I was drawn to make a special visit to my spiritual home, Brunton Park. Curiously and somewhat spookily, the next first-team game was against another of Bob's old charges, Bury. It was due to be played at Brunton Park on Saturday 7 February 2004. I made it my goal to be there, not in any professional capacity, but as a supporter on the terracing. The drive north was typically mind-numbing. The M6 offers little in the way of interest until you reach out beyond Lancaster, then it gives up some of the most incredible rural scenery as the Lake District spreads out across the horizon. As the remoteness of Carlisle, the Border City, hits you, it seems a million miles from the grim, grey monotonous conurbations you pass through and espy along the route from Birmingham to Lancaster. Carlisle truly can be a place to behold. As one hack once said to me: "It's grim up north, with the exception of Carlisle that is. Carlisle is the treasure buried deep within and protected by the hills and mountains of the Lake District."

Carlisle may not be the place of hidden wonders of which he spoke, yet to me it means a great deal, not only from a football perspective, but also by virtue of the fact that it is the place of my birth and where I spent my formative years, a place where my family roots are firmly embedded. Eventually, some 330 miles later, I pulled up outside Brunton Park, paid my admission fee and entered the ground. In the most dramatic of weather conditions – howling gales, driving rain, sleet and snow – the match unfolded before just 4,594 hardy souls. It was anything but a memorable football spectacle as a struggling bottom-of-the-table Carlisle defeated Bury 2-1, a result that would have greatly pleased Bob. It's not that he held no passion for Bury. No, it was solely down to the fact that Carlisle United, being his most favoured club, was struggling at the foot of the Third Division and faced the serious consequence of relegation from the Football League. They needed every point they could get, and points were all that mattered to them in February 2004. Bob, I resolved, would have been proud of that gritty performance from the team.

The game over, I once again tucked my face into the sanctuary of the warm woollen blue-and-white-striped scarf that was wrapped tightly round my neck, protecting me against the elements and the freezing probing fingers of Jack Frost himself. I must have looked a rather lost and forlorn figure as I quietly shuffled away from the Paddock area of Brunton Park and out on to Warwick Road. Outwardly, I was quietly satisfied that on the football front, at least, Bob's legacy of simple football and a team-based fighting spirit had not been lost or forgotten. Much of the talk on the terraces that day had been respectful of Bob's sad passing. I had listened intently as groups of supporters discussed their own special memories of the man and the manager who had served the club so well. The overarching theme of such discussions arrived at a similar conclusion: Bob Stokoe was a man of the people, he was what football people of the north ably describe as "a real football manager". I knew exactly what they meant. I had said my spiritual farewell to Bob at Brunton Park.

Just what is it that makes a real football manager? When you look at the current-day archetypal football manager or coach standing in the touchline technical area, suavely dressed in a three-piece designer suit (or a navy-blue trenchcoat in the winter), complete with silk tie, patent leather shoes and no doubt wearing the most expensive after-shave, you could be forgiven for believing that football is no longer the game it was in Bob Stokoe's day. These men, leaders is how they would wish to portray themselves, all too often act like some superior beings as they relay instructions to the players on the pitch. They seem emotionally detached from the fervour on the terraces as they concentrate and formulate football strategies. The limit of their passion is hardly visible at all. The occasional bit of pointing this way, then that, a few hand gestures, a wink of the eye or a nod or shake of the head, is as far as many allow their feelings to show. These days it is far more chic for a coach (in the higher echelons of the game it seems they no longer use the term manager) to portray absolute self control, displaying little in the way of emotion as they believe this can be construed as a weakness. With cold and calculating exteriors, coaches such as Sven-Goran Eriksson and Jose Mourinho seemingly have nerves of steel and emotions as cold as ice. You'll see no spittle in the corners of their mouths as they blaspheme at the match officials or players.

The increase of foreign managers, or coaches, into the once beautiful British game has effectively reduced the opportunity for locally grown managers to rise through the ranks and into the top jobs, unless of course one has a sponsor. It is a matter of opinion as to whether foreign managers are better than their British counterparts. Certainly some lower League clubs have found to their peril that overseas imports with romantic or impressive sounding names are out of their depth in the British game. Those that do rise to the top on these shores are generally heavily subsidised with huge transfer kitties and armed with an address book full of international players' agents, all keen to supply on demand highly-paid overseas footballers. At a price, of course.

A far cry, indeed, from the last few decades of the 20th century, when football managers openly wore their hearts on their tracksuit sleeves, when the boss showed his true colours, defiantly yelling at his team of players to work harder, push harder, and generally motivating them in an attempt to squeeze out that last ounce of energy. Health-wise such behaviour isn't good for the manager, but that's football. Such displays of real passion motivate supporters and unite emotions. Over the years there have been some tremendous exponents of emotive management from the touchline. The most notable in recent times has to be Martin O'Neill, who literally lives and breathes every challenge with his players, and mentally kicks every ball, too. Barry Fry was another who couldn't resist touchline antics, sprinting 20 yards before punching at the air and leaping in delight, all this to celebrate his team scoring a goal.

Without doubt, the most memorable and iconic image of a managerial celebration in the history of the English game belongs to Bob Stokoe, when he took to the Wembley pitch after the 1973 FA Cup final. Dressed in a cream mackintosh, red tracksuit bottoms and a trilby hat, Bob danced his way into history. On hearing the whistle signalling the end of the encounter and a famous victory for his team, Bob manically ran across the width of the Wembley pitch at record-breaking pace for a 43-year-old, in an outburst of emotion one seldom sees in public. His path led him to his heroic goalkeeper, Jim Montgomery, who in reward for his endeavours in the Sunderland goal that day received a huge loving hug from his presumably out-of-breath manager. That final whistle initiated a smile upon Bob Stokoe's face that was broader than the Tyne Bridge. For him it was a personal and very special moment. It was the moment an entire nation (outside of Leeds, that is) took the charming northerner to their hearts and praised his manner and, more importantly to him, his team.

Part of the reason a nation took to him that day in the spring of 1973 was because his demeanour was in total contrast to that of his counterpart, Leeds United's Don Revie, who strutted around Wembley as though he owned the place, tending to ignore Sunderland's part in the event. Inwardly, Revie was the cocksure manager who relied heavily on superstition. He played the media game well, apparently preferring a supercilious attitude to hide his weakness and that of his team. Don't get me wrong, Revie was good at his job, and Leeds on their day could be formidable opposition. Calculating and experienced bruisers, they would destroy the opposition at the first sign of vulnerability. The one flaw they possessed was a weakness to perform in key games and that included finals. Bob Stokoe, meanwhile, was honest. He cared little for what others thought of him, he wanted to be comfortable. The fact that several million television viewers saw him let loose his emotions and show the pride he had in his team was undoubtedly the last thing on his mind. That moment was for him, his players, and the 40,000-odd Sunderland travelling supporters to share.

This book is all about that pride and passion, emotions that Bob took with him from club to club. This is a football biography the likes of which you will probably never have read before. It's about a man who achieved virtually everything that he wished for in the game he loved so much. It's about a man who spent most of his professional career in the lower reaches of League football, working on a financial shoestring. Yet this same man offered advice and inspiration to some of the world's greatest players and managers. As Bob so often told me during interviews and social chats: "It is great being northern and it's something to be very proud of. Football is very much part of northern life and culture. It has certainly played a huge part of my life and I am lucky to have been so involved in it for as long as I have."

If you want to read about the managers with a multi-million-pound transfer kitties, and the financial clout to sign any footballer on the planet, then this book may not be for you. This book is about the real world of football, where little or no money exists, where transfers are negotiated and agreed in transport cafés on the A1, where the managers often have to clean the toilets, sweep the terracing, cut and water the pitch, even write the programme. It's the story of a real football player and manager, who could and would turn his hand to almost anything. This is the football story of Bob Stokoe, warts and all.

The majority of this work was compiled in conjunction with Bob and principally consists of his opinions, memories and personal recollections of events. It draws on interviews that took place between Bob and myself and have been collated over a period of two decades. Some are controversial, but then Bob never shied away from anything in football. Those who knew him were unanimously agreed that he was as honest and genuine as they come. I was fortunate enough to meet and get to know him. I like to think we not only struck up a friendship but also that we held a mutual respect for one another. Bob, like so many managers of his era, did not trust the media. At our first meeting to discuss the possibility of a book he told me that he wouldn't talk about his personal and family life. This was something he firmly insisted should remain private and out of the public eye. I agreed.

Once we had overcome the initial sparring about what format the book would take and what content was necessary – that it was to be football only – he soon relaxed, speaking quite openly about the great game. I could now begin to understand this hero of the north east community as I gently probed for further details of some of the anecdotes he recounted. He was without any doubt a fine man. A gentleman to the staff of every football club he served and in later days to the staff who cared for him. He made time to talk football with those who asked his opinions, and treated everyone's opinions with healthy respect. In the latter stages of his life, despite his failing health, his memory was as vivid as ever as he recounted some truly unforgettable tales, his wit always dry but unfailingly razor sharp.

I made a promise to Bob while talking to him over a game of golf on the Hexham course, long before his untimely passing. I told him that this book would be published and it would serve as a positive and lasting legacy for all he achieved during his lifetime in football. I promised him I would pull no punches. This, then, is that volume. I make no apologies for the honest and candid comments contained herein, as brutal as they may seem to some. This is how Bob Stokoe would have wanted it. A playing legend at Newcastle United and Bury, a managerial messiah at Sunderland, a performer of miracles at Carlisle United. Dedicated, genuine and honest, devoutly honest, at Blackpool, Rochdale, Bury and Charlton Athletic and everywhere else he served or played, Bob Stokoe was, indeed, all things to many people. He was a true leader, an ambassador and more importantly, he was a truly nice person, too. I still miss him.

Let the story begin . . .

1 Taking The Mickley

*L*ife in the north east of England between the world wars has historically been portrayed as both rough and tough. The area is littered with working-class heroes, the majority of whom found fame through a sublime talent for kicking a tin can, or anything else capable of being lashed with a hobnail boot, between goalposts, be they represented by a pair of jumpers, a couple of sticks or even bricks. Football was a preoccupation with virtually every young boy or man in the area. In fact, it still is. Heaven help you if you were in goal back then. Trying to prevent the tin can, jagged edges and all, from hurtling past you and into the make-believe net could be hazardous to say the least. Several would-be goalkeepers were injured or maimed by such a deadly missile, yet like goalkeeping legend Bert Trautmann, who famously completed a Wembley FA Cup final with a broken neck, the young stalwarts of those days would play on, putting team loyalty above everything else, even their own health. That's how Bob Stokoe learned his trade, kicking tin cans, stones or any other generally inanimate object that would suffice as a makeshift football.

For the young Robert Stokoe growing up in the village of Mickley, south of the River Tyne, in a family that had virtually always been associated with the coalmining industry, football became a natural way of life from an early age. "For me, all I really went to school for was playtime and the use of a well worn leather football – or 'casey' as we called it because it was encased in leather – that had been used in the school yard for donkey's years. It had a leather lace running through it to hold the rubber bladder inside. The bladder was inflated with a bicycle pump and that inflated the hand-stitched leather casing. When it rained the leather absorbed the water and it became heavy. I remember heading a saturated ball once. It very nearly pushed my head down into my shoulders, that thing was heavy I tell you. At the end of games I would have huge red welts across my forehead as a result of my heading the ball where the lace was. I was always very careful about going near it again with my head when it was wet. I would spend many an hour polishing dubbin into the leather casing, trying to make it supple and watertight. The leather was so badly worn and scuffed on the school ball that its texture was more like coarse-grained sandpaper. The problem was that leather footballs were so expensive back then and few of our families could afford to buy one outright, so the school ball was popular, being all that was available to us."

The tall youthful and energetic Robert Stokoe was as fit as they come. He enjoyed distance running and was once described by one of his teachers as having the stamina and strength of a mule and the pace of a whippet. He would stubbornly run for ever. "It wasn't as if I trained to be a runner, I much preferred to kick a football about and run at the same time. I was one of those boys who enjoyed most sports. I tended to be good at most of them but football was my best. I have never lost that competitive edge to my personality and I still enjoy most sporting events, especially those with round balls, from football to rounders to snooker. Running, I enjoyed that because it was clear cut, you either came first, or you didn't. Winners don't come second, it's a philosophy I have used all of my life in virtually everything I do."

The High Spen area is littered with youngsters who have succeeded at football, hence many role models existed throughout the generations for lads like Bob Stokoe to aspire to emulating. "I once read somewhere that any club wanting a decent footballer should shout down a mine-shaft in the north east and one would come up. Football was the game everyone wanted to play; High Spen even had a ladies team that would give most all-men sides a run for their money. I remember everyone talking about the great High Spen school team of 1931. They were outstanding and won just about everything locally, and that includes the County Cup."

Scouts from pretty well every northern club would often turn up and watch any of the High Spen teams in action, taking away a long list of players they felt able to meet the rigours of the professional game. The school team of that era was selected and managed by a committee consisting of a Mr N Smith, Mr Colling (whose family was to forge links with Sunderland AFC), Mr Davidson, Mr Emmerson and Mr Waters. "It's kind of funny because despite the quantity and quality of the players from the area, there was always talk of one player who never pursued a career in the game. I don't know whether it was just talk or make-believe or what, but I remember hearing about this one player, Henderson was his name. They say he was the best of the lot, better than the Milburns or any other footballer hailing from the north east, but he never went on to play professionally and preferred to play for the sheer enjoyment of it all.

"From my own perspective there was one outstanding family of footballers in the north east. That was the Milburn family." The first north-eastern footballing Milburn was Jack, who featured regularly for local club side Shankhouse, and also appeared for the county, Northumberland. These were the days when football wasn't regarded as the sport of the masses, but a relatively new activity when it came to competing leagues and regular fixtures. A few years later and Jack was followed into the game by the uncompromising stalwart known simply as 'Warhorse' Milburn. He was regarded as a tough and unorthodox style of footballer, renowned for his strong challenges and never-say-die spirit. 'Warhorse' certainly seems to have had plenty of stamina as he fathered 13 children, several of whom went on to play football at a reasonable standard. One of his children was known as John Thomas 'Tanner' Milburn and the lengthy family tree was extended when 'Tanner' had four sons and three daughters. Inevitably, the boys followed the family career and played football.

"Jack and George Milburn were the obvious players everyone talked of locally as they had played for Spen Black and Whites and then signed for Leeds United, as did their brother Jimmy. Stan Milburn, meanwhile, appeared for Chesterfield and Leicester City. With the exception of Stan, they were a lot older than I was but what they achieved in the game provided something that every young man in the district aspired to. Not joining Leeds United (although Leeds was to be one of the clubs that looked at signing Stokoe as a young player – *Paul Harrison*) but actually getting a contract and being paid to play football for a big club.

"The most famous of the Milburn lot without any doubt was the 'Ashington Flier' as we called him, better known nationally as 'Wor Jackie', Jackie Milburn, the cousin of the four football brothers mentioned earlier. Jackie was the odd one out in the family as he went on to become something of a goal-scoring phenomena on Tyneside. As a skilful attacker, a centre-forward, he stood out among his peers. He remains the best footballer I have ever seen and certainly the best I played alongside. He possessed every skill a good centre-forward needs: strength, power in the air, poise, timing and a killer instinct in front of goal.

"His football cousins were strong, and I mean physically strong and rugged full-backs that you wouldn't want to upset during a game, yet off the field they were down-to-earth people and very gentle folk. To be honest, the entire family were all very decent and, whenever they could, many of them would come down to watch us play at Spen Juniors, where they would cheer us on. It gave everyone playing and in the community a real lift. I suppose when you look at the Milburn family you have to take into account the Charlton brothers, too, Jack and Robert (Bobby).

"With such a history, it was wonderful being an integral part of the High Spen region's football culture. Today some people back there say that I am the most famous of all residents to have lived there and the best footballer to come out of the village. I'm not so sure about that, I always felt as though I was learning my trade from better players around me. The truth is that we learned so much there, not only about football but about responsibility and life in general. Back then there were regular accidents down the coal mines, friends would lose family members. It was like a vicious circle: as one died another went down to the coal face and so life continued.

"One of the things that will forever remain with me is the spirit of the place. The entire community would mourn, rally round in support and take care of the bereaved family, or celebrate successes. It was an accepted way of life, and being part of something like that at an early age really helps build character, trust and honesty. Yes it was tough, and it often made you realise just how fragile life is. I'm certain the tragedies of life associated with the coal pit made me appreciate everything I achieved in football and in my life outside of the game all the more.

"When you look at the High Spen area from a football perspective, there were a lot of successful junior teams in the one area. Spen Lilywhites would play on Barlow Fell close to Pawston Birks Farm. Spen Blues were another club, they played near the Institute. Spen Reds had a pitch above Towneley Terrace, and I think the Towneley team played there too. Without doubt though, High Spen Black and Whites were thought to the best club in the region, and they had a real reputation for finding the best footballers. I remember being told how other teams in the north of England despised playing against them as they were such a strong all-round team. I remember Arthur Eggleston, who would play as an inside-forward, either right or left and he also played at right-half, coming down to watch us. Arthur was a skilful player with a real turn of pace, and he read the game as well as anyone I know. He had played for Bury and Plymouth Argyle and scored plenty of goals, finishing up at Sheffield United. I was playing at centre-half for Spen Juniors at the time, not that I wanted to. No, I wanted to emulate Jackie Milburn. He was only six years older than me but was scoring goals for Newcastle and getting all the glory.

"At half-time in this particular game, Arthur comes over to me and says: 'Look Robert, the centre-forward is pulling you about all over the place. Make your mark on him, stand your ground, stand slightly off him and then you can read what he is going to do. Don't always watch the ball, read the game, it should be easy for you and you can do it..' Arthur coached me during the second half and, sure enough, after about ten minutes I had the centre-forward in my pocket. It was something I remembered throughout my career and when I reverted back to centre-forward I always tried to foil the centre-half by getting behind him. It worked, too.

"Another lad I got to know well, and played quite a bit of football with, was Johnny Grant. He was a bit older than I was but he was passionate about football and would join in with us younger kids. Only if we had a ball, mind! He was a wing-half and had a local nickname of 'Slasher' because of the tough and rugged tackling style he engaged in. He was signed on by Everton and then moved to Rochdale and eventually ended up at Southport. You didn't mess about with Johnny Grant. He would physically take you out of the match at the first opportunity, so it was always a case of not giving him a chance to do that. It was an influential learning curve having all these great footballers around to pit your wits against. I was very lucky really.

"Many years later I bumped into Johnny Grant and the first thing he did was to remind me how he had kicked me ten feet in the air during a kickabout. It was because I kept beating him to headers, using his broad shoulders to lever and support myself above him. It was like taking candy from a baby. He wasn't as quick as me and I kept it up for most of the game. Later he somehow managed to get behind me, slashed his right leg out and scooped my feet from under me. I shot up in the air just as I was about to kick the ball. It bloody hurt I can tell you, I was in so much pain. When I looked down and saw that my football boot had come off in the challenge and lay on the grass I was, for a few moments, certain that he had taken my right foot off with it, such was the pain. Not wanting to show weakness, I had the magic sponge treatment, which involved nothing more than a freezing cold water-laden flannel, and was soon on my feet again. I played on, keeping out of the bugger's way until after the game, when I tripped him (from behind) as we left the field. He cut his knee in the fall. We shook hands after that and 'Slasher' never did me again, thankfully. That was Johnny for you, not the sort of player to forgive anyone on a football pitch, yet off it a fair sport.

"They were great times. High Spen played a huge part in my football education and I remember how thrilled I was when I first signed for Spen Juniors. It gave me the ambition to go as far as I could in the game. To be honest, I never quite fancied a life down the mines. It was dangerous back then and a few Stokoes had lost their lives over the years as a result of coal pits. I wanted to make sure I wasn't another of those statistics. Many of my pals had a life in the pits forced upon them through family economics, the simple need to put food on the table. So from the day I signed for High Spen I put every ounce of energy and commitment into forging a football career for myself.

"When the war broke out in 1939 it was a terrible time, not only for us kids, but for families and communities, too. The fittest men went off to face the hostilities, while as I remember some stayed behind and kept the mines running. There always seemed to be a terrible atmosphere about the place, the whole country. It was strange because everyone tried to get on with their lives in a normal fashion. We still played football but every so often our games would be interrupted by the wailing of an air-raid siren. To this day, I still hate the sound of them awful things.

"With folk getting more and more reclusive as the war continued I got to spend some time on my own. I had an old solid rubber ball and that ball became my best friend. Throughout the daylight, for hours on end I would kick the ball against a brick wall, any wall would do. I would chalk marks on the wall that defined defenders or the goalkeeper. The ball wasn't a regular football size, it was only the size of a cricket or a tennis ball, yet it provided me with so much pleasure and really allowed me to hone up my ball control skills, my shooting and heading accuracy and my passing. I got to be so good with it that when it came to kicking a proper football again it took a while for me to get used to the bigger regulation-size football and for a minute or two I would struggle to get into my game.

"After the war things got back to some normality and football becoming a major focus for northern communities. Inter-village games began to take place, as the act of bonding communities commenced, distracting folk from the damage and destruction that had been caused across the north east as a result of the war. By now I had moved out of the playground games and was competing and playing in some of the grown-ups' kickabouts. I moved back to my preferred centre-forward position and generally seemed to score in most of the games I played in. It wasn't as if I was selfish when I got the ball, I was raised on the team ethic and the simple push-and-run style of play.

Of course, my solitary aim when I got the ball was to score a goal. I quickly realised that the easiest way to do that was by playing the passing game and finding space in the opponents' penalty area. I would lay off passes to wingers or inside-forwards and move into space. It was the players that featured around me who created the goal-scoring opportunities, I was just good at finishing chances off.

"There was one game against an RAF team played near Middlesbrough; I scored four goals and, to be honest, I should have put away a few more. Bob Downes was one of the inside-forwards I played with that day. He was quick, a real livewire, but could he finish a move and score? He couldn't hit a cow's arse with a banjo, honestly.

"Anyway, after this particular game these two sinister looking blokes in overcoats and trilby hats, who had been watching us, called Bob over as we tramped off the pitch. A few of us thought it was police catching up with Bobby; he was a bit of a card, always chasing his fortune in an easy way. We got back to the changing room (there was just the one for both teams) when Bob walks back in all smiling and happy. He looks over at me and shouts out: 'Robert, yon two fellas out there want to speak with you now, can you gan out to see them right away?' I thought he was kidding me on and told him to bugger off. He walked right up to me and said: 'Bob, if you don't go out there now you will regret it for the rest of your life. They are from a proper football club!' I went out and introduced myself, and it turned out they were scouting for Leeds and Middlesbrough. I told them they would have to wait on and come up to see me at my home. I never heard from them again. Bob went for a trial at Leeds but didn't sign for them. He said the players were full of shit and didn't make any effort to make him feel welcome. It was my turn to tell him that he would regret it.

"My boyhood dream was of starring for Newcastle United in front of a packed St James' Park. I wanted to play alongside Jackie Milburn – that was my goal, I wasn't interested in playing for any other team."

Bob's dream came true in the summer of 1947 when he was approached by someone who had contacts at Newcastle United. He was told that the Magpies had been watching him for a while and were interested in having a better look at him. Would he be interested in going for a trial at St James' Park?

"It wasn't the first time that Newcastle had a scout watching High Spen, I just never thought they were looking at me. As it happened they had done most of the business side of things, sounding out my family and getting reports back about everything, including my attitude and manner off the field. They really looked closely at the new talent, wanting players with a good temperament and a level head.

"The trial was a game with several local players featuring; I recognised a few as I had played against them, and so I knew strengths and weaknesses. There was also a fair few of Newcastle's lesser-known reserve players. It was a huge affair to me, yet in the bigger scale of football matters it was a low-key affair. Holding trials was something Newcastle United and other big football clubs did once a month. I played at centre-forward and although I managed to score I was marked out of much of the game by a brute of a centre-half. This bloke was more fat than muscle, yet he used his frame well and throughout the game continually knocked me off the ball. I was getting a bit frustrated as I desperately wanted to prove myself to the watching trainers. One of them called me over and told me to use my head, literally. He said to think about how I was dealing with this type of player. I realised that there was a double meaning to his advice. It was in the air that I excelled, he (Lard Arse) obviously couldn't jump very high as he was a fat lump. Within minutes, a cross come over, up I went and headed the ball into the goal. As I ran back to the centre circle I stood on the fat lad's foot and gently whispered in his ear that I thought he was a fat oaf. He got so riled that he was almost in tears, he lost it completely, and every time I got the ball he would waddle over to me and try to hit out at me. I made sure he never got close enough. After the game we came off and I was called in by a couple of trainers who chatted with me about how I thought I had done. One of them told me he had seen everything that had gone on with the centre-half. I thought I was done for! Thankfully he thought it was comical and said I dealt with it positively and that was good. I couldn't believe it when they invited me to come back for another trial.

"At the second trial, the quality of player seemed to improve. Lard Arse was gone and, to be honest, I thought everyone looked good. I worked my socks off for the entire game, scoring two goals with my head, and I also found myself back defending at corners. I won everything in the air. After the game I was called to an appointment at St James' Park in September 1947. I still wasn't certain that I had done enough to earn a contract.

"When I got to the football club I was greeted by the manager, George Martin, who politely introduced himself to me. He told me about his plans for the first team and how he desperately wanted promotion. Looking at me straight in the eye he said: 'I've heard an awful lot about you, young Stokoe. You have the build of a footballer, now let's see if you have the discipline to develop. I want you to sign for us.' You can imagine how good I felt. I was offered a contract with the club and a starting wage of a full £3 a week. I was rich! To be honest it wasn't anything to do with the money, I would have played for nothing if George had asked me to. It was the pride of representing Newcastle United. The thought of pulling on that black-and-white-striped shirt filled me with excitement. Thereafter I was given a whistle-stop tour of the ground, shown around the changing rooms and introduced to so many folk that I couldn't possibly ever remember who they all were or what they did. I was shaking with both pride and excitement. I couldn't wait to see all my mates and family to tell them. I had made it, I had really made it, I was a professional footballer."

2 Life on the Tyne is all mine – all mine

*N*ewcastle boss George Martin had joined the Magpies on 20 May 1947. He was the club's third full-time manager, replacing Stan Seymour and earning a three-year contract worth £1,250 a year with a £250 promotion bonus into the bargain. Martin was a straight-talking Scot with more than a hint of artistic talent – he often turned his hand to sculpting and was also a highly praised singer. Above everything else, though, he was man who possessed an outstanding football brain and determined organisational skills. He had breezed into St James' Park on a mission – to get the club back where it belonged, in the First Division. As a player he had been versatile and talented, appearing for Hull City and Middlesbrough, and he had also won promotion to the top flight with Everton in 1930/31. As a manager he had spent time at Luton Town and had identified and produced young local talent, an ability that had caused the Newcastle board to select him as opposed to the other candidate for the post, Don Welsh.

The new manager had a serious job on his hands. The Newcastle team was clearly a tired one, with some big personalities in the changing room questioning his every decision. Martin, though, would have none of it. He was the manager, and he picked the team. In fact, it was the first time in Newcastle's history that team selection wasn't by committee and full autonomy had been granted to the manager.

He knew exactly where things needed to improve. Several months later first-team regulars like Roy Bentley, Charlie Wayman and Tommy Pearson were sold to Chelsea, Southampton and Aberdeen respectively. When Len Shackleton, who had requested a move, was sold to Sunderland for a then-record fee of £20,050, Martin had amassed a total of around £40,000 in transfer fees and set about changing things around. In came goalkeeper Jack Fairbrother from Preston North End and forward George Lowrie from Coventry City, while other players like Bobby Cowell, Benny Craig and Bob Fraser were given an opportunity to prove their worth.

"George Martin wasn't the sort of man you questioned; he knew precisely what he wanted from the team. Although I didn't know it at the time as a junior professional at the club, there was a lot of dissent in the dressing room. Some players like 'Shack' needed a fresh challenge, their presence was undermining a lot of what the manager was doing. I watched closely and learnt a good deal from George Martin. I saw how players respond to different managerial styles and how to motivate, manage and get the best out of people. As juniors George told us that he was building a team around players like Joe Harvey and Jackie Milburn because they were the perfect professionals, they trained and worked hard for the club both on and off the field. Oddly enough they are two of the greatest names to be associated with Newcastle United. George was a learned man."

Another player Martin identified and brought to the club was Lancashire-born wing-half Frank Houghton. "I remember Frank well; he was a workmanlike footballer who was always on the go. When we trained Frank would be there working with us, coaching us and giving advice on how we could improve our game and chances of a first-team call-up. There was one game at St James' Park in my first season at the club during which he showed all the grit, determination and physical endeavour expected when you turned out for Newcastle

United. The game was against Sheffield Wednesday and was a promotion clash. Over 66,000 were inside the stadium that day and the gates had to be locked well before kick-off. Sheffield took the lead through a penalty and we looked really vulnerable as they came at us. Then Geordie Stobbart pulled one back for us to level matters. Joe Harvey gave us a lead and we were cruising to victory. The stadium was a cauldron of noise and you could hardly hear yourself think; then late on you could have heard a pin drop when Sheffield equalised, making it 2-2.

"Frank Houghton pushed forward with hardly any time left on the clock. With a drop of his shoulder and a shimmy he was past a defender and hammered the ball into the net. The place went wild as a win all but assured us of promotion. The referee had got his whistle in his mouth when Frank turned up in the Sheffield area to score again. The momentum of his run saw him collide with the 'keeper and a goalpost, and he went down. The poor bugger had broken his arm and his leg had a gaping wound, but still he managed to celebrate.

"After the game Jackie Milburn and Joe Harvey came out to see some of us clearing up the ground. They told us that to play for Newcastle you were expected to run through brick walls for the team, just as Frank Houghton had. The funny thing about Frank was that he seemed to court personal disaster. A while later he contracted tuberculosis and was very ill with it. The club sent him abroad for the best treatment, to Davos in Switzerland. He was out of the game for a fair time and by the time he got back things had progressed again. I was in the first team, he moved to Exeter City and soon broke his leg in a practice game, it was an injury that finished his career. It's things like that you remember and you realise how short a career football can be from a player's perspective.

"After the Sheffield game we clinched promotion back to the First Division in London, at the home of FA Cup semi-finalists Tottenham

Hotspur. Even though we finished as runners-up to Birmingham City, the end-of-season celebration was fantastic. Newcastle people know how to party and they did that summer, I promise you. I did enjoy those formative years at Newcastle. Fair enough, the sweeping and clearing of the terracing and replacing churned-up divots in the pitch wasn't the most popular aspect of the junior's professional life, but we got on with it, understanding that it was character building. I got to train with the first team and always put a lot of effort into the practice matches. As a set of reserves at Newcastle we were doing all right, too. In fact, we won the Central League championship in 1948, topping Manchester United. Everywhere you looked there was quality. Ron Batty and Charlie Crowe were local lads who went on to make names for themselves in the first team and then there was Tommy Thompson, who could finish as well as Milburn when he was in top form. Ernie Taylor was another who graduated through the juniors and reserves. These lads were dedicated and extremely committed footballers.

"There was a part of me worried that as a centre-forward I would have to oust Jackie Milburn from the shirt, and anyone knowing Jackie and the club would realise that such an opportunity was never going to occur. As well as Jackie there was his understudy, a centre-forward called Andy Donaldson, who was lethal. Despite this I kept my head down and continued to work hard. George would come and watch us play in the local leagues and always offered positive advice. It got to the stage where I would have done anything to please him as a manager, which was the very mentality and discipline he had said he expected at our first meeting. I was scoring a lot of goals back then and I suppose got a bit carried away with myself when I was told that two Division Three North sides, Gateshead and Carlisle United, were interested in signing me. Both had been put off by George and no one formally said a word to me. I was desperate to play first-team football, so I took the bull by the horns and knocked on the manager's office door. As I walked in, George was sat at his desk and casually looked up at me and said: 'This had better be important, Robert. I am a busy man, you better hadn't be in here looking for a transfer!'

"I didn't know what to say. How could he know my reason for being there? I asked him about the interest from other clubs, he denied it and duly informed me that he would not be releasing me from my commitment to the club. I thanked him, turned on my heels and left the oppressive office, closing the door behind me. As I walked away from the ground I did wonder why I had bothered going to see George in the first place. Jackie Milburn was standing by the main road and he called me over. I told him about the Gateshead and Carlisle rumours and what I had just done. Once again I received more excellent advice. 'Bobby, you get to learn a lot in this game. One of the main things to remember is never ever listen or respond to rumours. They generally have an ulterior motive. Until the manager tells you otherwise, you are a Newcastle United player. He'll be watching you closely now, testing you, checking your commitment and loyalty. Dig deep and do it not only for Newcastle but for your family.' I felt ten feet tall and very proud."

The following season saw a rejuvenated Newcastle back in the top flight, achieving a creditable fourth position in the League, having actually topped the division pre-Christmas after a 1-0 home victory (courtesy of an Ernie Taylor goal) over Everton. The team spent much of the season in second place and looked every bit potential champions. In January and February of 1949 came three influential signings: the Chilean Robledo brothers, George and Ted, arrived from Barnsley and Bobby Mitchell joined from Scottish club side Third Lanark. George Martin had been watching Mitchell for some time and saw in the skilful winger a man who could consistently deliver the balls for Milburn to score. Despite this relative success, many players were unsettled and it was reported that 16 handed in written transfer requests as in-squad squabbling once again reared its ugly head.

"It was obvious that some players were unhappy at being left out of the team. George tended to chop and change the team in an effort to keep everyone happy, I suppose. We had a trainer, Norman Smith, who was one of the best I have ever known during my time in the game. Norman would temper the unrest and talk many of the disgruntled players down. He continually told me to stick at it. Norman held the belief that I would make a better centre-half than a centre-forward. I denied him such speculation as back then centre-halves were all square-shouldered and thick-set, which clearly I wasn't, so I continued to do my best to prove myself a centre-forward.

"It seemed to take forever, but I eventually got my chance to pull on the famous black-and-white shirt in earnest. It turned out to be the best Christmas present I could have hoped for. It came in 1950 when the team wasn't playing too well. Earlier that season we had been beaten 7-0 at Tottenham and things didn't look promising. Despite that we put a run of results together leading into the December, and then when it became clear that George Martin would be leaving, it sort of knocked us for six and we fell away again.

"I was devastated by the news that George was leaving. I had spent three years under his charge and had worked my way through the ranks to the verge of the first team. I did wonder if it would all slip away for me again. Once more I went to speak with George in his office, but this time I was more direct and asked him if it was true that he was leaving. 'You been listening to rumours again, young Stokoe?' he responded. The advice Jackie Milburn had offered me years earlier rang in my ears. I asked the question again, he refused to answer, so I asked him where it left me as I was so close to the first team. 'Maintain your discipline and commitment, now get out, I'm busy here' was his response.

"At least I knew that he was leaving yet I didn't dare breathe a word of it to any of the other players. Gossip was strictly taboo in the dressing room, especially the kind that could cause unrest. Anyhow, it became clear that everyone knew he was moving to Aston Villa and he eventually left on 15 December. There has been much speculation down the years as to why he left the club. Certainly he had lost the respect of some of the players, but they were the ones who couldn't hold down a regular first-team spot. The mainstays of the first team, people like Frank Brennan and Joe Harvey, spoke highly of him. The interference from the boardroom didn't help matters. Stan Seymour, as genuine and honest as he was, was an autocrat. He wouldn't leave George alone and always tried to tell him how to do his job. I think, with all things being taken into consideration, that was why he joined Aston Villa.

"Without his influence, a disappointing performance and defeat at Everton two days before Christmas 1950 saw the team slip to fourth in the League table. Next up on the fixture list was an away trip to table-topping Middlesbrough at Ayresome Park.

When Ted Hall, the club secretary, asked me to go and see Stan Seymour after a training session following the defeat at Everton, I thought my time at the club was up.

Some of the older, more experienced pros at the club, like Joe Harvey, referred to Stan as 'the boss' so as I entered the manager's office, I followed suit. Stan had again taken over the responsibility for first-team affairs. 'Bobby, I'm playing you in the forward line against Middlesbrough on Christmas Day, can you handle that? You will be travelling and training with the first-team squad from now on. You have earned your chance, now take it and let's give Middlesbrough a match to remember and beat them.'

"Once again football had proven me wrong. Now here I was being given my big chance in the first team. The rest of the team were bloody good to me. George Robledo reminded me that to play for Newcastle's first team you had to be very special. Bobby Mitchell and Joe Harvey told me to do the easy thing, not to get over excited and to play the simple ball. In the dressing room before the game I was itching to get out and get at Middlesbrough. I was reminded that as a centre-forward I was pivotal to every attack we made. Then it was time to run out on to the pitch. I think more than anything I remember the noise, it was frightening. Someone, I'm not even certain who it was but they clearly recognised that I was awestruck, told me to block out the noise and concentrate on our team's voices. The weather was cold and it was horribly damp. As I stood there looking at the faces of the packed Ayresome Park crowd I recalled the days when I kicked that rubber ball against the wall, dreaming of making my Newcastle debut. I looked down at my shirt, shorts and socks. This was it; my time had arrived.

"The game went by in a flash. 'Boro were strong and resilient. Everything we threw at them they soaked up and came back harder, more determined. I was struggling to win anything, then I heard a voice cry out from the sidelines: 'Bob, pull off the centre-half, get behind him, he's bossing you too easily.' I had forgotten the basic rule taught to me many years previously at High Spen. I managed to find a bit of space and calmed myself down. It was the situation, as opposed to the game or any player, that was actually bossing me.

"It was a typical north-eastern grudge match. I was getting kicked all over the place. I had to earn my respect, it didn't come free. I managed to start winning a few of the high balls, flicking on some headers to our wingers, and my confidence began to grow. Suddenly it became easy. I was holding the ball and laying it off, just as I had been trained to do. I forced the 'keeper into a few saves with some speculative efforts when perhaps I should have passed, yet nobody complained. We continued to press forward and really tested the home side's defence, which stood resolute. During one foray, a loose ball in the Middlesbrough penalty area bounced right in front of me, and I managed to force it towards the goal. My view was blocked by the defence desperately trying to prevent me from scoring. The next thing I knew was a mighty cry of 'Goal' that came from the terracing. I looked around and saw my smiling Newcastle team-mates hurtling towards me, skipping and jumping for joy. I still wasn't certain that I had scored a goal. It was a quite incredible feeling, better than anything I had experienced in the game up to that point. Unfortunately we lost the game 2-1, yet it was a debut to be proud of. What a Christmas present.

"Afterwards in the changing room, I was told by the rest of the lads that I had been dominant in the air, winning just about every ball that came my way. The Scottish international Frank Brennan told me I defended corners as well as any centre-half he had seen. I reminded him that I was centre-forward and was promptly advised that he knew a good centre-half when he saw one. Frank Brennan was someone I hugely respected, a tough and straight-talking Glaswegian. He was a massive figure of a man, standing at 6ft 3in in his stockinged feet and weighing in at about 14 stone of pure muscle. Frank rarely failed to win a challenge against anybody.

"I will always remember sitting down with him in a café in the centre of Newcastle after training. He said he was feeling a bit peckish and a few of us, Bobby Mitchell, Joe Harvey and myself, went to this greasy-spoon place and sat down to order. I was still not a first-team regular at that time. I had played in a few games and the lads had welcomed my company and accepted my future potential, so I was now one of them. Anyway, we get sat down and big Frank picks up the menu and orders two meals for himself. I said nothing as it wasn't my place to question his appetite or eating habits. The rest of us had a butty (sandwich) while Frank wolfed down both platefuls he had ordered and then had the cheek to have a desert to follow. I was to find out that this wasn't unusual for the 'big fella' yet despite all he ate he rarely put on an ounce of fat. He was fighting fit and could run as fast as any centre-forward. His metabolism must have worked overtime to keep him in the shape he was. In training he would make time to show the more inexperienced how to get the most power into a header and how to time our tackles. He would even give a few trade secrets out about opposition players and what wound them up. That always came in useful.

"But I think the main thing I learnt from Frank was humility. You are never too big or important to remember your roots. He always spoke fondly of his upbringing and of his time with his first club, Airdrie. I once asked him about a confrontation he had with the Blackpool player Stan Mortensen in the tunnel at St James' Park. He told me: 'Mort's a decent bloke, a good footballer, but he is a bit of a moaner. As soon as the game kicked off he was at it, moan, moan, moan, telling the ref how I was thumping him from behind when I tackled him and pulling on his shirt. All true, of course. Anyway, he wouldn't shut up and as we left the pitch he pinched my arse. No one does that to me. So I put him against the wall and simply smiled at him. He kept well away from me after that. We did shake hands after the game but that's not what people remember.'

"I recall when Frank had the big fall-out with the club. It was around 1955/56, what a torrid time that was. Frank was a clever man and he invested his money in a few things over the years, including a sports shop in Gallowgate. We would pop in to help encourage his trade. He was still playing at the time and the business was to be a source of income after he finished at the club. It was doing very well, people reckoned it was doing better than Stan Seymour's and that's when the trouble started. The first thing I knew about the problem was when Frank let on that his wages had been cut down without any good reason. He went to the manager, Dug Livingstone, and was told to discuss it with Stan Seymour. Frank was having none of it and pushed his playing contract under the noses of the club directors, pointing out his legally binding salary. The club wouldn't back down either and put him on the transfer list.

"We as a group of players were worried, who wouldn't be? There was no loyalty in what Newcastle had done and no reasoning behind it either. A few of us told Frank to get the Players Union involved, and so Jimmy Guthrie became embroiled in the situation. It was embarrassing, the press got hold of it somehow and the directors were publicly lambasted for their behaviour. The people of Newcastle grouped together and held public meetings announcing their support for the player, hundreds of letters were sent in to the club asking them to reconsider the situation with Frank and the local press published several articles in which they more or less pleaded with the club to keep him. It wasn't to be and Frank moved on to North Shields. Before he left he told me that I should never trust an employer, they push you to give every last drop of energy and professionalism, then dump you when your time is served. 'Football club directors,' he told me, 'are the most insecure men in football, not good enough to be players or managers and not confident enough to be honest to themselves. They take the glory and shy away from the defeats.'"

That Brennan made a huge impact on Bob Stokoe as both a footballer and as a person is without question. The youngster admired Brennan's honesty and dedication to the game and his open relationship with supporters. The brutality and harshness of Brennan's treatment by the Newcastle board of directors made a lasting impression on him and in later years he, too, was to suffer from the whims and fancies of directors and club officials. Having broken into the first team and made a real impression, the desire to remain as part of the first XI week-in and week-out drove Stokoe to push himself harder.

Unknown to him at the time, in Stan Seymour he had a great admirer of his tenacious desire to succeed at all costs and of his fight-to-the-death attitude for the greater cause of Newcastle United. Seymour promoted him to the position of the first team's 12th man, albeit there were no substitutes back then. It meant that should any player drop out through injury (goalkeeper excepted) then he would be looked at first with a good chance of replacing them in the team. Such a position required a variety of football skills, and in later days such a footballer would be termed a utility player. In training matches he would find himself playing on the opposing team to Jackie Milburn. This was not only so that he could profit from seeing how the centre-forward pulled defenders first one way, then the other, and how he would trick them with his ball skills, but also to aid his development defensively.

"I can't precisely recall when it was, but the boss asked me if I would drop into the wing-half role for a time. It was a position that was alien to me and although it did allow me some freedom to get up to the attacking end of the pitch, invariably it meant much defending, too. Then one day in training I was pitted as centre-half against Jack Milburn. I don't know what came over me or how it happened but I dominated him, read every move he was going to make and countered it. The bugger still managed to get a couple of goals, though, and that pissed me off! After the game, he (Jack) came up to me and said it was the best piece of defending he had ever encountered from a centre-half. I thought he was having me on and thought nothing of it, then Frank Brennan told me that he could do nothing but admire the way I played and read the game, adding: 'You'll have to fight really hard if you want to take my place in the team, I'll tell you.' I told him I was up for the fight and he winked and told me to keep up that kind of spirit.

"It was an uncanny transformation. Suddenly I enjoyed playing at the back as it gave me so much more freedom and time. The aerial stuff came naturally to me. Without doubt I benefited from having such quality footballers around me. Playing against the likes of Milburn, Mitchell and Robledo every day helped to hone my skills to an even better standard. It was a fantastic time to be part of Newcastle United. That team was exhilarating. It was exciting; it had pace, power and delivery, and it also had 11 level-headed footballers who rarely panicked and ultimately, when the big games came around, rarely failed to aspire to success.

"One of the greatest achievements I had up to that point in my career was being selected as part of the first-team squad for the 1951 FA Cup final at Wembley stadium. The boss had a quiet word with me and told me what was expected of me, and that the rest of the team felt I was the best suited player to be 12th man. What an honour it was." Despite not appearing in the final, Stokoe was very much included in everything the team did off the field and he took part in the build-up and training sessions. "Oh, it was magic, you know. We were all treated to smart blazers with the club badge on the pocket,and trousers and shoes. There was no expense spared with top hotels and guest appearances in and around London. Never before had I been part of something so special."

The final itself was against the mighty Blackpool, fielding the legendary Stanley Matthews, a player who desperately wanted an FA Cup winner's medal to cap the wonderful achievements he had attained in his football career. As it was, the final played out in favour of the Magpies and Matthews was outshone on the day by Milburn, who fired two second-half goals that are still to this day the talk of Tyneside. The first came following a mistake by Matthews himself when, during a Blackpool attack, he pulled the ball back to a Newcastle defender. In a swift counter-break, Milburn received the ball just inside his own half and galloped towards George Farm in the Seasiders' goal, then thumped a powerful shot past him and into the net.

"I think my main memory of that game, and it was an exceptional cup final, was Bobby Cowell's clearance early on in the game. It was breathtaking. It was still 0-0 at the time and Stan Mortensen had powered a bullet-like header towards our goal. To everyone in the stadium, it was a goal. Then up popped Bobby, our right-back that day. Somehow he not only got his head to the ball, but managed to lift it from beneath the crossbar and up and away to safety. I remember Norman Smith, our trainer, turning and telling us to look at the reaction of Mortensen and some of the Blackpool players. Mortensen was holding and shaking his head in disbelief, other players were congratulating Bobby on an incredible piece of defending. Stan Matthews said that the incident swung the game and had Cowell not cleared then Blackpool would have won, that's how important a clearance it was. After the game it was all celebrations and we were treated like royalty back in Newcastle, with a bus ride through the streets of the city as we paraded the cup. I'd never seen so many people take to the streets as I did that day. Everywhere was a sea of black and white. It was emotional stuff and a few us shed a tear of two of joy.

"If pressed I should say that the Newcastle side of the early 1950s was the best football team I have ever seen. There was so much quality, starting with goalkeeper Jack Fairbrother, who was later replaced by an even better 'keeper in Ronnie Simpson. Bobby Cowell was another local lad who done good, having joined the club after the war, before my arrival. Then there was Alf McMichael, an Irish-born full-back with a mean and dry sense of humour that kept everyone laughing. Bob Corbett was another local full-back who stood out. Charlie Crowe was a wing-half who loved nothing more than to run at the opposition; he was a decent tackler, too, and would often show me how to win the ball in just about every possible scenario. Right-half Joe Harvey was perhaps one of the most underrated players of his time; Frank Brennan was the rock at the centre of defence. As for the Robledos, George was quick and skilful as an inside-forward whereas Ted was reliable as a wing-half, often referred to as 'Steady Teddy.' Bobby Mitchell was just sensational, an excellent professional with ball skill that could match Matthews, or anyone else in the game throughout the world. Willie Foulkes used to play off Jack Milburn and tease defenders, winger Tommy Walker was a rare talent whose crossing and delivery of the ball was inch-perfect every time, and there was inside-forward Ernie Taylor, who was actually sold to Blackpool shortly after the 1951 final. It was an incredible set of lads and I haven't even mentioned half of them."

With such an abundance of talent at St James' Park it was a difficult situation for the young Stokoe to find himself in. As a result, he missed out on another successful FA Cup final in 1952, when Arsenal were beaten 1-0, thanks to a George Robledo goal.

"It was disappointing not being able to break into the first team and missing out on another final, of course it was, and yes, I was bitter about it. I thought I had done enough to push for a regular starting place. It was Frank Brennan who was keeping me out of the team. I felt deflated as I had played second fiddle, if you like, to players like Milburn, Harvey and Brennan. I began to think I was never going to be a regular in the first XI, so I slapped in a couple of transfer requests. Not because I wanted to leave or anything; no, it was petulance on my behalf. I wanted to let the boss and the club know I wasn't going to put up with continually being the 12th man.

"One of the funniest and most memorable trips I ever had with Newcastle United came in 1952 when we went on a pre-season tour of South Africa. We played something like 16 games while we were out there, it was really exhausting stuff. I remember at the airport asking Frank Brennan where his luggage was. He opened up his jacket and pulled out a toothbrush informing us that he travelled light!

Flying back then wasn't anything like it is now. In order to get to South Africa we had to stop over in Tripoli. On the flight over there one of the plane's engines made a banging noise and the whole aircraft lurched. We were told that the engine had broken down – but not to worry, we could still land on one engine! I wasn't the only one shitting myself on that flight, I can tell you. Even the toughest of men had a look of panic in their eyes. We managed to land safely and all was well. The tour itself was arduous. We stopped at a place called Kano. What a god-forbidden hole that was, filthy and a hovel. None of the players or club staff was happy with that place. Thankfully once in South Africa we were treated like heroes and spoilt by everyone we met. They seemed to think it right to lavish us with gifts that consisted mainly of trinkets, alcohol and smokes."

Rumours of other clubs' interest in taking Stokoe away from Newcastle continued to surface and by 1953 he had submitted three separate transfer requests. It wasn't as if he had been forgotten and left in the wilderness – each request was dismissed by the club. "The first time I asked for a move, trainer Norman Smith had a word with me. He told me to retract and withdraw it, as one day I would be pivotal to the club's success, adding that first I had to learn my trade. I left it a week or so, then withdrew it. Stan Seymour was pleased when I told him and, shaking me by the hand, said I had made the right choice. It was hard to believe, yet I trusted Norman Smith's word implicitly." When wing-half Joe Harvey retired from the playing side of the game in 1953 and took up a coaching position at the club, it provided an opportunity that Bob Stokoe had waited for and seized. While appearing more frequently, he still wasn't getting the amount of first-team football he craved for, hence came further transfer requests. The problem was that the centre-half role coveted so keenly by Stokoe remained with Frank Brennan, a situation that continued until the Scot lost his grip on the position, mainly after the arrival of a new manager, Dug Livingstone, who had previously been in charge of Belgium's international side.

The new manager had been brought in to change things around. Stan Seymour wasn't seeing eye to eye with several first teamers and unrest swept through the club. Livingstone could see that some of the team's ageing stars were tiring and that the side desperately needed an invigoration of new talent to freshen it up. It was Livingstone, who had a wealth of defensive playing experience with Glasgow Celtic, Everton, Plymouth Argyle, Aberdeen and Tranmere Rovers on his playing curriculum vitae, who provided Stokoe with the opportunity to make the centre-half position his own.

"Dug Livingstone was an upbeat sort of man, laid back and calm and full of life and energy. It was just what the club needed. He wasn't scared of upsetting anyone and let the players know who was boss, although the directors did still tend to interfere. They had their favourites who they felt should be playing, but Dug would have none of it. He picked the best team from the best players and I'm pleased to say I was one those he regularly selected. I felt saddened by what had happened to Frank Brennan and met with him before he officially left the club. I wanted to apologise for taking his place in the team. He said: 'Don't ever apologise for achieving something. You have shown a bit of loyalty to this club and if anyone deserves a crack at wearing my shirt it is you. Now remember, if the ball is in the air in your half, it's your responsibility to win the header, win the ball and clear it. Don't ever put the ball back towards your own goal – never, that's a sin. Always clear it away from the Newcastle goal, that is all you have to remember and you will do well.' I informed him that the centre-half shirt was now mine and laughed off his suggestion that I may ever clear the ball back towards my own team's goal. We left it at that.

"Prophetic words indeed, as on 30 April 1954, in a game against Tottenham Hotspur at White Hart Lane, I hit a back-pass towards

Ronnie Simpson. It was just before half-time; I was being put under pressure, having miscontrolled a ball to my feet and, what do you know, the Spurs forwards were on to me in a flash. I panicked and thought the easy option would be to give the ball to Ronnie to punt up the field. In my haste I overhit the ball and it sailed straight past an unprepared Ronnie Simpson into the net to give Tottenham a 1-0 lead. I wanted the floor to open and swallow me up. What a dreadful moment, the lowest point of my playing career. It really hurt scoring that own goal. The rest of the team were great, telling me that everyone makes mistakes and to forget it, these things happen. All I could think of were the words and advice of Frank Brennan – never kick back towards your own goal. Lesson learned."

A year later and it was but a distant memory as Stokoe, now a regular in the starting XI, appeared in his first Wembley FA Cup final. The 1955 final had been reached the hard way and had taken its toll on some of the players. "It started off well enough, we beat Plymouth and Brentford fairly comfortably, then we met Nottingham Forest. It was bloody awful stuff in the first game at the City Ground. We managed to pull off a 1-1 draw but we were very lucky to escape wth that. At St James' Park in the replay they shocked us and managed a 2-2 draw, that being after extra time, so it went to another replay. We won the toss of a coin to have it played at our place, and again it went to extra time before Alan Monkhouse scored the winner for us. Next we had Huddersfield Town, who gave us another battle but we came through, drawing at their place and winning the replay in Newcastle 2-0. Now we had reached the semi-final and the draw had been good to us. We were paired up against York City, a Division Three North team punching well above their weight to get so far in the competition.

"The semi-final was played at Hillsborough and York gave us a real shock. They had a forward called Arthur Bottom, who had scored seven goals in the competition leading up to the semi, and he gave us a torrid time. The worst part of it was that every time I went near him for a challenge he would throw himself to the floor and the referee would award a foul against me. I told him him what I thought of him and that while I was marking him he had scored his last goal in the competition for that season. He laughed at me and swopped positions with another of their players, so Jimmy Scoular was now marking him. A slip-up in our defence let Arthur get away and he lifted the ball over Ronnie Simpson into our net. 'Stokoe!' he shouted. I looked across at him and he winked at me as he made his way back to the halfway line. It was one-apiece and moving towards full time when Bottom very nearly grabbed a late winner, but Ronnie Simpson somehow managed to get down to clear his header off the line. The referee blew his whistle and we all thought he had given the goal. The York City fans were celebrating. Then he awarded a free-kick to us for a foul on the 'keeper. Bloody relief that was.

"In the replay at Roker Park, Sunderland, we turned them over 2-0 and we were finally at Wembley. It must have been one of the longest FA Cup runs I can remember. Dug Livingstone hadn't helped matters by chopping and changing the team around, either. A few players who warranted a place would suddenly find themselves dropped. My good friend Ivor Broadis was one of them, and Dug also dropped Jack Milburn from the final, only to be overruled by the directors.

"Our opponents at Wembley were Manchester City, and I was facing tough opposition in the shape of Don Revie, a much-vaunted centre-forward who was strong both on the ground and in the air. Never had I heard a player moan as much as Revie did. Even before the game had started he was talking up the referee (Mr Leafe), telling him he always suffered greatly against rough centre-halves who kicked lumps out of him. Jokingly I asked him out loud if he was referring to me as a rough centre-half. He looked embarrassed and kept his head down, never once making eye-contact with me.

"The game had barely started when we went 1-0 up through a Jackie Milburn header, only for Bobby Johnstone to equalise before half-time. My battle with Don Revie turned out to be a non-event as I won everything above him in the air and took every ball off him on the ground. Not once did I foul him or kick or push him. He was calling me all the bastards under the sun, but I never let it wind me up and kept smiling and laughing at him. He called Jimmy Scoular some things and all, but soon shut up when Jimmy threatened to kick him so high that he would end up swinging by his shirt collar from one of the stadium flagpoles!

"Before half-time one of the City players, Jimmy Meadows, had turned quickly and his knee had gone. There were no substitutes then, so City played with ten men in the second half. Bobby Mitchell had the freedom of the pitch and destroyed them with his tantalising skill and trickery. In the end we were 3-1 winners and what a feeling it was to hold aloft the FA Cup at Wembley stadium. One of the few Manchester players to congratulate us was Don Revie. He admitted I had outplayed him and wished me well for the future. I reciprocated the comment. Afterwards, there was a huge celebratory dinner at the Savoy hotel in central London. What an event that was. Us Geordie boys living it up in the posh surroundings of the Savoy, now that really was something special. The following day, the Sunday, we went to the London Palladium, taking the FA Cup along with us. There we met Max Bygraves, a real highlight. He was thrilled to get his 'hands'* on the trophy.

"Another highlight of that year for me was the four-match continental tour including a game against Atletico Madrid. It was stifling hot and the entire trip saw us bond as a unit. Some of the attendances we played in front of were huge and more partisan supporters I have never seen. It was intimidating at times, even though they were friendly fixtures. The stadiums we played in were in a different class to what we had in England. It was the best tour I ever went on as a player."

* *Hands* was the title of one of Max Bygraves' best-known songs.

3 **Talk of the Toon**

*I*t would be all too easy and desirable to say that from 1955 Bob Stokoe enjoyed a successful half-decade as the principal bulwark of the Newcastle defence and served a lengthy stint as club captain. However, typical of his football life, such years were dotted with trials and tribulations. Not least in August 1956 when in a game against Sunderland at Roker Park, played in a tremendous thunder-storm and lashing rain, there was something of a spat in the player's tunnel.

"I normally kept my cool when I was playing, but derby games are a bit different, especially those involving Newcastle and Sunderland. Both see each other as the arch rival. On this particular day we had beaten them fair and square (2-1) at Roker Park. There was lot of needle in the play and some of their forwards were goading us, particularly me. The conditions didn't help proceedings as players slid into tackles on a wet surface and clattered into one another. A certain Sunderland player, who shall remain unnamed, did for me right at the end of the game. He took me clean off my feet and could have broken my ankle. I jumped up and went nose to nose with him, calling him a clown for such a reckless challenge. In response, he poked his index finger into my cheek and called me a 'Newcastle ponce', telling me he would sort it out after the game as I clearly had a problem with him. It was all something and nothing, emotions were running high. I laughed at him, reminded him of the score and who was winning. When the referee blew for full-time I made my way off the pitch and into the players' tunnel, where four or five Sunderland players started having a go at me, again calling me names and pushing me about. I admit I really lost my temper. There was a lot shoving and more crude name-calling from all parties. I managed to extricate myself from the situation and get into the Newcastle dressing room.

"Naturally we as a team were exuberant. We had won our local derby game on away territory. We sang a few victory songs, nothing outrageous really, just celebrations. I got dressed and made my way out of the reception area. As I was leaving the ground through the car park a few of the Sunderland players were outside and again started on me, name-calling mainly. I walked up to the group of them and calmly informed them of the final score. I shouldn't have done it, I should have walked away, turned the other cheek, but this lot deserved to have their noses rubbed in the final scoreline. The next thing I know there has been a real song and a dance made about the whole affair. A local journalist tried to make it out to be more than it was and all he really achieved was to inflame the matter. Unknown to him, the players concerned had already kissed and made up.

"Down the years a lot of memories have stuck with me, and one of the greatest games I recall being involved in was another FA Cup tie, this time with Manchester City in 1957. It was a third-round replay on a cold and wet January evening in Manchester. We expected City to come at us in the opening 20 minutes or so and had prepared ourselves for a dogged battle of wits. As we were about to come out on to the pitch Len White turned to me and said: 'Let's have a big game from you Bobby. If you play well, we all do.' It motivated me and I went round the rest of the lads trying to gee them up. As we thought, City flew at us, tearing down the wings and firing cross after cross into our penalty box. One cross flew over with pace, and as it was dropping quite quickly, I sensed a City player coming in behind me. Seeing that

I had no cover elsewhere, I met the ball firmly with my forehead expecting to see it fly over the bar. Instead it nestled in the back of our net, another own goal by Stokoe! Once again the players rallied round and tried to keep my chin up. To be honest, there was hardly any time to think about the error as City were soon at us again. We were being pulled all over the place defensively, and soon the home team had moved 3-0 ahead. In what has to be one of the greatest comebacks of all time, we went into a 5-4 lead and clung on to win, but not before City gave us another fright and almost equalised with the last touch of the game. I was exhausted. It had been one of my poorest performances in a black-and-white shirt, yet we had won.

"Afterwards I was told that England manager Walter Winterbottom was at the game, apparently looking at me! It never sat comfortably with me that I never got a crack at playing for England. I know plenty of people in the game who believed I should have been given an opportunity. Despite that, every time I met Walter he seemed at a loss as to what to say to me. I always felt that he thought himself a cut above and he really wasn't, nor had he any right to think that way. It didn't help that I once bumped into him at Molineux, home of Wolverhampton Wanderers. In general conversation I queried his England team selection; nothing derogatory, just an innocent off-the-cuff remark. He seemed flustered by it and clearly didn't know how to respond.

"Looking back, that probably cost me any chance of a call-up. I have to say that if the stuffy attitude displayed by Walter Winterbottom that day was anything to go by, then I was better off out of the England picture. I know that with the honest and genuine opinions I hold, and openly discuss, I would have fallen out with a few people. From all I heard the entire England set-up of that time involved a fair bit of sycophancy. If you didn't continually feed egos then you were likely to be blackballed.

"From 1955 onwards the Newcastle team never quite matched their previous success. Charlie Mitten was introduced as team manager in June 1957 and almost immediately found himself in the midst of issues within the club, as Stan Seymour, William McKeag and himself begged to differ on a number of important matters, not least who should be playing where. The team vacillated between mid-table and the lower reaches of the old First Division.

"Football was put into perspective on 6 February 1958 when the Munich air disaster occurred. The accident killed many Manchester United players and other people I knew. A few of us got emotional in the dressing room at training. All those young lives being taken, it was a true tragedy. It was a black day and black period in everyone's life. Few were untouched by the Munich disaster and the whole of Newcastle went into mourning. The people up here are respectful to any sort of human tragedy. A memorial service was held at the Central Methodist Church in Newcastle a few days after the crash. I went along with Jimmy Scoular, Len White and Albert Franks as representatives of Newcastle United Football Club. It was a very sombre affair, meticulously respected by all who attended and there wasn't a dry eye in the place. Occasionally I look back on that tragedy. The sorrow diminishes but never truly leaves you. I knew most of them lads; it was terrible devastation."

A few years later and Bob Stokoe's playing days at Newcastle United were over, perhaps hastened by an on-the-pitch scuffle with his own team-mate Jimmy Scoular. "Jim could be an obnoxious so-and-so and sometimes got the devil in him, not playfully but maliciously. He was an arrogant bastard at the best of times and was well known for splitting the Newcastle dressing room, telling tales and causing trouble and the like. He was a selfish man who expected junior players to bow to his greater wisdom and experience. He never seemed to understand that respect had to be earned.

"In this one game he really pushed my patience to its very limits. He was messing about with the ball, dwelling on a pass and missing the obvious ball, and as a result of his messing about we missed a couple of decent goal scoring chances. He didn't seem to give a toss whether we were winning or losing, and wanted to do things his way. I was having none of it. I marched up to him and told him that I thought he was greedy with the ball and that he was a prima donna. He replied, calling me a tosser or something equally as eloquent, so I responded likewise. Next thing we were at each other's throats, it was all a bit silly. No punches were thrown but only because we were held back by other players. It can't have done the reputation of the club, nor of either of ourselves, any good. I apologised to the club immediately after the game. Jim never once said sorry – that's the kind of person he could be, not just to me, to anyone."

Not too long after that transfer moves were afoot. Scoular went to Bradford Park Avenue in January 1961 and Stokoe to Bury in April 1961 as part of a £24,000 exchange deal that saw John McGrath move to Tyneside from the Gigg Lane club.

Newcastle United minus Bob Stokoe were relegated at the end of the 1960/61 campaign.

"I was heartbroken to be leaving St James' Park. Norman Smith had taken over as the new manager and he had been a colleague of mine in his days as first-team trainer. I don't think he really wanted me to leave. However, he had wanted John McGrath and Bury had asked for a suitable replacement at centre-half, so that was me. I knew I had made a mistake with the Jimmy Scoular situation, and I also realised that I was being made something of a scapegoat because of the team's poor performances during 1960/61 season. I felt like Frank Brennan and a few other players before and after him must have felt when they left the club – discarded, tossed away like an old rag.

"Still, I wasn't about to let it get me down. I knew I had a lot left in me and had aspirations to achieve and do well for a different club. Bury suited me fine. It was a typical northern working-class town, not too dissimilar to Newcastle in many ways. But unlike Newcastle, its fans knew the harsh reality of football, life at the bottom end of the League where the only big-name signings are on the advertising hoardings, where free transfers often mean just that – no signing-on fee or contractual adjustments or additions. I was relishing the move and new challenge. As for Newcastle, they could go fuck themselves as far as I was concerned when I left. They had a reputation for ignoring player loyalty, though looking back I can see that I was actually ready to move on."

The hurt felt by Stokoe over the manner of his release cut deeply at the emotional strings which had tied him to the St James' Park club. It was now battered passion, and while the hurt would subside with the passage of time, the emotional detachment his release had enforced upon him was never likely to be fully repaired. Bury Football Club were to get the better part of the deal. Soon they would have a new and focused captain, a man on a mission to do his best for them.

4 I can manage that Gigg

*S*o it was that Newcastle manager Norman Smith called his old friend into his office and informed him that Bury were interested in his services. "As we sat there, Norman looked me straight in the eye and said: 'Bob, you have served this club well and we have shared some great times together on and off the field. I have been watching the lad McGrath at Bury; he's a good 'un, a centre-half. You know how these things work. I need to make my own mark on this team, impress the directors and bring my own players in. You would do the same in my shoes. Bury have asked that you are part of the transfer deal. I have told the board I'm prepared to let you go. It's in your best interests to move on. I think you have a lot of football left in you and it's an opportunity for you to gain experience somewhere else. Bury are a fair club.'

"I was stunned to hear him say those words. He could never know how much he had hurt me. I had been through a lot at Newcastle, from a junior right through to first-team captain, and now it was over. I wasn't about to show my disappointment at being pushed out, so at once I jumped to my feet, shook his hand and said I would go down and speak with Bury. Norman looked a relieved man, and I know from conversations we had later in our careers that his hands were tied. It had been the directors who insisted on releasing me as they didn't want too many centre-halves at the club, added to which it saved them forking out more cash on the cost of the transfer. The same day as I agreed to leave Newcastle, I called David Russell, the Bury manager, and asked him what it was all about. He was enthusiastic and had a pedigree few managers outside the First Division could match."

Russell's playing career began at Dundee, followed by a move to East Fife, where he was a Scottish Cup winner in 1938. He later moved into the English game with Sheffield Wednesday, featuring in every match for the Owls in the 1938/39 season. The interruption of the war effectively ended his playing career as he retired before the conflict was over. Moving into the training and management side of things, he found himself acting as trainer for Odense FC of Denmark and was to later coach the Denmark national team for three years. He arrived at Bury as coach in 1950 and moved up into the managerial role, replacing John McNeil in November 1953.

"Bury had always been a decent team and had spent a hell of a long time in the top two divisions of English football, competing with some very big clubs such as Liverpool and West Ham." They were, in fact, relegated from the Second Division at the end of 1956/57 and had finished fourth, tenth and seventh in the Third in the following seasons leading up to the arrival of Bob Stokoe.

"I arranged to meet with the manager and one of the directors the following day. They offered to come up to Newcastle to speak with me, but I didn't want any Newcastle influence getting involved, so said I would go down to Gigg Lane. When I got there a few fans were milling about the place and spotted me in the car park. I nodded and bid them good morning. It was humbling, to say the least. The pair of them came directly over to me, shook my hand and almost begged me to sign for the club. Cheekily I asked them who their best players were. 'It will be you, that's if you sign for us, Robert' they remarked. There was something about the Gigg Lane ground that attracted me to the club. It was no St James' Park yet it felt comfortable. I made my way to the darkly lit reception area and was greeted by a man who never spoke, shook my hand and led me through to some back offices where I met the manager and Major George Horridge, the chairman of the football club. The smell of stale cigar smoke filled my nostrils, a smell I had become accustomed to at Newcastle, where to smoke a cigar was viewed as a sign of affluence!

"Dave Russell at once put me at ease by telling me that Bury wanted me, needed me in fact. He led me through the dressing rooms, down the players' tunnel and out on to the pitch, reminding me of some of the great names who had played at the ground in years gone by. I laughed out loud and told Dave that he had nothing to worry about. I was keen to join and he did not need to sell the positives of the football club to me. The one question I did ask related to his and the directors' aspirations for the team and the club. He told me: 'We want to get back into the Second Division, then take it from there. It would be good to get there as soon as possible.' That was all I needed to hear. After a whirlwind tour of the ground I was taken on a busman's tour of the sights of Bury, given a meal and offered terms that were, as I remember, better than I had anticipated, about seven guineas a week, added to which I was team captain.

"I remember making my way back up to the north east, filled with satisfaction that the move to Bury would benefit all concerned. I spoke to Norman Smith and told him I had accepted terms and would be signing on a date mutually agreeable to both clubs. 'That's tomorrow then, Bob. You have to go back down tomorrow and sign. We have agreed a package that involves you and £24,000 going to Bury in exchange for John McGrath.' It was another metaphorical kick in the teeth – Newcastle couldn't actually wait to get rid of me. Despite that, I wished Norman every success and said that I looked forward to the day when I was facing his team as I would do my level best to beat them. I think he swore at me, I'm not certain, as I was out of there, eagerly anticipating the new challenge ahead.

"The following day I was told that Bury wanted me as soon as I could get there – they even offered to pay my train fare and would have me collected by taxi. It was Friday 10 February 1961, and as I put pen to paper I wondered how John McGrath was feeling at Newcastle. There was no time for sentimentalities, though, as I was informed that I would be leading the team out for a League game at Watford the following day. I hurriedly got changed out of my suit and into the training kit, and went out to meet my new team-mates for the first time. Bury had some decent players in their ranks, including wingers Bill Calder and Johnny Hubbard. Then there was Don Watson, some attacker he was, and Bill Holden, too. Everywhere I looked there were footballers who wanted to achieve something for Bury Football Club, and now I was added to those ranks.

"That first game, at Watford, was a tough one; they were fighting for promotion along with us, Walsall and Queen's Park Rangers. With the defence conceding seven goals in the three games prior to my arrival I wanted to organise us defensively. We worked damn hard and earned a draw. It all seemed to come together at once, as after my arrival we didn't lose another League game all season, a total of 17 games, and we only conceded six goals during that spell. We won promotion with three games of the season still remaining, after winning 1-0 at Bradford City through a Bill Holden goal. The championship was won by the following game, a 3-0 home victory against Hull City. Not since 1894/95 had any Bury team won a championship.

"It didn't end there, either. On 4 April Don Watson netted our 100th League goal of the season, against Grimsby Town at Gigg Lane, and the celebratory champagne began to make frequent appearances in the dressing room. Bury scored a total of 108 goals that season, beating the previous club record of 94 set in 1958. We were treated like heroes everywhere we went, the club house was always busy and you could never spend any money as supporters were always there wanting to toast you and buy you a beer. At the end of the season, Dave Russell called me into his office and told me that everyone at the club appreciated my input and said the manner in which the championship was won was down to me. I told him he was wrong, it was a team effort, a real achievement, and that he should savour it as much as he could because the hard part was following that success the following season, back in the Second Division.

"The promotion had a double meaning to me as it gave me the chance to pit my skills against Newcastle, who had been relegated from the First Division along with Preston North End. To be honest I had the grin of a Cheshire cat all that summer. The season I had been released Newcastle had been relegated, while the club I join won promotion via a record-breaking championship success. Despite that, I still felt some sympathy for the Newcastle supporters and for their manager, Norman Smith, who found himself jettisoned in June 1962 after just nine months in charge. They all deserved better treatment than they got. Some friends told me that Joe Harvey was coming into Newcastle as the new manager. I affirmed the belief that Joe would do well as he was a passionate supporter of the club and knew only too well what was expected of him. I also learned that my replacement, John McGrath, had struggled to settle in at the back. I decided to get in touch with him and offer some words of support and comfort. I never knew whether he got my letter or not as he didn't respond. I decided from that day forth to be indifferent to what was going on at Newcastle United. Putting it simply, they were just another one of my employers."

The following season saw little in the way of transfer activity at Gigg Lane. Boss Dave Russell was prepared to give the Bury team who had achieved so much the previous season the opportunity to prove themselves at the higher level. "We got a bit of a shock when in our first game of the new season we were taken apart and beaten 3-1 by Norwich City at Carrow Road. We played it a bit naively, I thought, trying to defend in numbers and break with pace. It wasn't the style we were used to. I always remember the feeling in the dressing room after that game – the manager was really downbeat about the performance. I thought: 'To hell with this, let's get some fire in the belly and get people believing in themselves again.' I stood up and reminded the players that we now had two home games to win. We actually won the next four games and that put us second in the table. The manager had gradually got me doing more of the dressing room pep talks. I knew that something behind the scenes was wrong but didn't say anything about it. Dave looked disheartened by it all and had lost the fighting and inspirational spirit that had impressed me when I first arrived at the club.

"Typical of me, once again I took the bull by the horns and confronted him, asking him what the problem was. The poor sod, he told me that he was disillusioned by the lack of real investment in the playing side of things. One director had seemingly made a flippant comment in front of him, implying that it might be good for his career to move on soon. He had made the fatal mistake of going to the supporters seeking validation which, as a result of the team's inconsistency and therefore the inability to stay away from the relegation zone, had not been forthcoming. Dave then began to analyse things too deeply, even comparing attendance figures to previous years in a desperate attempt to prove to himself that he was successful.

"The day I had been looking forward to since the season started was not long in arriving. On 14 October 1962 we were facing my old club, Newcastle United. I had a word with our manager in the build-up to the game, informing him of the relevant strengths and weaknesses of the Newcastle team and how we should play them. I needn't have bothered because he ignored everything I said! A 4-0 hammering by Luton the previous week had again seen his managerial qualities called into question in the boardroom. He desperately needed a result from the Newcastle game to instil faith in his ability, not only at director level but with the club's support, too. He was actually persecuting himself, yet we as a set of players had the self-belief that we would get through the season without being relegated. Clearly, the manager didn't quite believe that.

"The pre-match banter with the Newcastle lads was lively, to say the least. I had received a nice greeting from a few of the visiting supporters outside the ground, and inside they were as vocal as ever. Joe Harvey had a beaming smile on his face when I bumped into him. 'I got it Bob, I got the job' he said, almost whispering it to me as though it was a secret. I wished him well with it, telling him to remember his roots and not to get carried away with the importance of the position. I have always believed that the most important people at any football club are the fans. Without them and their support the game would be lost. Once you lose the faith or trust of the fans, then you are finished. No matter how hard you try, you might as well pack up and move on. The board of directors may make a public statement backing you, but that's only the death knell sounding.

"In the dressing room before the Newcastle match, our manager looked to be a bag of nerves, his team talk proving anything but motivational. I was upset because I had so desperately wanted to put in a performance against my old club, who I believed we could have beaten had we played our usual attacking style. No, the manager changed things round again. This time it was a backs-to-the-wall, defend-at-all-costs tactic. The result was embarrassing to say the least – we were slaughtered 2-7 on our own ground. The fans voiced their concerns, demanding that the manager should stand down. After the game we held a post mortem-type discussion over what went wrong, and why. While nobody actually said it, I think we all thought the same thing; the manager had failed to address key areas such as how to stop Newcastle playing their pace-driven pass-and-move game. Joe

Harvey told me afterwards that he thought we had played like headless chickens, running round without any focus or understanding of what we should be doing.

"As the weeks went by after the Newcastle debacle our results and performances barely improved. There was the odd decent win, like the 2-1 victory over Lancashire rivals Preston at Deepdale, but overall we were struggling. It's easy to say after the event, but the writing was on the wall for Dave Russell. He had been given the tip-off earlier in the season that he may need to move on, and since that time he had seemed to lose some of his passion."

After a 2-0 loss against Huddersfield Town on 2 December 1962, Russell shocked everyone at the club by revealing that he had accepted the manager's position at Tranmere Rovers, a club who played their football two divisions below Bury. The board of directors accepted his resignation without any further discussion. It was a somewhat acrimonious and indifferent end to his time at Gigg Lane. However, supporters recall all he achieved at the club with great fondness. It was to take him five years to achieve any similar kind of promotion with Tranmere.

"I was a bit cheesed off by the way Dave left us. He had really put himself into a no-win situation by being so successful. If I had been him I would have stayed on and faced my detractors. He blamed everything from attendances to lack of support at director level for the team's failings that season, the reality being that it was mostly his doing. Having said that, I can only thank him for taking the plunge and leaving Bury when he did, as it opened up a whole new career path for me. A few days after he left, as team captain I was called into a meeting with the Bury directors. The players wanted some answers about the future and to know when a new manager would be announced. I honestly walked into that meeting totally unaware of what was happening. Before I could ask the question regarding the manager, I was told by the chairman, Major Horridge, that the players had given me a 100 percent backing and supported my leadership credentials. A few of them had apparently suggested that I should be appointed as player/manager. I had no idea where the whole meeting was going until the Major asked the question: 'Will you take over as team manager but continue in your playing role? We believe you have the character to take us forward.'

"I was gobsmacked and didn't know what to say. I had been a player for a fair few years and, at 31, I was ready for a new challenge. I accepted the job without any hesitation. It was to be a decision that I would never regret and it provided me with some of the happiest times as a manager at any club I have served. My first task was to make sure we didn't get relegated. I was looking for a season of consolidation when I was captain. Now I was the manager my perception hadn't changed."

It was hardly the most auspicious beginning to a managerial career. In his first game in charge, Norwich City visited Gigg Lane and left with a 3-2 win as the Shakers dropped to 17th place in the table. "I laid into the team after that game. We didn't deserve to lose it. However, at the back we had left ourselves exposed as we chased goals, and Norwich punished us." A win at Scunthorpe United temporarily settled things down, though a greater storm was on the horizon. In a woeful period in January and February 1963, the team lost four consecutive games, conceding 11 goals into the bargain and dropped to 19th place in the division.

"I wasn't about to panic. Despite everything I had the belief that we could get out of the situation. I had one eye on the big game at St James' Park and told my players that I expected us to beat Luton Town, Middlesbrough and Newcastle United. I spent a bit of time with them individually, motivating and empowering them in their game. Wingers needed to use their skill and pace, forwards had to get in the opposition penalty area and cause havoc, defenders were told to stop opposition forwards fairly and at all costs. The rest was simple, push-and-run football. It's an easy game and I wanted the players to enjoy what we actually employed them to do, play football."

A 2-1 win over Luton Town provided a positive attitude for the next away trip – to the north east and Newcastle United. "I never slept the night before the Newcastle game. My wife, Jean, said she had not seen me so restless before. I had gone through every scenario with the players in the lead-up to the game and, to be honest, I was shitting myself. If Newcastle blasted us with another seven-goal salvo it wouldn't help with team confidence. When we pulled up outside St James' Park I desperately wanted us to come away with both points, but a point and a draw would do nicely. Joe Harvey almost blanked me when I walked into the ground, until I shouted out to him to get the kettle on. He stopped in his tracks and led me down to his office. 'Who would have believed this Bob? The pair of us, facing one another as managers of opposing sides. Don't worry, I'll tell my lads not to score too many, just enough to put you Lancashire lot in your place.' It was the perfect motivational speech for my pre-match team talk. I knew it was kidology but Joe was belittling our club, my club, my team, my players, how dare he!

"I sat the players down and told them what Joe had said about us, which got the very reaction I had hoped for. At once they became charged, inspired and desperate to beat the fallen big-time Charlies from Newcastle. Never did I envisage myself plotting Newcastle United's downfall, but that mattered little. I wanted what was best for Bury Football Club and the people of Bury. No one expected us to win or even get a draw; we proved them all wrong."

In an epic battle of David and Goliath proportions, Stokoe's minnows pulled off the performance of the season and ran out 2-1 winners. "It will always be one of the very best moments of not only my managerial career but of my entire life in football. To see my players respond so positively, fight like warriors and work as a collective unit was truly uplifting. I loved every minute of the game and it was nice to put one over on Joe, especially after his pre-match comments. I never did tell him how I got my team so fired up. That was destined to remain a Stokoe secret. The momentum kept going into the following game as we beat Middlesbrough 2-1, a result that moved us up to 16th place. We managed only four more wins from the remaining 11 games that season, but it was enough to keep us up and I was really pleased with the effort and commitment shown by everyone."

If the victory at Newcastle was one of the high points of his career, then equally as significant is one of the low points that also occurred that season. "I vividly remember the run-in. We played Leeds twice over Easter and everyone expected us to get relegated, but no one had anticipated that Leeds would be in a relegation dogfight with us. Don Revie was the Leeds manager and much was expected of him. As a player he had appeared for England and he had been responsible for the famous Revie plan at Manchester City, the team we (Newcastle) just happened to beat in the 1955 FA Cup final. The Leeds team of the early 1960s was desperately poor and Revie had clearly failed to inspire them. He knew and I knew that on our day Bury could beat them. My lads had enjoyed four back-to-back victories and had secured safety. Leeds, meanwhile, were still struggling.

"Before the game I did my usual bits and pieces – checked on everyone's fitness, gave a motivational team talk, had a chat with the chairman and directors, and welcomed visiting officials. The problem with Leeds was that Don Revie was a bit of a furtive character. He wasn't like other managers, not open and welcoming. Rather he was deep-thinking and moody. I always thought he was trying to get one over on me, playing psychological games and looking for a reaction. He was, I know, deeply superstitious. I couldn't be doing with that claptrap, that hocus-pocus and the witches' curse theory he later held about Elland Road. I don't think many could quite believe how far Don Revie went with his 'Leeds are victims' plea. It is football, it is about 11 men competing against 11 men, playing fairly, scoring goals and trying to win as many games as you can throughout an entire season.

"As I was wandering through the office area I noticed Don Revie in the corridor whispering to one of his club officials. I nodded an acknowledgement of his presence, but he chose to ignore it. I put it down to nerves and him being worried about his reputation as a manager should his side lose the game. As usual I intended to offer him a private drink in my office, as I did with all opposition managers, after the game. A few minutes later, as I was preparing myself for the game in my office, I again noticed Don Revie. The best way I can describe his manner is to say that he was skulking. Then there was a knock on the office door and in he walks. 'Hi Bob, you've had a good run of form recently, you are safe now aren't you?' I smiled and confirmed his point. He moved closer to me and quietly offered to give me £500 if we threw one of the two games we had against them.

"It took me a few seconds to take in what he meant, the enormity of what he was actually saying, so I asked him to repeat it. I think he thought I was overwhelmed by the money, and again he offered me the sum of £500 to throw one of the games. I jumped up, looked him straight in the eye and called him a fucking cheat and a disgrace to the game. He didn't seem to care and then proceeded to ask me if he could have a word with some of my players! By this time I was going ballistic and refused him all or any access to my players, advising him that if I saw him so much as looking at one of them before, during or after the game I would knock his block off. He was gently rocking from side to side on his feet and seemed totally unfazed by my response. He seemed unsure about what to say or do next. I confirmed to him that as long as I was in the game I would never do business with him. I added that I would make bloody well certain that everyone else knew that he was a cheat, too. He then said something along the lines: 'That's okay, Bob, I won't be at your level for too long. I can't see my team being improved by any of your players.'

"I was so bloody angry about it, and it still rankles with me all these years later. I really wish I had reported him there and then to the referee, though clearly he would have denied it. I think the worst part of it all was that up to that point, other than him being a moaner as a player, I had nothing against him. He was overrated, in my opinion, but that was hardly anything to condemn anyone for. But this showed me his true colours. I am devoutly honest. I never cut corners and always do what is right and proper. I cannot stand cheating in any form. It is wrong.

"Revie stepped out of my office, disappearing down the passage and into the visitors' dressing room. I looked out Major Horridge, our chairman, and told him what had happened. He was calm, cool and collected about it, advising me not to say anything to the referee as Revie and Leeds would simply deny it ever happened. The outcome, more than likely, would not reflect too well on us as a football club. He told me that the best way of getting back at him would be to beat Leeds fairly and squarely on the pitch. Good advice. I did want to tell my players what had happened but thought it unfair on them so kept my own counsel. As for the two games, we drew 1-1 at our place and I played out of my skin at Elland Road to make sure Leeds did not beat us. We drew 0-0. During the second game Revie would not make eye-contact with me and kept well out of my way. At the end of the game I saw him looking all forlorn and sad with himself. I was bouncing with confidence and joy and openly laughed at him. As I walked by, I called out 'fucking cheat'. He hung his head and moved away. I loved that Leeds result that year. Unfortunately they stayed up, though they did finish below us.

"I want to clarify that it wasn't Leeds United that I disliked or held a grudge against. No, it was Don Revie. What a silly man. I thought that the attitude of some of his players often reflected his personality, his desperation to achieve and to win at all costs. I often crossed swords with little Billy Bremner. On a couple of occasions he got into a verbal slanging match, accusing me of all sorts of things, all untrue of course. The funny thing was that when he became a manager at Doncaster, he changed into a more placid person. We discussed the Revie bribery incidents and he tried to tell me that Don Revie had the best interests of his club and players at heart, that he had meant no ill by it. 'No one ever got hurt by accepting a bit of money, now did they' he told me. I told him that such funds were nothing less than dirty money. Such was his devout loyalty to his one-time manager and leader that at no point would Billy Bremner accept that Revie had tried to bribe me to throw a game in Leeds' favour.

"I suppose I, too, was foolish in selling the details of the incident to the press in the 1970s. I believe there was quite a dossier collated on bribery in the game, not only involving Don Revie, but elsewhere, too. There's no room for it. Such despicable actions and the people concerned should be banned from the game for life in my opinion. I would much rather maintain my northern integrity by speaking the truth than selling my soul to the devil."

It should be noted that although Revie did successfully sue the newspaper for libel, he never went to court to try to clear his name. Subsequently this has left a stain on his character. When I interviewed Revie in 1978 he refused to talk about the matter or discuss Bob Stokoe in any depth, or any games Leeds had played against any of Bob's teams. 'Bob Stokoe's opinions and career are of no relevance to me. I don't care about him.' That was the sole response I received on the matter. Clearly emotions ran deeply between the pair and there was much in the way of disdain shown by both parties. While Stokoe had, as always, been honest, open and transparent in all he did and said, Don Revie displayed his private side and, in my opinion with some amount of dignity, maintained his own counsel. That the situation between the two men would never desist in its venom is now on public record, with countless works making mention of it. It is sad that two men, highly skilled in different ways, should have had such a long-lasting public disagreement. The simple fact of the matter is, of course, that Revie should never have made the approach in the first place.

"In the summer I was told by Major Horridge that I would have to largely rely on free transfers if I wanted to strengthen the squad. This was a phrase I was to become extremely familiar with during my time as a football manager. However, I had the contacts and was reasonably good at negotiating, so it wasn't a real problem to me."

The 1962/63 season was Stokoe's first full campaign in charge. The impression he made and impact he had on the club and the town were quite incredible. Goalkeeper Chris Harker had already joined the club from Aberdeen. Stokoe originally knew him from their playing days at Newcastle. A fantastic start to the season saw the Shakers win seven of their opening ten fixtures, twice beating Leeds during that sequence and thrashing Rotherham United 5-1 at Millmoor.

"I put the boys on to a different sort of training regime, made it more enjoyable for them and got the unity spirit and some bonding instilled in them. We were one collective body now, a team with a lot of spirit and big aspirations. I got the local community voluntarily involved in some of the ground repair work and cleaning, too. People could see the players training and working hard in all the elements. There were no prima donnas in that side, just one team with one common vision. For a time it looked likely that we could win promotion, but a 0-0 draw at home to Newcastle United was seen as a disappointing result and as we moved towards Christmas we suffered two further defeats.

"The big talking point of that season came on Boxing Day. At the time we were going through the Big Freeze, heavy snow and ice meaning that the majority of games were postponed due to the treacherous conditions underfoot." Bury faced Sunderland at Roker Park in what was one of the few games to go ahead that day. Playing for Sunderland was Brian Clough. He was a determined centre-forward who described himself as 'the finest goal-scorer in the country and one of the best the game has ever seen.' But Stokoe held little respect for such outspoken individuals and regarded them as clowns. He was keen to see his charges take full points off Sunderland, not least because they faced them again at Gigg Lane three days after the Roker Park encounter. "I never really got on well with Sunderland, not since my Newcastle days and the grudge games between the two north east rivals."

Rain had begun to fall on the snow-covered Roker Park half an hour before kick off, thawing the ground and creating slush. During some frantic exchanges, Clough latched on to a loose ball and moved into the Bury penalty area. Chris Harker was equally as committed to winning possession and left his line to collect the loose ball that was now out of Clough's control. Clough raised his knee as a barrier to prevent him from injuring himself in the inevitable collision with the shoulder of the onrushing Harker. There was a mighty crunch and both men went down, the ball spilling loose and Clough making a vain attempt to get up to retrieve it. He collapsed in a heap. Both players were injured. The Bury men, Stokoe included, rushed over to the referee and claimed that Clough had been out of order in making the challenge on the goalkeeper. The prostrate Sunderland striker lay in the slush and mud, his face grimacing in pain. Stokoe marched over to the player who was being tended by the trainer and club physiotherapist.

"The referee was overseeing what was going on. Chris Harker was hurt also, yet the referee only seemed concerned by Clough. I went up to him, tapped the toe of my boot against his shoulder and told the referee to make him get up as I thought he was only codding. I accused him of being a cheat and told him I thought the challenge was unnecessary and crude. He mouthed a real obscenity back at me, telling me to 'go and fuck myself,' so I again told him to get up and get on with the game like a man.

"The Sunderland fans were giving me lots of abuse but I ignored it. The next thing I see is Clough being lifted on to a stretcher and carried off the pitch. Apparently he had torn his cruciate ligament. We went on to win the game 1-0 and beat Sunderland 3-0 at our place a few days after. Little did I know that Brian Clough's career was all but ended by that reckless challenge. I think he did make an attempt at a comeback of sorts about 18 months later, but only played a couple more games. He was just 29 when his playing days were over.

"I never thought any more of it until some playing colleagues told me that he had been bad-mouthing me and asserted his hatred for me. I thought hatred was probably an exaggeration. It wasn't. Brian Clough never did forgive me for what I said to him that day, nor that it was my Bury team he had been playing against when he ended his playing career. Occasionally I would bump into him at grounds we both visited, but he avoided me like the plague. Eventually I bumped into him at Roker Park and asked him what his problem was. I hadn't caused the challenge, it was his own doing. He responded: 'You stay away from me, Stokoe. You are a nasty piece of work and I want nothing to do with you. Piss off back to the Fourth Division where you belong.' Naturally, I didn't just walk away. I got as close as I could to him and reminded him that he originated from the north east and should have the good grace to remember his roots instead of acting like some opinionated southern ponce. Well that was it, the profanities flowed from his lips and for the first time in my life I actually saw in his face the expression of a person who really did hate me. I will never forget it. I felt hollow and sad. It had gone too far."

My own interview with Brian Clough revealed little else in the way of detail, other than that he refused to even utter Bob's name or refer to him in any manner, shape or form. When I discussed Carlisle United he cut me short in mid-sentence and implied that I was going to lead on to a 'certain cheap manager.' I, too, saw in Brian Clough his feelings of animosity for Bob Stokoe. It was a shame as I always found Cloughie to be difficult yet charming. His personality, ego and self-confidence were well known and respected throughout the game. I had to promise him that I would not utter the name in his presence again or face permanent exclusion from Nottingham Forest's City Ground.

On the pitch Stokoe had the team charging towards Wembley, reaching the semi-finals of the League Cup only to be denied a place in the showpiece by a strong and clinical Birmingham City side, who prevailed 4-3 over two legs. An injury sustained against Chelsea in April 1963 saw Bob out of playing action for the rest of the season. His absence at the heart of the Bury defence was noticed, as the club slipped to a final League position of seventh.

"In the summer I signed Colin Bell on professional terms from the Horden Colliery Welfare club. He was a real talent, one of the best young players I introduced to the professional game. The strain of playing and managing was taking its toll on my body. I chopped and changed some of the playing staff, bringing in good, strong local players. It was something of an indifferent season where the word 'inconsistent' doesn't begin to cover our form. At one stage we were fourth in the League, yet we also had a spell at the bottom of the table. We lost 2-1 at home to Newcastle, then later in the season went to St James' Park and whopped the Magpies 4-0. Eventually we survived to fight another season in the Second Division, finishing in 18th place.

It was tough on me as not only was I committed to playing but also I had a major input in team selection, though the final decision was always down to a committee which consisted of the chairman, the vice-chairman and me. I really found that tough, since my belief was that I should be responsible for first-team matters.

"Three days after the season was over I decided to retire from the playing side and concentrate solely on the managerial commitments. It also gave me the opportunity to select my own team and to manage more tactically. It coincided with Major Horridge standing down as chairman. There followed another season of fighting off relegation, but young Colin Bell was in sensational form for us."

The local press described the Stokoe team as 'raw and full of youthful energy and skill.' "I think the perfect example of what I had built is the youth team. We entered them into a tournament in Dusseldorf, Germany, in the May of 1965. Eight of those players were below the age of 20, yet had had Second Division playing experience. I was extremely proud of what we achieved at Bury, and shall never forget Major Horridge for giving me my first managerial appointment. Now, in the summer of 1965, I was being courted by the south London side, Charlton Athletic. The thought of moving and living in London filled me with horror, yet the Charlton position provided all the challenges I was looking for to take my career to the next stage.

"On 11 August 1965, with just ten days to go before the first game of the season, I formally tendered my resignation from Bury Football Club. I had advised the directors of my intentions a week or two earlier and had recommended a couple of people to them as suitable replacements. They actually appointed one of these a few days after my departure. His name was Bert Head."

5 Down in the Valley

*T*he move to London SE7 was not a straightforward one. Highly regarded in the north of England, Stokoe now had to prove his worth and cut his managerial teeth in an altogether different environment from what he had grown up with and was used to. "Charlton were a well respected football club. A previous manager, Jimmy Seed, had worked wonders there and was regarded as the best the club had ever had. Naturally I wanted to make my mark but Rome wasn't built in a day and I understood that a long-term restructure was the best option since there was no money for me to play with in the transfer market."

The Addicks, under Stokoe's predecessor Frank 'Tiger' Hill, who had gathered experience at Burnley, Preston North End and Notts County before moving to The Valley, had achieved very little during his four-year tenure. Initially he saved the club from relegation to the Third Division after succeeding Jimmy Trotter in 1961, and then led them to 15th position in the Second. But Charlton finished third from bottom in 1962/63, and although there was a brief renaissance to fourth place in the following season, they slumped back to fifth from bottom in 1964/65, Hill's last term at the helm. Clearly they were a long way off being promotion candidates and under Hill the football wasn't pretty, resulting in a dreadful dip in the seasonal average attendance figures, from 18,283 in 1963/64 to 13,065 the following season. Such matters have a serious impact on the financial implications at a football club. Hence Hill, only 18 days before the new season commenced, was called into the office of Mike Gliksten, the Charlton chairman, and sacked.

"I felt a bit for Frank Hill. He was a combative half-back in his playing days and a very good motivator of his teams as a manager. Frank would call it as he saw it and while he got his players wound up before a match, he wasn't the best communicator, often upsetting them by calling some of them idle and lazy. Nothing wrong with telling the truth! One player he really couldn't handle was Stuart Leary, a South African centre-forward who was as good as anything outside the First Division. Leary scored the goals that saved Charlton from relegation. With other clubs sniffing around and trying their luck to entice him away from The Valley, he asked for a review of his weekly wages for the following season. Frank apparently went up the wall and told him that any contract offer would be less than the one he was on at the time. You can only imagine what was said and how the player reacted. It was still being discussed when I got there a few years later. The long and short of the matter was that Leary left the club and joined another London side, Queen's Park Rangers, a situation the fans were none too pleased about.

"My own situation was that Mike Gliksten had made contact with me and asked if I would interested in joining Charlton. He said he had been impressed with what I had achieved with a tight financial budget at Bury. Charlton could offer me more support in the transfer market and because they were London-based they would highlight my managerial skills to a whole new audience. It was all very different from what I was used to. There was lots of buttering-up talk and, looking back on it now, sycophancy reigned. I fell for his patter. For a young man – he was just 25 when I joined the club and had been chairman for about three years up to that point – he certainly talked a fantastic game and knew where he wanted to lead Charlton Athletic.

He was also elected to the Football League management committee, which at his age was an achievement in itself.

"It was bloody difficult to leave what was, comparatively speaking, rural tranquillity at Bury for the urban environment of south east London. At Bury there seemed less of a competitive nature about the manager's role, whereas in London you were forced to always look on how other London club sides were doing in comparison to your own achievements. I'll be honest, I thoroughly liked Charlton Athletic Football Club and rate their supporters as the best in London. As for London, I didn't like it all, it's the sort of place that's great to visit but not to live in.

"I remember taking a look at the playing surface on my first day at the club. When Bury had played there the pitch had always seemed bog-like. I like everything to be right at a football club. If we provide a good playing surface and a good infrastructure throughout the club, then we can expect the players to understand how important their skill and performance is to the overall aspirations. They have no excuse for not consistently producing a good quality of play. Putting it mildly, the pitch at The Valley was at times like a heavily abused park pitch. I wasn't alone in voicing my concerns over its condition. Other visiting managers had at different times called it dangerous and a quagmire, including me when I was at Bury. I had felt so strongly about the dangers that I got the Bury chairman to write to the Football Association and Football League and to Charlton Athletic themselves to highlight the dangers.

"There were just a few days before the season kicked off, so it was too late in the day to change but I wanted to know the groundsman's opinion on what was causing the problem and what he was doing to remedy the situation. He was a Canadian, and as I walked the length of the pitch with him he seemed preoccupied with telling me how he came to be at the club. I have to say, although he seemed very knowledgeable, much of what he offered was ephemeral data and I hate people trying to bullshit me. I talked to many people, experts who dealt with turf and pitch maintenance, and asked our groundsman to come up with some solutions along the lines they had suggested.

"He never did. It was by pure chance that another club employee, assistant trainer Charlie Hall, told me that he didn't rate the groundsman, and that the fellow had, in fact, claimed to be an expert in ice-rink maintenance. Grass and turf were providing him with a whole new set of problems. Charlie told me that he knew someone who would be keen to have a look at the pitch and could do a far better job of preparing and looking after it than the current incumbent. So I was introduced to Maurice Benham, a die-hard Charlton fan and season ticket-holder since the 1947 FA Cup final. Maurice was my kind of man. The minute I met him I knew that his commitment to sort out the pitch was not only professional but also born out of his passion for the football club.

"Before I could do anything I had to get rid of the other groundsman – that in itself wasn't easy and took three attempts before he eventually got the message! The first time I spoke to him I baffled him with my knowledge of pitch drainage, the fact of the matter being that it was Maurice who had told me about this. I pointed out that I appeared to know more about pitch quality than he did and told him that perhaps he wasn't the right person for the job. It seemed to wash straight over him. The next day I complained about the cutting of the surface. It was uneven, with clumps of grass everywhere. He blamed the tractor and the cutter so I told him they were simply machines, operated by a human being, and that it was his fault. I told him to leave the club. The next day he was back again, trying to sort out the mess he had caused. I lost it with him and told him to clear his things and not to come back unless invited. The poor sod stood there and cried.

It didn't have any real emotional impact on me. I had lost my patience with him and shook my head in despair. He wrote me a letter of apology, which was nice, then proceeded to tell me how he wouldn't want to work for anyone like me again. Thank heavens, I say.

"I was truly concerned about the state of the pitch and while I respected Maurice I felt it only fair on both the club and the grounds-man to give him a six-month trial period during which I expected to see some improvement. Maurice was out there first thing in the morning until last thing in the evening, tending to every blade of grass, each one cut and trimmed as if by a barber cutting hair. As I recall, he had learned his trade in the RAF and offered an altogether more professional service and attitude. Within a few months he identified the major problem with the pitch as coming from an incorrectly fitted drainage system. Maurice was a real personality and we would spend hours over a pot of tea talking football, players and personalities. He was to be the best signing I made at Charlton and he was a great servant to the club over the next 20 years."

The following season got off to the worst possible start for Bob Stokoe. Two disappointing results at Bolton Wanderers (4-2 defeat) and at Plymouth Argyle (3-0 defeat) caused immediate pain as the team struggled to make any impact under the new manager. "I remember my first competitive game in charge quite vividly. Burnden Park has never been a favourite stamping ground for me. In an early Bolton attack our goalkeeper, Mike Rose, took a bad knock and he couldn't carry on. I talked to full-back John Hewie and told him to take over in goal. I made football history that day when I sent on Keith Peacock as substitute. It was the first time ever in a competitive League fixture that a substitute had been used. I had tried to bring in a mixture of experience and youth and gave young Alan Campbell, one of our colts, his first start. The goalkeeping setback knocked us completely out of our stride and we lost 4-2.

"There was a huge amount of work needed to get the team and the club into good shape. Too many players were coasting through games, so I stepped up the training, introduced more running and gym work to improve fitness and stamina. I wanted to add some needle to the training games, so took the decision to get involved myself. I would really mix it up with them. I wanted to see passion and a winning commitment. Anyone turning up late for training or for not, in my opinion, trying their utmost would be reprimanded and issued with a forfeit, generally press-ups or an extra run. In some cases it would entail helping the groundstaff clear up.

"Footballers have a tendency, if you allow it, to become lazy away from the pitch and to expect others to do the mundane tasks for them. Granted, some footballers earn a right to respect, but some of the Charlton players I inherited needed a reminder that they were fortunate to be in the game at all. There were a couple of exceptions. Young Mike Bailey and Billy Bonds were clearly players with a bright future in the game. I rated the pair of them very highly. Bonds, in particular, was always going to be a bit special. Bailey had already played for England, so was something of a seasoned professional.

"We got off to a stuttering start but after three straight home wins in September, in which we totalled 12 goals, I thought things were actually beginning to improve. I was wrong. After we beat Carlisle 4-1 at The Valley in the League Cup it all went sour and other than a 3-2 home win in the League, also against Carlisle, we didn't pick up maximum points again until the beginning of February 1966. The fans were on my back, telling me to get back up north. I was at a real low point in my football career. In December I appointed Charlie Hall as trainer after our regular trainer, Jock Basford, moved on to Exeter City, warning me before he went that I had bitten off more than I could chew at Charlton Athletic and to get out while I could. I always respected Jock yet felt he couldn't deal with my disciplinarian style. He was more of a pal to the players and was too lenient, whereas I was raised with – and strongly believed in – self discipline. It is something that will serve you well in life.

"During the awful run of results that we had endured for about four months, the morale of the first team dropped, and some of the attitudes in the dressing room didn't help. I wasn't afraid of confrontation and on many an occasion tore into players after or during training, and at full time after games if I thought they deserved a bollocking. One player reported me to the club chairman, saying that I was bad for the club and had not got a clue about management. When I found out I hit the roof and called him to a private meeting to try sort out his problem. I emphasise, it was his problem, not mine, not anyone else's. Typically, he withdrew into his shell when I confronted him and asked him why he had gone behind my back. At one point he even denied it. I despise liars, too. This should be an honest game with honest players and managers respecting an unwritten code of conduct. The player didn't stay with the club beyond that season."

With the fans vociferous and on his back, and the board of directors beginning to ask pertinent questions about why the team was struggling so badly, Stokoe once again took the honest line and said that he needed to bring in fresh faces to add to the calibre of the squad. "It wasn't rocket science. Anyone who watched us could see that in certain positions we were weak, and that it was always the same players who were giving 100 percent in each game. I told the directors that we needed to plunge into the transfer market and received the shock of my life when they told me that other clubs had been enquiring about some of our players.

"Now there was a number of players I would have wanted to get rid of. In fact, I would gladly have driven them personally to the other clubs in order to get shot of them. However, no manager likes to lose his best players or his most reliable players. So when the chairman said to me that Mike Bailey was attracting attention, and that I could spend some of any transfer funds received, I was forced to think about it. Bailey was an honest player, too good for the level he was playing at. In February 1966 I took a call from Ronnie Allen, then manager of Wolverhampton Wanderers. He was enquiring about young Bailey. 'How much will you take for him, Bobby?' asked Allen. '£40,000 and not a penny less' was my response. There was a moment or two's silence before Allen said: 'Okay, we will have him then. Can you send him up here so we can speak with him?' It was one of the most straightforward transfer deals I have ever completed, but afterwards I felt as though I had made a big mistake by selling our star asset. To be fair to the player he deserved the opportunity to play at the best level the game could offer and, to his credit, he went on to play most of his football in the top flight."

The resultant publicity the transfer aroused was bad as the media and the fans expressed their fears that the club lacked ambition. They were in no mood for sympathy. Stokoe had just sold one of the club's crown jewels. As far as the fans were conerned, the sale of Mike Bailey was solely down to the manager. In their opinion it showed his lack of ambition and inability to manage top-quality players, and he was publicly condemned for it.

"It wasn't nice. Some evenings I would sit on my own, thinking about what was being said about me, the questions being asked about my ability. Worse still, it became clear to me that there was, indeed, a north-south divide and I was bearing the brunt of all the so-called bad things the north stood for! It was a soul-destroying time and I had few people I could talk to about how I felt at Charlton. To be fair to the club, I tried to mask my feelings of hurt and get on with the job. I hadn't even got through one season and I felt I was being hounded out by certain elements within the staff who leaked everything I did to the press. Many a night I sat in tears, questioning why I had taken the move. A few phone calls from friends within the game helped to get my focus back. Folk like Jackie Milburn, Joe Harvey and Bill Shankly all told me to dig in and manage how I saw best, and not to listen to the hurtful and divisive comments. Shanks actually told me I should root out the mole in the camp and get rid of him. The problem I faced was that there were several untrustworthy moles. Shanks' solution to that being: 'Trust no one except your own family.'

"Curiously enough, between February and April 1966 the team hit a rich vein of form, losing just one game in nine, winning six of them. The one game we lost was against Bury 3-0, and some idiots in the press questioned my loyalty and asked whether I played the wrong tactics against Bury. These comments were tossed at me to put me on the spot. I threw them back with a response which left the journalists in no doubt as to where my loyalty lay, clearly stating that as so far as football reporters went, their knowledge of the game was non-existent and if they thought I was dishonest in any way then I would sue them for slander. They apologised for the flippant remarks there and then. There are only a handful of reporters, journalists or football writers I hold any respect for and will talk to openly, and none are from SE7."

A final league position of 16th was attained and that seemed respectable enough after his first turbulent season in charge at The Valley, although some supporters still questioned the manager's leadership ability. Some quite ridiculously claimed him to be tactically naïve. But if Stokoe thought things were bad then, by the end of the 1966/67 campaign they were to get a whole lot worse.

"Football, considering it is such a popular sport, can be a lonely and mad game. As a manager, your every move is analysed and assessed by the self-proclaimed expert pundits on the terracing. At Charlton I was finding it like being the sole piranha in a goldfish bowl.

People didn't want me there and gave me little room for error. The Mike Bailey sale would continue to haunt me during my entire spell at the club. There was a certain section of the support which didn't like my style. Some of these people wandered around the club on non-match days as though they were officials. I threw three of them out after seeing them in the office area. For years they had been given the run of the place, but that wasn't going to happen any more, not while I was there.

"As a result of my obstinate attitude towards these few I had abuse hurled at me in the street and in the clubhouse. During games they would spend 90 minutes calling me names until I confronted them, in public of course, after a game. I simply asked why they bothered coming to games if they were so negative about everything. The next thing I knew, journalists were on the phone trying to put words into my mouth, insinuating that I was ostracising supporters and had lost the plot. Charlton were good about it all and knocked back such suggestions. I was even given the dreaded vote of support by the directors.

"The season was memorable for the side being non-effective. We struggled to make any impact on the League and seemed to stagnate. My frustration spilled out when, as a result of a shortage of players, I was forced to turn out for the reserves as a centre-half along with coach Malcolm Musgrove and assistant trainer Peter Angell as wing-halves. It was a pathetic situation in all honesty. I had retired from playing more than 12 months earlier. At my insistence the reserve team had started and joined the Midweek League, pulling out of the Football Combination altogether. This, I proclaimed, would make it easier for us to staff such games. Now here was I putting my playing boots back on!

"I told the chairman and some of the directors exactly what I thought of the situation regarding our playing strength, and true to form they claimed to understand, telling me to get on with my job. This was despite the fact that two of them had clearly lost the desire to admit my presence at the club. The chairman, to all intents and purposes, was supportive and despite Charlton having a further season where the status quo had been maintained, he wasn't critical of what I was trying to achieve. I was given the all-clear to bring in players, so in an attempt to placate the masses I opted to bring back fans' favourite Eddie Firmani. To this day I don't know what it was that inspired me to bring him back to the club. He wasn't a player I particularly admired, yet the club needed someone to hold their focus, and Firmani was greeted like a hero returning from a successful battle.

"After the last game of the season, a 1-0 victory against Birmingham City, the chairman once again called me to the inner sanctum of the boardroom. There he advised me that the club had accepted a fee of £49,500 for Billy Bonds. I was gob-smacked because he was a priceless asset to the club. Yes, I had mooted the point that he could be worth cashing in on as we attempted to rebuild the squad, but at that fee we were giving him away. I expressed my dissatisfaction and was told in no uncertain terms that club finances were not any concern of mine. You can imagine how the supporters and the local press took the news. Having already had my name dragged through the sewer system of SE7, I was well prepared for this latest mauling. I tried to divert the criticism back on to the directors. However, their press machine was far more potent than my own and, once again, everything was my fault. I offered to resign from my position but was told that such talk was to be ignored, which I took as a compliment. In fact, they meant what they said. All such talk would be ignored, though some of them clearly wanted to see me resign.

"Despite the constant feeling that the Sword of Damocles was swinging above my head, I tried to get on with the task I was charged with, that of rebuilding the team. That summer the chairman released funds for me to spend. I brought in Theo Foley, a vastly experienced coach, from Northampton Town, to support me. It was Theo who recommended inside-forward Graham Moore to me and I signed him in May 1967. The following June I secured the signature of England schoolboy and youth international wing-half Paul Went from Leyton Orient for a then-club record fee of £24,500. At last, I was expressing myself and my confidence was returning. For the first time since arriving at Charlton Athletic I felt as though I was truly building my own team from players I had selected as opposed to those I had inherited or had been forced upon me by other sources.

"We faced a bloody awful start to the season, two home games and three away. There seemed to be a lot of attention being placed on the away fixture at Crystal Palace in September which was seen by fans as one of the big games of the season. In the opening game we were unfortunate to lose 3-2 to a physically strong Derby County team at the Baseball Ground, and then we then had consecutive draws, in one of which we picked up a good point at Millwall. But in a home game against Cardiff City I felt some of the fans turn against the players. We should have won the game but ended up drawing 1-1 with plenty of booing coming from the terracing. In the dressing room I sat the players down and reaffirmed to them that we had started the season better than our previous three, we looked strong at the back and were, in fact, proving difficult to beat, always a good sign.

"Afterwards I noticed Eddie Firmani chatting to a couple of the directors and at the time thought nothing of it. Then over the following week I witnessed further discussions, so elected to enquire what it was all about. Incredibly, I was told to stop being so fucking paranoid! But a couple of my players told me that Firmani had been ordered to keep an eye on the dressing room and to act as a link between club officials and players. I asked Eddie outright, and he denied it. I don't blame him really because he was put into an unfortunate position that tested his loyalty. I won't deny it, I was pissed off with him and the directors for being so underhand and playing so dirty. My players didn't know what to do or say. It was clear that the writing was on the wall and my days at the club were numbered. Foolishly I was the only one who hadn't seen it coming.

"The day before the Crystal Palace game I heard that some of the players had been spoken to by the directors and that questions had been asked about my standing at the club. To be honest I don't know what was said in those meetings. It was all very cloak and dagger and had an air of mystery about it. What I do know is that in the dressing room at Selhurst Park before the kick-off, I gave my worst pre-match talk ever. I wasn't focused on the game. My mind was preoccupied with all the talk circulating that day, stories that involved my dismissal. A couple of journalists asked me for a quote. I didn't know how to respond to the enquiry about whether I was to be sacked that day. I felt impotent and had no control over what was happening regarding my future. I blurted out some nonsensical response about concentrating on the game, reiterating that I was northern and proud, and what will be, will be.

"We lost the game 3-0, and the fans' response was typical. 'Stokoe out' they continually cried. After the game I became a non-person, everyone ignored my presence, no eye-contact was made with directors or club staff. It was over, I knew it was. It had been my intention to resign, but that would have shown defeatism and I wouldn't allow that of myself. So when the chairman told me I was being relieved of my responsibility with immediate effect and thanked me for my efforts, I simply asked him to fulfil the financial side of my contract. He agreed and I left The Valley in somewhat acrimonious circumstances. I think I said goodbye and good luck to about half a dozen members of staff and the majority of my team. There was not one good luck message from the boardroom and it was with some satisfaction that I bumped into two directors in the club car park. 'Gentlemen', I shouted to them, and they looked up in my direction. 'Go fuck yourselves with your inflated egos.' I wasn't proud of my departure but it sure as hell made me feel good for the rest of that day.

"That was it, I vowed to myself that I would never manage a London or southern-based football club again. I recalled Frank Brennan's comments to me about not trusting or putting faith in football club directors, and once again his advice rang true. I was out of the game for the first time since I was a young boy and I didn't like it at all. Inside I yearned for the opportunity to get back into management and to prove to Charlton Athletic, and to all those who doubted my ability, that they were wrong. It was a dear friend, Matt Busby, who offered me support, advising me to take some time out to get over the Charlton Athletic experience once and for all. He told me to wait until the right chance at the right club came along. Little did I know then that I was still highly respected for my ability and that my time out of the game was to be a brief one, indeed. Within four weeks I was back in the manager's seat, this time at a great little club called Rochdale."

6 **All roads lead to Rochdale**

*T*o most outside the region, Rochdale is hardly a place renowned for its football prowess and profile. Despite it being depicted satirically as a Lancashire backwater by many comedians and football pundits, it is, in fact, a pleasant town with a good football support that is hardened to the often toiling nature of lower League soccer. With an area population of approximately 200,000 there can be no doubt that the football club does well to attain the attendances it does achieve.

Rochdale FC was founded in 1907 and originally joined the Manchester League for one season, thereafter becoming a member of the Lancashire Combination in 1908. Having unsuccessfully tried on several occasions to gain access to the Football League, Rochdale were eventually invited to join the Third Division North in 1921. The club's first Football League game ended in a 6-3 victory over Accrington Stanley on 27 August 1921 played before a home crowd of 7,000. It was one of the few highlights of that inaugural season as the team finished bottom of the table and was forced to apply for re-election, which was successfully attained.

Few realise that the Dale have enjoyed a more than reasonable element of success since then. Back in 1962, when Tony Collins was manager, they reached the final of the new-fangled Football League Cup, then in only its second season, where they fell to Second

Division Norwich City, losing both legs of the final, 1-0 and 3-0 respectively. Despite the scorelines suggesting a comprehensive victory for the Canaries, the contest was much closer than it seems. Rochdale were, in fact, the first team from the basement division to reach a major final, in itself no mean feat.

As a result of that success and some improved League positions, the board of directors offered Collins a five-year contract in January 1963. A final League placing of seventh at the end of that season augured well for the future, even though the average attendance fell. The continuing improvement couldn't be sustained and soon Rochdale were again struggling at the wrong end of the table. In September 1967, with the Spotland crowds expressing their discontent, Tony Collins tendered his resignation, which was accepted. The situation worked in favour of Rochdale as word reached Bob Stokoe that the club was looking for a replacement manager.

"I knew Rochdale quite well from my days at Bury. They were a decent club with a loyal fan base. I knew the previous manager well, too. Tony was a good man who worked hard for the club on a very limited budget. His problem was that the success in the League Cup had brought about an air of expectation in the region and people expected promotion to follow in the next couple of seasons. When it didn't, the club and the support became demoralised. He did well getting a five-year contract out of them. No one ever offered such a long term commitment to me!"

After an informal chat with Rochdale chairman Fred Ratcliffe, Stokoe soon found himself discussing terms with the club. "Fred Ratcliffe was a real down-to-earth and sensible man. He had a real passion for the football club, his enthusiasm rubbed off on me and I was only too pleased to join them and to work for him." The new manager was formally revealed on 23 of October 1967. "We beat Barnsley 1-0 at Spotland and I was sat in the stands. I had popped into the dressing room for a quick chat with the players before the game, just to confirm who I was and that I was looking forward to taking the club forward. In the stands I felt relaxed when all of a sudden out of the blue the Tannoy announcer revealed to the crowd (3,368) that I was the new manager of Rochdale FC.

"Suddenly I became the focal point of every supporter in the stand. The majority were warm and welcoming, while others tried to tell me what a huge task it was going to be to get the team to play decent football. I said very little in return, but privately agreed with many of the comments. It was as difficult a public relations situation as I have ever encountered. Sometimes you just can't say what you want to, and I wanted desperately to tell these supporters that I would get rid of the dead wood and bring in footballers who were motivated and wanted to play for Rochdale.

"I wanted to make the team much more resolute and determined, and on my first day at training I really let loose at them, accusing them of being wimps and cowards. I wanted them to speak up and challenge me. That way at least I would know that they cared. Not one of the buggers said a word and I thought to myself: 'Christ, what have you taken on here, Bobby?' In goal we had little Les Green, a great shot-stopper and a huge personality. He was one of the few playing assets I had when I joined. The chairman had already told me that money was tight and I may have to sell if I wanted to bring anyone in. Same old story. I have yet to meet a chairman who says that the club is well off. To be honest, I expected a bit more from the players I inherited. There was a lackadaisical attitude among them that was hard to shake off. Without any shadow of a doubt they had become a team of losers. The most difficult thing was trying to field a consistent team. It seemed that every week we had a new injury or I had to drop someone for lack of effort or for being plain useless in a game. I told the team that I wanted more.

"The cup competitions often provide extra revenue, especially when one of the bigger teams is drawn. We pulled an away tie against Tranmere Rovers in the FA Cup. We were thrashed 5-1 and I was so angry that I couldn't speak to the players afterwards. They had let the club down, let the supporters down, let the town down and, from my perspective worst of all, they had let me down. At the next training session I had them running and running until they were fit to drop. This was followed by a gruelling and lengthy seven-a-side game, gym work, then crossing, defending and shooting practice. I know I was worn out, so I'm certain the players must have been. I wanted to teach them a lesson – let me down and you will suffer."

With both the FA and League Cups gone for the season, the team were left with some minor cup competitions, the best of these being the Lancashire Cup, where Manchester United were the opponents. "It was great stuff. The Lancashire Cup offered us the chance to pit our wits against some of the best teams in the country. Manchester United were a big shout. They were without doubt the best footballing side in the country, if not the whole of Europe, during that era. They won the European Cup in 1968, beating the Portuguese giants, Benfica, 4-1 in the final at Wembley stadium. Matt Busby, soon to be Sir Matt, was a real gentleman and a sport. He would attend as many games featuring his Manchester United teams as he could.

"We managed to draw at Spotland and got a replay at Manchester three weeks later. That game was abandoned due to some bloody terrible weather in Manchester. I understand why it is known as the rainy city. We were 1-0 down at the time so it was something of a blessing as far as we were concerned. Eventually we got the game played in January 1968. It was a match I shall never forget because my team simply capitulated. Up to that time in my career I had never seen a team of players put in such an inept performance. We lost 7-0, having fallen behind after just 15 seconds. Five of the goals conceded were, in my opinion, the fault of one player, Brian Eastham. I had played in the same team as Brian at Bury. He was an average sort of player, nothing inspirational, but steady. Tony Collins had brought him to the club in the summer from Toronto Falcons. In my thoughts he added little or nothing to the quality of the team; however, his experience would surely help the more immature players. I picked him against Manchester United hoping that his knowhow would help us out defensively, but what I saw made me shudder. He strolled around the pitch hardly breaking into a trot, and his performance that day was one of the worst I have ever witnessed from a professional footballer. Time and again he was caught in possession and out of place, his passing was inept and his confidence looked completely shot.

"After the game I told him I wanted him at Spotland first thing the next morning and to come to see me in my office. He told me to fuck off and that he wasn't about to take the blame for the result or the team performance. I reiterated, in my own inimitable style, that he would be waiting outside my office first thing the next morning. I had a quick word with the chairman and told him that I was going to sack Eastham as his attitude both on and off the pitch was abysmal and he was not adding any value to the team. What do you do in a situation like that? Brian, at Bury, was a thorough professional; now he was a totally different player and personality. It seemed to me that during his time away from Bury he had picked up all kinds of bad habits and traits. The net product was that he never kicked a football again for me or for Rochdale. I sacked him.

"As you can imagine, the press loved the story and made many additions to it, making it into something really lurid. I knew that a few of the local hacks spent many days trying to dig up dirt on both Brian and myself, though none was forthcoming. In that sense, Brian was professional. He didn't like what I did, yet at the same time he knew

I wasn't about to change my mind on the matter. I would never question his integrity as a person and he deserves respect for the way he handled the situation. A certain faction of the club's support was put out by my actions, however. But I stood my ground and confirmed that Brian was released in the best interests of Rochdale Football Club. Over the weeks that followed I suffered one hell of a lot of abuse from this minority group. I was inflexible where this was concerned and stood my ground against the amateur critics. As I have said previously, I am an honest person and I do things in a genuine and open manner. I expect footballers playing for me to put in a lot of effort. Any footballer who doesn't, or cannot match that commitment, gets but one chance with me."

The quality of the football improved slightly, but not sufficiently to keep Stokoe happy. "We were making silly and costly mistakes in defence, while up front the majority of the goals were coming from Joe Fletcher. I had a talk with the chairman and asked him if he would release funds for signings. I wanted to bring in a wide man to help supply ammunition for our centre-forward. I knew that Bolton were looking to offload Dennis Butler, and he was just the sort of player we needed at the club. The chairman asked me how much money I wanted and I told him a couple or three thousand pounds. The reply was typical – you will have to sell and cover the costs.

"I remember speaking with Len Richley, who had been secretary at Bury and was to be my assistant manager at Rochdale. I was thoroughly pissed off by the situation. The only decent player we had worth anything like that sort of money was our full-back, Laurie Calloway, and I didn't really want to sell him. Len told me that he would speak with Bolton to find out what the lowest fee they would accept for Butler would be. I felt impotent and was genuinely worried that without strengthening the team we would find ourselves again applying for re-election, something the club had endured in the previous two seasons. Such a situation would not reflect well upon me as a manager and I could be facing the sack after less than a season in charge."

Faced with such a debilitating disaster, Bob Stokoe dug deep into his experience and took control of the situation. "I spoke with Bolton manager Bill Ridding and laid my cards on the table. He was more than understanding, and told me that two other northern clubs had enquired about Butler. My worry must have been obvious on the phone because Bill then said that I could have him for £1,000 providing the player accepted terms. I agreed there and then and asked him to send the player to see me at Spotland. The chairman wasn't too happy but I told him not to fret and that he would have his money back in no time. Thankfully he backed me.

"Dennis joined us and gave us fresh options, and I felt confident that we could climb away from the bottom end of the Fourth Division. I also managed to get money to sign Billy Rudd from Grimsby Town for £1,500. Both sales were ultimately financed by the sale of Laurie Calloway to Blackburn Rovers for £5,500, much more than I expected to get for him, so it was excellent business for the club and the chairman was pleased with my wheeling and dealing. Now I had to satisfy the fans."

The impact of the new players was substantiated by results on the pitch. Four straight draws in March were followed by an outstanding 2-0 away win at promotion-chasing Chesterfield, then came another victory against a team looking for promotion, Bradford City. There followed a run of four straight defeats, leaving Stokoe's side struggling and staring at re-election. A decent 2-1 home win against Halifax Town was followed by the most important victory of the season, 1-0 at Workington, with one of Stokoe's new signings, Dennis Butler, scoring the all-important goal. A final League position of 19th was attained and re-election avoided.

"It was a huge relief to finish above the bottom four places and we only just managed it. After the season I sat down with Len, my assistant, and we drew up a list of the players we felt would help us to climb the table the following season. We both realised that we would have to sell half-decent players to release cash for us to manoeuvre in the transfer market. To some extent our position was made easier when the chairman informed me that the Derby County manager, Brian Clough, had enquired about our 'keeper, Les Green. I told the chairman to tell him to fuck off and to come through the proper channel, that is the manager. Then, after a few seconds, I asked the chairman to tell him that Green would cost £8,500, a price I knew he wouldn't want to pay. To my horror, Clough accepted the fee and so Les Green moved up to Second Division football.

"Now we didn't have a goalkeeper, but we had a bit of money to spend. Some people say I was frugal, but I would rather get a player in for a lower transfer fee and give him a decent regular wage than give a lump-sum transfer fee to a football club. I was on the phone eight hours a day, and brought in for free my old goalkeeping chum, Chris Harker, from Grimsby, and a talented youngster, Matt Tyrie, from Burnley, as his junior.

"Other free transfers followed. Full-backs Vince Radcliffe and Derek Ryder were recruited, while winger Norman Whitehead arrived from Southport. Vinny Leech (an ex-Newcastle player) and Joe Ashworth also joined on free transfers. In fact. the only outgoing money was the £1,000 spent on Stockport's Colin Parry. I wanted to bring in a blend of experience and young tenacious players. Certainly on paper we looked strong enough to hold our own, but I still had only 15 players at my disposal. I wanted to make this team feel special, unique in the history of Rochdale FC, so to get the supporters onside, too, I brought back a plain playing kit, blue shirts and white shorts. I am a great believer in doing things the easy way, and the new kit and the new team went down well. It was the dawn of a new era for the football club."

The season got off to a decent start, with the team unbeaten in the opening seven games, six of which were drawn and five of which finished 1-1 with Steve Melledew grabbing the vital goal every time. "There was a lot of pressure on our front men to deliver and I could see that they would need help as the season progressed. In September I got wind that Mansfield centre-forward Terry Melling was unsettled, so I offered £1,000 for him. In his debut game we beat high-flying Bradford City 6-0, a scoreline and victory that back then was something most Rochdale supporters were not used to. We really were looking like a very good football team, there was a buzz about the place and we no longer felt or performed like perennial strugglers. I was very pleased with what we had achieved and recognised that if we could sustain our efforts then promotion was a real possibility.

"One afternoon the chairman called me to his office. I hated these situations. It generally meant that some other club had put in an offer for one of our players or, worse, that I was facing the sack. As I wandered across the pitch to the office area beneath the stand, I wondered to myself what it could be. I knew on this occasion that it couldn't be the sack, so I talked myself into believing it must be a player sale. When I reached the stuffy boardroom Fred told me to sit down and take the weight off my feet. He offered me a tumbler of whisky, but I declined. He looked more serious than I had ever seen him and I asked him what was troubling him. He replied: 'Bobby, you know how much we value you here at Rochdale, you have done a fantastic job of work here and I think we all know that we are going places with you this season. Our fans worship you, the players commit to your every instruction. You have made this into a proud club.'

"With so much glowing testimony coming my way, I asked him if he was going to give me a pay rise. 'No I'm not, Bob, I only wish I could afford to. I would do anything to keep you at this football club.' 'What precisely do you mean by that?' I asked. By now I was certain that he was going to dismiss me. 'Bob, we have had a telephone call about you. It was from another football club in the Second Division, Carlisle United.' 'What do they want?' I asked, knowing the answer before I had even finished asking the question. 'You' said the chairman. 'But I don't want you to go; I want you to stay here where you belong and to see us promoted. I have put Carlisle off by telling them that you are settled here and wouldn't consider moving to them. Have I done the right thing? I felt it only honourable to let you know what I have done.'

"Suddenly I felt empty. Everything I had done in my brief time at Rochdale had led me to this point in my life. I wasn't too pleased with what the chairman had done and after contemplating in silence for a few moments, I looked up at him and his face was bearing a grin broader than that of a Cheshire cat. His head was nodding almost uncontrollably. I was enraged and said to him: 'How dare you block my career without first speaking to me? I do my best for you on a shoestring budget and you cannot even muster an ounce of reciprocal energy when it comes to supporting me.'

"Poor Fred, I can still see him yet, standing there, gobsmacked, his face ashen. I stood up and walked out. He followed me and asked if I wanted him to get back on to Carlisle. I told him it was too late and that the damage was probably now done. I went down to the dressing room and sat on my own, contemplating my next move. Should I stay with Rochdale or should I let Carlisle know I was interested? Len Richley came in to see me and asked what was up. I told him: 'The sodding chairman has stitched me up like a kipper, telling Carlisle I wasn't interested in a move to them as manager.' Len was typically calm and asked if I really fancied the Carlisle job. It was a pointless question, he knew I was ambitious and would jump at the opportunity to manage a decent Second Division team again. I knew Carlisle well enough to know that I could do a job for them. My old mate Ivor Broadis was a local man, he knew the club inside out having once managed them and played for them in two separate spells. Len advised me to keep my cool and to stay put for a few days to see how things mapped out. We both went away, our minds focused on different things; I couldn't get Carlisle United out of my mind, while Len was thinking about taking my job if I did move to Brunton Park.

"The next day Len came rushing over to me. I was taking part in training and was a bit worn out if the truth be known. 'Boss,' he said excitedly to me, 'Carlisle United are on the telephone for you, can you call the Carlisle club secretary?' I made my way to my office wondering if our chairman had agreed anything with Carlisle since we last spoke. I can still remember the number I dialled to this very day: Carlisle 26237. Making the call, I spoke with a very intelligent and respected man called David Dent. David was the Carlisle secretary and had made a real name for himself as an efficient and motivated manager of club business. He was to become well known to me both professionally and personally and is in my opinion the greatest football administrator in the entire history of the game.

"Shortly I was speaking with the Carlisle chairman, an enthusiastic man called George Sheffield. Few chairmen throughout my years in football have commanded instantaneous respect; George Sheffield was one such man. He was a straight talker and honest man, in the same mould as me. 'Bob, we want you to come to Carlisle. I've got rid of Tim Ward, waste of bloody space that he was. He didn't have the mind to take us forward, not like you. I see a bright future for you and you can help yourself by joining us.' I asked him if he had spoken with the Rochdale chairman. 'Of course' was the reply. So I agreed to meet and speak terms at Carlisle. I went to see Fred to thank him for getting back to Carlisle. He wasn't happy, the truth being that he hadn't got back to them, which left me in something of an uncomfortable situation. I insisted that he did and asked him to do so with some haste, because if he refused me the opportunity I would resign and walk away. He called me back and asked me to sit down while he made the call. After a few minutes it was agreed; I had Rochdale's support to speak with Carlisle United.

"It wasn't that I desperately wanted to leave Rochdale, I enjoyed it there. But this was a good opportunity for me to get back into the Second Division and perhaps reach the First Division. Deep down inside I also relished the opportunity that a Second Division club could offer of facing Charlton Athletic again. I was treated despicably there and wanted to show those southern prima donnas that they were wrong to ditch me and replace me with the bible-puncher Eddie Firmani." It was a personal grudge that Stokoe was to harbour for many years.

"The funny thing about the Carlisle job was that the previous boss, Tim Ward, rang me and tried to put me off going there. He said the directors were little more than a bunch of country yokels with stitched-up pockets, meaning that there was no money there. I remember him telling me how verbally vicious the fans could be and how he had suffered from their torment of him for over six months. 'It's not a nice place to be, Bob, and there is nowhere to hide' he told me. Quite why any football manager would want to hide I couldn't understand, but it perhaps indicates how the barrage of abuse that Tim believed he was subjected to had affected his confidence and self-esteem.

"It wasn't a straightforward move to Carlisle; there was a lot in the way of discussions about my contract. Originally the money was less than I was on at Rochdale and at Charlton and Bury before that. It really was poor. My wife, Jean, told me not to commit to anything until the money was right. She was great at keeping me straight.

Eventually we agreed a figure and some additional expenditure for travel and removal expenses. With something of a heavy heart, I went in to speak with the Rochdale chairman for the last time. We shared a drink and he wished me well, adding that he didn't know what Rochdale would do for a replacement. I told him there and then that there was just one man who could finish the job I had started, and to appoint Len Richley."

There can be no doubting that Bob Stokoe held a real affection for Rochdale. He had, after all, transformed the team from perennial strugglers to promotion challengers in less than a full season. The players he brought in, (almost an entire team) were there because of him. That he was respected, even revered, by his team is without doubt.

"I recall going to speak to the players to break the news to them that I had agreed to move to Carlisle as manager. It was dreadful. The look of absolute despondency upon their faces will be a sight I shall always remember. 'Are we coming with you, Boss?' was the unanimous response. A Royal Automobile Club road map of the north of England was produced from a bag and handed to me so that I could see where Carlisle was. It was a sad moment and as I shook every player by the hand, I genuinely wished them good luck and future success. Finally I turned to Len and let him know I had put in a good word for him. 'I know, Bob, that's the next thing I want to tell the boys. I'm their new boss. So hurry up and clear off.'

Len was a good man, a proud and honest Geordie who hailed from Gateshead. His name was actually Lionel but he didn't like it when you called him that, so he had adopted and always introduced himself as Len. He was one of the most trustworthy people I knew in the game. Unknown to anyone at the time he was to lead Rochdale to promotion that season, a great achievement by anyone's standards. Sadly, a couple of seasons later, there was some backbiting going on at the club, with interference into the playing side of affairs by what I can only describe as non-football people – I'm talking about directors. I think Len had lost the support of the boardroom and once that happens it's a slippery slope for any manager.

"Football club directors are a breed unto themselves. Once you cross them you are more or less done for. They have a knack of undermining you and rubbishing your credibility, not only within the football club but within the town or city where you ply your trade. Look at any club manager who gets the sack. Rumours are generally in circulation about him, away from the club, long before the axe falls. It's almost as though, as a manager about to be sacked, he is the last to know. That's because he is so wrapped up in trying to make it work. The directors feed scurrilous tales to sources they know will pass it on because it helps validate their decision to get rid.

"I reckon I must have been the only person in the whole of south east London and Kent who wasn't aware that I was to be sacked by Charlton Athletic. Tim Ward told me the same about his time at Carlisle, how the directors of that football club had effectively began to ignore him, treating him like an outcast and creating an insecure environment, his only route of communication within the club being through the ultra-professional David Dent. It's not that I don't like directors, but they should really stick to doing what they do best, whatever that is, and keep their noses out of the playing side of the game."

7 Doing the Brunton beat

*I*t is often said that some things in life are down to destiny. Most certainly Bob Stokoe's arrival at Carlisle United in October 1968 was significant as it was the beginning of a special football relationship that was to be spread over three different decades. "If there is one football club that is closest to my heart, then that football club is Carlisle United. Carlisle is a lovely place filled with lovely, passionate people. They know and understand their football, too. You would expect them to with previous managers of the club including such eminent names as Bill Shankly, Ivor Broadis, Bill Hampson and Allan Ashman.

"When I joined the club they had gone 11 League games without a win, and were sitting bottom of the Division Two table, having amassed just four points all season. The only success the loyal fans had witnessed was in a League Cup tie against Cardiff City at Brunton Park which they won 2-0."

A couple of weeks later the cup run was abruptly ended when Leicester City won 3-0 at Carlisle. The poor run of League form had seen heavy back-to-back defeats, including 5-0 to Crystal Palace at Selhurst Park and 4-0 at home to Norwich City. It was a dire time to be a supporter of Carlisle United. It was, in fact, the season when the author was first introduced to "real-life" professional football, my first game being a 0-0 draw at home to Huddersfield Town, the last League point that then-boss Tim Ward would win in his time at the club. I can well recall the cries of "Ward Out" emanating from the terraces at that stage of the season, which was only August.

"When I joined Carlisle the team was in complete disarray – no motivation, no discipline and a real lack of belief and confidence. The supporters were at the end of their tether and were beginning to turn against some of the players. All the signs were readily visible that this was a team and a club going backwards. George Sheffield was a man after my own heart, plain speaking and ambitious, but on a shoestring budget. I didn't really go much on the other directors, although Andrew Jenkins was always supportive of me and if I am honest he was to become one of the few directors in football for whom I held a healthy respect. Even though we did cross swords occasionally, he was always a fair and genuine man.

"As so often happens in football, I had been interviewed for the position as manager and then had to participate in a strange test of my managerial ability. It transpired that the club wasn't quite ready to reveal me as the new manager. There were one or two other issues to be sorted out first, mainly surrounding the sacking of Tim Ward, contractual obligations and the like. In the meantime I was to remain in the background, gathering information on the players and staff and working on my plan of action.

"I met with the trainer, Dick Young. What a man he was, passionate and devoutly loyal to Carlisle United. Dick gave me the rundown on the team and the characters within the boardroom and the club. Getting back to this test of my ability, I was pretty shocked by the whole thing. However, the directors had told me to watch and report on the team from the stands at Deepdale, Preston. It was a 2-2 draw and I thought to myself: 'This team have the best centre-forward in the Second Division – that was Hugh McIlmoyle – and they aren't using him to his strengths.' To be fair they did work hard as a set of players, but there was little team ethic visible to me. I told the directors what I thought and was formally given a contract at the club. I remember thinking to myself: 'Bloody good this, I have left Rochdale and now they are testing me to see if I know what I am doing. Club directors, of all people, asking me to justify how I would manage and run a football team – bloody idiots! I came close to telling them to shove it, but there was something about Carlisle that was different. I really wanted the job, though I wasn't desperate, and I was very pleased to get it.

"It had been decided that I should take over for the home game against Bolton Wanderers. I wanted it all kept low-key and few if any of the local or national press had any idea what was going on. I had been meeting with Dick Young and asked him to say nothing to the players. I wanted it to come as a complete surprise on the day of the Bolton game. Dick told me that they would shit themselves when they found out who the new manager was, as I had a reputation for being a touch on the hard side. Too right as well, I would give this lot a real kick up their backsides to wake them up.

"My first meeting with the team came pre-match in the Central Hotel on Victoria Viaduct in Carlisle city centre. It was a venue where the team generally met up and enjoyed a good meal consisting of steak. I was waiting for them in the lounge. I will never forget the look on a few of their faces when Dick Young revealed to them: 'Chaps, this is Bob Stokoe, our new manager.' Talk about shocked, there were a few long faces, I can tell you. Some of them knew that I wouldn't carry passengers and so they would have to buck up their ideas if they were to have a future at the club with me as manager.

"I knew a couple of the players. Hugh McIlmoyle was a centre-forward most managers would have loved to have at their club. If played properly he was lethal in front of goal. He was a leader on the pitch and someone the fans held in high respect. I told everyone before the Bolton game that they had to prove themselves and that I thought they were all decent footballers. However, the team was in a rut and it would take a huge effort from all of them to turn things around. Frank Barton was a player I really liked amd who was hugely underestimated. He was full of skill and could finish as well. I told him to go out and run at the Bolton defence whenever he could, and to feed big Hugh with as many crosses as he could. We drew that game 1-1. A few days later we went to Oxford and won our first League game of the season, Chris Balderstone getting the all-important goal for us. I treated the players to an impromptu reward on the journey home. We stopped off at a pub and had a pint to celebrate."

Despite that result the team remained at the bottom of the League, although the performance was not of a struggling side. Three days later Blackburn Rovers were beaten 2-0 at Ewood Park courtesy of two McIlmoyle strikes, and this was followed by a 1-0 home win over Blackpool when George McVitie hit the winner in front of a crowd of over 10,000. It must have been with some satisfaction that the club directors listened to the Brunton Park crowd rejoicing and euphorically chanting the new manager's name. In tremendous form, the team remained unbeaten under Stokoe until 21 December, when Blackpool avenged their defeat earlier in the season, winning 1-0 at Bloomfield Road. It mattered little for Carlisle, who now sat comfortably in 12th position. It was quite an incredible turnaround. Both on and off the field the club looked to be heading in the right direction.

"I knew that some motivational needs had to be implemented, both on and off the field. For a start the players had lost self-belief. They wanted to be winners so I had to instil a winning attitude in them. It didn't make me popular with them when I called them crap or useless to their face, but it had the desired effect – they didn't want to suffer my wrath again so they upped their performance accordingly. The supporters were as enthusiastic and loyal as anywhere in the world, but no one had given them anything to shout about. I won the supporters over fairly swiftly, not only by creating a winning team, but by making their ultimate hero, Hugh McIlmoyle, the team captain. Hugh knew the game as well as anyone on the pitch, he always gave 100 percent and the rest of the team respected him, so it was a natural progression. The fans loved it, too.

"We drew Chelsea in the third round of the FA Cup that season. It was a filthy day at Stamford Bridge. Chelsea were a First Division team and no one gave us any real chance of beating them on their own soil. But we matched them in every department, albeit they had quality players such as Alan Birchenall in their team. Their superior finishing outfoxed us on the day as we went down 2-0, but by no means was it an emphatic Chelsea victory. I was proud of how the team had risen to the challenge and had worked together. I told Dick Young after that game that I thought this team, with a few decent additions, could put together a real promotion challenge for First Division football. He agreed and we talked of how effective Chris Balderstone and Tommy Passmoor had been, and how in Stan Ternent we had a gritty, determined footballer who couldn't accept defeat, a real motivator both on and off the field. Stan and I didn't always see eye to eye, maybe because we were both tough and honest. I respected him, though; he was a leader and worked his socks off for Carlisle United."

The revival of club fortunes continued and at one stage of the season the team sat in seventh position and looked likely challengers for promotion. However, a dramatic collapse in form, with five defeats from the remaining seven games of the season, ended all such speculation.

"The squad that first season was too small. I had asked a lot from the players from the moment I arrived and they had given me and the supporters full commitment. It was a disappointing end to the season, but when you consider that we had been bottom of the table since about the end of the first week in September, we had done bloody well overall. I had talked to the chairman about bringing a few extra players in after the Chelsea FA Cup game, players who would help us push on, but I was told that I would have to sell if I wanted to increase the size of the squad. I wasn't prepared to split what was the makings of a really good team, so decided to stick with the players we had and to enhance it during the summer.

"I had a few players in mind that I would have liked at the club, and one of these was the striker Bobby Hatton. Both Dick Young and myself had been to watch him play on a few occasions while he was with Northampton Town. I liked what I saw in Bob; he was determined and a fighter for lost causes, too. I had a chat with the chairman and he told me that he thought Hatton would be out of our price range and not to bother. So I asked if he would pay him a wage if I could get him for less than £10,000. 'You won't get him for less than £10,000, Bob, don't waste your time. But if you do get him for less then we'll have him.' I love a challenge, so I got on the phone to Dave Bowen, the Cobblers' manager. Dave was a lovely man and a pleasure to do business with. I told him I was interested in taking Bob Hatton off him. To my surprise, Dave told me that his board of directors had advised him that he would have to sell if he wanted to bring in any new talent. Not only that, but he wouldn't be guaranteed to get back the amount of the received transfer fee to spend, the underlying message being that the club desperately needed cash.

"Dave had rejoined Northampton in the May of 1968, having previously been the manager from 1959 to 1967, taking the team on a fantastic journey from the Fourth Division to the First and back again. Since then two managers had come and gone. Now he was back he wanted to make his mark and again build his own promotion-winning team. In business you have got to make some tough decisions, and as lovely as Dave Bowen was, I knew a deal was there for the making and taking. So I offered up the names of several players who I thought would do a good job for Northampton. Dave liked what I was saying but continued to remind me that he had no transfer funds. I, too, pleaded poverty, albeit this was no untruth, and offered him just £8,000 for Bob Hatton. The phone went silent for a few minutes, I could hear Dave taking a few deep breaths. He accepted my bid on the proviso that the directors agreed to it also. They must have been desperate because within minutes the deal was accepted and I got the player signed up on a two-year deal. To this day, it ranks as one of the best pieces of football transfer business I have ever achieved.

"I moved a couple of players on, good footballers who had in my opinion seen their best days at the club. Peter McConnell moved to Bradford City, Gordon Marsland to Bristol Rovers and Eric Welsh to Torquay United. It upset quite a few fans that I had allowed such players to go and I received a couple of silly letters telling me that I needed loyal players at the club. I replied to every letter I received and thanked the fans for caring so much, explaining that I didn't need to justify my decisions, but to trust my judgement. In-coming players, along with Bob Hatton, included Derek Hemstead from Scunthorpe United and Willie O'Neill from Glasgow Celtic. I didn't want to upset the status quo of the team, yet there was a definite need to enhance it and the people I brought in did just that. Derek, in particular, was a steady and reliable full-back, while Willie was striving to make a name for himself in the game. He was more of a flair player and I thought he would complement Chris Balderstone's style perfectly.

"I asked the directors to change the club's crest on the players' shirts, too. My intention was to bring the club, the players and the supporters closer together, uniting them under one term. I utilised the old Latin term *Unita Fortior* (United Strength is Stronger). This sat below a new fox-head badge that was specially designed. It looked great in itself, but the badge took up a fair bit of room on the shirt and it looked a bit unsightly, to be honest." Stan Ternent once told the author that it was like playing with a saucer over his left tit. It could, one imagines, have caused severe nipple rub. "I cannot ever remember anyone asking me what the Latin term was or what it meant. The local press never grasped the logic behind it. A bit too advanced for them back then, maybe?"

Early season form was less than spectacular as the team struggled to get into their stride. Two wins from the first five League games of 1969/70 took us to eighth place in the table, but the goals simply weren't flowing from the McIlmoyle and Hatton partnership. It wasn't until September that Hatton broke his scoring duck, bagging both goals in the 2-1 home victory over Hull City. A week later he scored another brace in a disappointing 4-2 defeat at Millwall. We played Leicester City at Filbert Street soon after we were stuffed at The Den. I was still seething with the players because we had held a 2-1 lead at half time and threw it away by some sloppy defending and a lack of concentration. I told them I wanted more from them and expected better at Leicester.

"I got it, too. Hughie McIlmoyle had promised me 20 goals that season, and he scored both in our 2-1 win over the Filberts. He was outstanding that day and with a little more luck he could have scored more. We systematically took Leicester apart. Before the game I had told my lads that Leicester were nothing but a team of overrated players who couldn't cut it when the going got tough, and that seemed about right. When we got back to Brunton Park I was told by our chairman that Middlesbrough had put in an offer to buy Hughie McIlmoyle. I told him to tell them to go and shove it. Hughie was a major part of my team-building plans and I wanted him to stay. With him in the team we could possibly win promotion to the First Division."

Incensed, Stokoe turned his back on the conversation and walked away from it. "The chairman followed me, and further informed me that Middlesbrough had actually offered £45,000 for the player. That was a lot of money to Carlisle United Football Club. I told him that if he sold Hugh for that amount he was cheating the player and the club out of a lot more money. I told him that in my opinion Hugh was worth at least £75,000 on the transfer market. I pleaded with him not to sell the player, but I was told that he and the directors would have to do what they thought was best for Carlisle United. Angry and disappointed doesn't begin to tell the story of how I felt about this situation.

"The newspapers had got hold of the story of Middlesbrough's bid from somewhere and I telephoned the local rag and asked if they had set the rumour mill going. They denied it, of course they would, but inside I knew that any journalist worth his salt would sell the story to one of the nationals. Hugh approached me in training and asked me if what was being said about him being transferred was true. I told him that I didn't want to sell him; it was the directors of the football club, our employers, who were negotiating the sale. I felt for the player. It was clear to me that he didn't want to leave Carlisle. He could see we were building something special, the fans worshipped him and he had a real pride about representing the club. It reminded me of my days as a player at Newcastle, when I was sold against my desire.

"The next thing I knew was that Middlesbrough had come back to our directors with a firm offer of £55,000. The daft lot that they were, they accepted it without even trying to squeeze more out of 'Boro. I couldn't believe it. Hugh was clearly our best player and here he was being removed without any real consultation with either myself or him. Football club directors back then were just like accountants, making a profit on the books was all they cared about."

Hugh McIlmoyle himself did everything he could to deter Middlesbrough from signing him. He added all kinds of extras to his contract, but Boro were determined to recruit him and agreed to such notions as the player remaining in the city and doing weekly training sessions with Carlisle. Hugh told the author: "I didn't want to leave Carlisle, I loved it here and felt as though I was being pushed away. It seemed that everything was taken into consideration except what I wanted." Hugh played his last game for Carlisle that season in a 1-0 win over Preston North End at Brunton Park, a result that moved them to seventh in the League table.

Prior to his departure and unknown to anyone at that time, Hugh McIlmoyle ignited the fuse that was to lead Carlisle United on an adventure the likes of which had never previously been seen in their history and has never been repeated since. Two McIlmoyle goals in the 2-0 victory against Huddersfield Town, on a dark and sultry September evening at Brunton Park before 11,198 spectators in the Football League Cup competition, sparked a run that will long remain in the minds of club officials, players and supporters of Carlisle United. It was to be, at that point, the club's greatest achievement as the Stokoe magic began to show itself and the team became transformed into a genuine force within the game.

On 24 September 1969, just 24 hours after Hugh McIlmoyle departed to Teesside, Blackburn Rovers arrived in Carlisle as League Cup third-round opponents. It wasn't the first time the teams had met in the competition. In 1967 Carlisle had thrashed Rovers 4-0 at Brunton Park; now the visitors were keen on revenge and played out a pre-match war of words based wholly upon the loss of United's star player. The Carlisle boss was in no mood to make light of the matter.

"The Blackburn manager was Eddie Quigley. He called me on the Monday afternoon before the League Cup game and to begin with I thought it was a genuine social call. However, he suddenly began to mock me about the sale of Hughie McIlmoyle, asking how I thought it would affect us as a team. He was making light of the matter and said he thought we would be a spent force. I blew my lid and told him that the day when Blackburn Rovers could ever be regarded as a force would be a long time coming, especially with him as boss. I ended the call abruptly but before replacing the receiver I informed him, with more than a touch of devilment, that I would look forward to seeing him at the game the following evening.

"The first thing the next afternoon, Eddie called at the ground to see me and apologise. I told him I would accept it and shake hands with him after the game. He told me that I had a reputation as being tough and had an attitude that put a lot of people's backs up, adding that he could see why this was so. I reminded him that I wasn't there to be his friend or his chum, I was paid to be manager of Carlisle United. My sole aim was to get my team to beat his team and every other team we played. He shook his head from side to side as though he couldn't believe what I was saying and he shuffled off muttering something to himself.

"I could never understand managers playing psychological games with other managers. The whole thing was daft, especially as there was only a handful of managers, people like Bill Shankly and Matt Busby, whose word and opinion I would accept and appreciate. I knew I could be brutally honest. It was the only way to be in my opinion, open and frank. That way nobody misinterpreted what you said. If people couldn't handle that then it wasn't my problem. I have mellowed over the years and am now perhaps much more accepting of other people's ways, but back then I was in my prime, with a huge amount of ambition and a determination to win and make my team winners, too. Also, I could never stand rudeness, and Eddie Quigley had been rude to me and my club.

"You can imagine how I felt when Blackburn scored to take the lead in the game that followed. Eddie gave me a nod and a wink as a signal of his team's superiority. At half-time I had a go at my players in the dressing room. They looked lethargic, almost as if they believed they were a worse team without Hugh McIlmoyle. I had a quiet word with Bobby Hatton and told him to make a bloody nuisance of himself in the Blackburn penalty area. Likewise I told our flying winger, George McVitie, to run at the full-backs, to get to the byline and to pull the ball back into the penalty area as often as he could. It worked – we came out like a steam train at full throttle and really tore at Blackburn. We overcame the hurdle of their 11-man defence and created several chances, two of which we finished and won the game 2-1.

"Afterwards Eddie Quigley came up to me, shook me firmly by the hand and said: 'You are a bastard of a man, Stokoe, but you are a winner. Good luck to you, I really do wish you well. I will be plotting to avenge this defeat for the remainder of the season until we meet again.' I had no idea how important that win was to prove. My players bonded that evening, at times we looked as though we were on a higher plane altogether than Blackburn. Our second-half play was calm yet exciting. Dare I say it, we didn't miss Hugh McIlmoyle too much."

The draw for the fourth round of the League Cup couldn't have been tougher for Carlisle United. We were paired with First Division Chelsea at Brunton Park. The Pensioners, as they were then nicknamed, had already knocked out the competition favourites and reigning League champions Leeds United, having drawn 1-1 at Elland Road, then won comfortably 2-0 at Stamford Bridge. Chelsea, by virtue of that victory and some decent League form, automatically became the new favourites to win the trophy.

"In preparation for the Chelsea tie we won just once in four games, a 2-1 victory at Watford. It wasn't good, and to make matters worse Chelsea were on a strong run, losing only once in ten games. They were regarded as one of the best teams in the country at the time." In fact, they were to finish third in the First Division, losing only eight times all season, and won the FA Cup. Truly this was a very good team that faced Carlisle.

"The pre-match preparation and build-up was phenomenal, the whole city went football crazy. Everywhere I went there was the blue-and-white of Carlisle United on display. Shops had window displays that included rosettes, scarves and photographs, there were Carlisle United cakes (buns with blue-and-white icing) and a local butcher even created Carlisle United sausages! We were inundated with press enquiries. I found it hard to get any space to gather my thoughts and my right-hand man, Dick Young, did really well to respond to most of the probing questions asked by the hacks.

"I don't know what it is about football journalists. They can be bloody inventive with transfer talk and tales of managerial sackings, yet when it comes to asking sensible and interesting questions they seem to have a void in their vocabulary. It rarely happened in my experience. Once again the Hugh McIlmoyle transfer came up. Dick dealt with it firmly and with some dignity. I remember him responding to the very delicate suggestion that goals had become scarce since Hugh had left the club and that Bob Hatton seemed to be struggling. He told the gathered group of reporters, all anxious for a slip of the tongue and an admission that it was a mistake to sell Hughie to Middlesbrough: 'Hughie McIlmoyle was a great goal-scorer and footballer for this club, but he's moved on, gentleman. It's time you did, too. Have you not noticed that we have a cup-tie to focus our attention upon? If you would like to ask any questions about that then please feel free to do so. If not, then I'm too busy to talk about someone else's footballer.'

"Dick was a great man. He is up there among the elite, most knowledgeable people I have ever known in football. I came to rely upon him a great deal and welcomed his input into team tactics and options. We tended to bounce ideas off one another, new ways to develop players through different training techniques. So when Dick came to me and said that he was worried that an in-form Chelsea would do us over, I really took it seriously.

"Neither Dick nor I ought to have worried. When the players came in for training the day before the Chelsea tie they were clearly very focused and had been running through the various strengths and weaknesses of Chelsea themselves. The fact that Dave Sexton, their manager, had belittled us in the press, asking 'Where is Carlisle?' and 'What league do they play in?' helped further motivate the players, not that they needed any more winding up. Collectively, the team I put out that night was the most focused and self-believing bunch I have ever had. They were utterly fantastic. For all the Chelsea fighting spirit, my lads had enough fire in their bellies to match them in every department and ultimately to see them off completely. A beautiful strike from the foot of full-back Derek Hemstead was enough to see us through to the next round. It was a marvellous feeling and in the dressing room there was an air of self belief emanating from the players, who realised that on their day they could beat anyone. The celebrations throughout the city were memorable that night and for a few days afterwards.

"In the quarter-final we faced Oxford United, who then had Gerry Summers as their manager. He was a softly spoken man and a bit of a wolf in sheep's clothing. There was an undercurrent to his personality. In the dressing room he could and would really lay into his players, yet his public persona was so much different, almost quiet and unassuming. He knew the game well and was a good coach. I always found him welcoming.

"When we arrived at the oddly formed Manor Ground he was more than gracious with his compliments about how we had beaten Chelsea and how we really should beat Oxford United. I didn't fall for any of it. As it was, Oxford really tested our determination to progress in the competition, and we had our goalkeeper Allan Ross to thank for keeping Oxford out. We earned a 0-0 draw and I mean earned. It was much tougher than the Chelsea tie, mainly because we had become the team to beat. At Carlisle in the replay, Oxford defended resolutely, hardly creating a chance, and thankfully Chris Balderstone tucked away a penalty for us. We went on to win the game and the tie 1-0."

It was quite incredible stuff. Carlisle United had reached the semi-finals of the League Cup for the first time in their history. They were just 180 minutes from a Wembley appearance in a major cup final. Fate is a cruel thing, for standing between them and the Wembley dream was First Division side West Bromwich Albion, managed by Carlisle old boy Allan Ashman. "I groaned when I heard the draw but I really fancied us to get to Wembley. In the other semi-final were Manchester United and Manchester City. I had wanted City as I knew they were definitely beatable, then I hoped to face West Bromwich Albion in the final. I would have taken real satisfaction from beating an ex-Carlisle manager in a Wembley final.

"As it was, Allan knew a lot about Carlisle, he knew the undoubted spirit the club possessed, he knew many of the players. West Bromwich Albion was not the draw I had wanted at this stage. I used the Ashman link to get into the players psyches. Some of them held the man in much awe. Never being one to stand on ceremony, I rubbished him and his current team. A few of the players understood why I did this, others couldn't and one actually came up to me afterwards and asked why I had said all the derogatory things about Allan. That was typical of the type of personality in a player that Allan liked, and when I told the lad that Ashman would be rubbishing me and our players, he was disbelieving and seemed quite surprised. I left the dressing-room inspiration to a couple of the other more seasoned players.

"The game at Carlisle should have seen us capitalise on the majority of possession we had. My players were all over the Albion lads like a rash. We closed them down, gave no space or room for manoeuvre and played them off the park. Unfortunately we had just one goal to show for our efforts. As we headed down the players' tunnel I heard a few harsh words spoken by Allan Ashman to a couple of our players and thought to myself: 'Ouch, I bet that's hurt them.'

"The mood in the dressing room wasn't one of elation. Although we had won the first leg, it was certain that Albion would pressurise us for the full 90 minutes at the Hawthorns. I told the team I was proud of them, and this was greeted by a united cry of 'Cheers, boss.' I remember a couple of them saying that Ashman was something of a twat for what he had said and how he had behaved towards them. Apparently he had referred to some of them as second-class crap. The tide had turned and I could feel the determination in the players' hearts to go out to prove him wrong.

"In the second leg, for the first 45 minutes we looked capable of holding Albion off and winning the tie. The players had responded positively to the comments of Ashman. I almost leaped out of the stadium when a Bob Hatton header beat John Osborne in the Albion goal, but unfortunately the ball struck the inside of a post, rolled along the goal-line and was eventually cleared to safety. I firmly believe that if that ball had gone into the Albion net, we would have gone on to win the game and taken our place at Wembley. At half-time we were level on the night, effectively 45 minutes from an appearance in the League Cup final.

"As it was, Ashman swapped about his line-up for the second half. He introduced a wiry winger to the game, Dennis Martin. That bastard tore at us like a terrier down a rabbit hole. Single-handedly he ended our challenge as my tired players, who had given their absolute all, had no answer to his pace and skill. We capitulated and lost the game 4-1 and the tie 4-2 on aggregate. It really hurt. In the dressing room afterwards there wasn't a dry eye to be seen. Dick Young was really upset. He, more than anyone, deserved success that night. As it was, the fitter (not the better) team won through.

"Later in the dressing room Allan Ashman entered, his hand outstretched to me. 'Sorry Bob, better luck next year' he said patronisingly. Tommy Passmoor was nearby and quietly but firmly told him to 'piss off'. Allan didn't quite know how to respond. A few players shook his hand, but the majority were too upset to care about what Allan Ashman thought or felt. I honestly believe Allan himself was sad to beat us. He was a shrewd man and tended to make sly little comments in order to provoke a response from his players, whereas I would tell them straight. I was pleased for him that Albion went on to win the competition. They beat Manchester City in the final and Allan sent Wembley tickets for the players and staff at the club, a genuine touch and show of emotion."

In the FA Cup, United again showed their resilience and ability to challenge with the best teams in the country. In the third round, First Division Nottingham Forest were held to a 0-0 draw at the City Ground, before being beaten at Brunton Park 2-1. In the fourth round Aldershot surprised the Cumbrians, fighting out a 2-2 draw before losing 4-1 on their own soil in front of a Recreation Ground record attendance of 19,138. In the fifth round, fate again conjured up a Brunton Park return for a former Carlisle man. This time ex-player Hugh McIlmoyle and Middlesbrough were the opponents. A packed Brunton Park, equalling the record attendance figure of 27,500, set in 1957, cheered the team on.

"The Middlesbrough tie was great stuff. Our directors were really enjoying every minute of it, what with a record attendance and record gate receipts for them to pore over. I knew where the 'Boro threat was likely to come from. Obviously the Hugh McIlmoyle link had filled column inches in most northern newspapers, but I knew there were other threats in that team. John Hickton and Derek Downing had that killer instinct about them, too. Stan Anderson, the 'Boro boss, was a man I knew well. He had a way of getting the most out of his players and I was certain he wouldn't allow his team to underestimate Carlisle. The noise the supporters made that day was incredible. I can't remember a noisier crowd in all my time at the club.

"We won a corner and 'Tot' Winstanley (so called because of his aerial ability and his giant-like appearance) fired in a header and the whole place erupted. I tried to get the message out to the players to stay calm and focused. Dick Young had just said to me that if we could hold on for the next 20 minutes then we would win through to the next round, when Hugh McIlmoyle collected the ball. We backed off and off as he moved into our penalty area. I remember thinking how quiet the ground had suddenly gone as Hugh drifted left of the goal, forced wide by Terry Caldwell. The next moment he flicked a pass across to big John Hickton, who miskicked and the ball seemed to be bouncing aimlessly towards our defender Joe Davis on the goal line. The entire ground was willing the usually reliable Joe to hoof it out of the stadium, but he seemed strangely aloof to everything going on around him. I saw him do this strange jig with his feet and yelled out: 'For Christ's sake, clear the fucking thing, Joe!' Then the ball bobbled a bit and rolled straight between his legs into the net. The very thing we didn't want.

"Joe's panic attack caused our defence to become jittery and suddenly we couldn't find our own men with a pass. In the middle of the park 'Boro were running us ragged. I wasn't alone in feeling it all slip away that afternoon, some 27,000 other Carlisle supporters felt the same. It was Hughie McIlmoyle who was causing many of the problems. We were giving him too much space and treating him with far too much respect. In another flash of brilliance, McIlmoyle turned our defence again, flung a cross beyond our defence and Downing headed in at the back post. Disappointed but defiant, I praised each and every one of our players, and the fans clapped them off the field. They gave Hugh McIlmoyle a really good reception, too. That was great of them and I don't know many supporters who have shown such a dignified attitude in defeat, especially towards one of their ex-players who had essentially inflicted the damage against their team.

"If I thought I was disappointed then you should have seen Dick Young. He really took the defeat badly and the team seemed to sense they had personally let him down. It was no bad thing as it showed the respect they held for the trainer. Afterwards I had a quick chat with Hugh McIlmoyle. He was typically professional; he didn't gloat, nor did he appear happy at the result. Seconds later, I bumped into some of the directors. They were pleased as punch with the day's takings. A few of them were clearly upset by the result and our failure to get into the sixth round. I reminded them that the difference between the two teams was Hugh McIlmoyle, the very player they had sold against my will. It didn't go down too well, but the buggers deserved to know that in my opinion they had made the wrong decision. Not that they cared, mind you, some of them were too wrapped in themselves to worry about my opinions."

The remainder of the 1969/70 season petered out as mid-table obscurity was secured. In the summer, Stokoe provided the chairman with his shopping list of players he wanted to sign, and top of that list was the West Bromwich Albion flying winger, Dennis Martin. The directors extensively subsidised the transfer activity, with Martin arriving for a fee of £20,000. Manchester City striker Bobby Owen was also recruited, at a cost of £25,000, while John Gorman joined from Glasgow Celtic and Mike Sutton from Norwich City. To balance the books somewhat, out went local lad George McVitie, sold to

en Juniors in 1945/46; A youthful Bob Stokoe is seated on left of the picture, middle row.

A Cup holders Newcastle United line up before facing Real Madrid at the Bernabeu Stadium in
e early 1950s. Bob is back row, left.

R. Stokoe – cigarette card.

On tour in South Africa, standing outside a very large aeroplane.

In action for Newcastle United in front of a packed St James' Park.

colossus in Newcastle's colours.

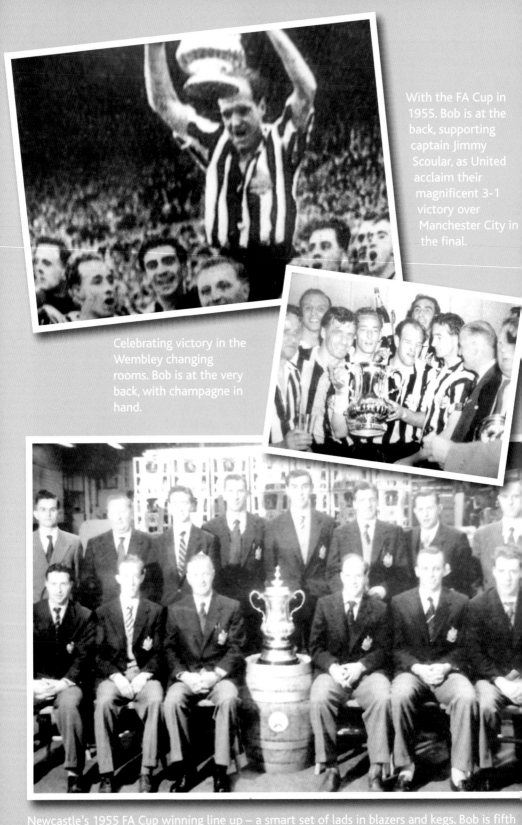

With the FA Cup in 1955. Bob is at the back, supporting captain Jimmy Scoular, as United acclaim their magnificent 3-1 victory over Manchester City in the final.

Celebrating victory in the Wembley changing rooms. Bob is at the very back, with champagne in hand.

Newcastle's 1955 FA Cup winning line up – a smart set of lads in blazers and kegs. Bob is fifth left, behind the Cup, with Jackie Milburn to his right. This was the club's third FA Cup victory in five years, 1951, 1952 and 1955.

rare colour photograph of Newcastle
aining in the gym. Bob is back row,
entre.

orthern and proud, leading Newcastle
nited out as their captain.

After leaving Newcastle, Bob had a short
spell at Hartlepool United before joining Bury
as player/manager. He stayed at Gigg Lane
from 1961 to 1965.

Moving down south, to manage Charlton — note the guy behind painting the crush barriers on the vast East Terrace at the old Valley.

Happy at Rochdale, where he was manager in 1967/68, and returned a decade later.

Carlisle training in 1969 — Bob is at the back with his coat and flat cap on.

concerned-looking Bob at Carlisle.

Anyone for golf?

he 1970 Carlisle line-up, without a badge on their shirts.

To the author, a signed picture of Bob Stokoe, circa 1970.

Happy at Blackpool after taking the job in December 1970, but relegation from Division One followed at the end of the season.

Training players at Blackpool to laugh.

Second Division Blackpool's Anglo-Italian Cup final line-up prior to the 2-1 extra-time victory over *Serie A* Bologna in 1971. Bob was extremely proud with this achievement, which upset all the odds and silenced the packed 40,000 crowd in the Stadio Comunale Renato Dall'Ara.

Bob's jig of delight at the final whistle in Italy was followed by skipper John Craven lifting the trophy.

Alan Suddick joined forces with Stokoe at Blackpool and produced a match-winning display against Bologna.

Sunderland in 1973.

Billy Hughes and Mick Horswill celebrate a goal in the 1973 FA Cup semi-final win over Arsenal.

The FA Cup Final in 1973 when Sunderland defeated the much-fancied Leeds United in one of the greatest FA Cup final upsets in history.

Jim Montgomery with the FA Cup. The
goalkeeper's double save in the final is one
of the most repeated Cup final moments
of all time.

Taking the Cup
home to an ecstatic Sunderland
in May 1973.

Showing off the Second Division trophy in 1975/76 with captain Tony Towers.

Newspaper coverage of FA Cup glory.

THEY'VE DONE IT!

Echo SUNDERLAND

SPORTS EDITION

MATCH PICTURES: PAGES 8 & 9

SATURDAY, MAY 5, 1973

CUP FINAL SPECIAL

orterfield the ero in glorious Wembley victory

SUNDERLAND 1 LEEDS UNITED 0

Binns

An Estée Lauder gift for you
Light and Lovely Colour Kit
When you buy any Estée Lauder purchases of two products or more

Blackpool and Carlisle legends, Stanley Matthews, left and Bill Shankly, right.

Back at Carlisle in 1984. Bob would return as manager to Brunton Park on three separate occasions.

Press coverage of Carlisle's successful 1983/84 season in which they finished 7th in Division Two, flirting with promotion.

Carlisle's squad in 1984/85.

CARLISLE UNITED

CLUB SPOTLIGHT

BOB Stokoe's Carlisle have come a long way since narrowly avoiding relegation last season.

Indeed, he is keeping a few bottles of champagne on ice to celebrate the Northern club's promotion to the Second Division next month.

Stokoe, who has managed six clubs, some of them twice since running his first club, Bury, in 1961, has every confidence that Carlisle will be in there at the kill to revive memories of their First Division glory days in the mid 70's.

They are bounding towards promotion on the strength of two shrewd signings by Carlisle's ambitious manager, namely Bob Lee, from Bristol Rovers and Bryan Robson, whom Stokoe drafted in from Sunderland towards the end of last season.

They had scored 22 goals between them by the middle of last month, and Gordon Staniforth and Paul Bannon offered valuable support with almost as many crucial goals.

Bob Stokoe is confident that Carlisle can go up despite hiccups in February and March when they lost momentum and sacrificed goal advantage in several games.

Fortunately, the Third Division is such a lottery that on the night second in the table Carlisle drew with strugglers Doncaster, leaders Fulham, were losing 3-1 to Plymouth.

Bob Stokoe is happy enough with the progress made this season. He says: "They're a decent bunch of lads, hard working and honest.

"The three points for a win system has encouraged us to play attacking football home and away. It's been a success as far as I'm concerned."

Stokoe still yearns for a Dennis Tueart, who used to snap-up half-chances to Stokoe's delight when he managed Sunderland, but he is realistic enough to appreciate that players in lower Divisions often compensate for a lack of outstanding talent with other worthwhile assets.

Peter Beardsley's (right) five goals boosted Carlisle before his transfer to Vancouver Whitecaps last month.

Money is so tight at Carlisle that Stokoe fears the future. If they win promotion, can they survive in the Second Division?

"Our average gate is 4,000 — and we're doing well," Stokoe points out. "We need more support and I'm hoping that our efforts to attract families to Brunton Park will succeed."

The future "frightens" Stokoe, who reckons it is only a matter of time before the Third Division is regionalised, part-time football is introduced, and a wage structure is worked out for players that is within the scope of the majority of clubs.

He is confident that he is doing as much as any manager to cope with the present situation which threatens the future of so many clubs.

"You often have to sell to survive. I don't want to, but that's the only way.

"We'll take our chances if we get promotion. I'm worried about football's future — but we're happy at Carlisle with the pro-

BACK ROW (left to right): Gary Watson, Bob Parker, Paul Haigh, Andy Collins, Tony Larkin, John Crabbe.
MIDDLE ROW: Dick Young (coach), Keith Houghton, Paul Bannon, Trevor Swinburne, John Pickering (now asst. manager at Lincoln), Tony Harrison, Bob Lee, Jack Ashurst, Herbert Nicholson (physio).
FRONT ROW: Mike Coady, Russell Coughlin, Bryan Robson (asst. manager), Bob Stokoe (manager), Gordon Staniforth, Alan Campbell, Jim Hamilton.
SEATED: Hugh McGrogan, Cliff Thompson (contract expired).

The last ever goal scored for Carlisle under Bob's management – Ian Bishop, right, netting against Oldham in 1986. Carlisle were relegated to Division Three that season.

With new signing, goalkeeper Barry Siddall, at Sunderland, when Bob returned as temporary manager in 1986/87.

Sad headlines, newspaper coverage 2004 in Sunderland, reporting Bob's death.

Sunder[land]

MONDAY, FEBRUARY 2, 2004

Call to build a statue ... outside Stadium of Light

MEMORIAL TO A LEGEND

By GRAEME ANDERSON

SUNDERLAND AFC was today urged to build a lasting memorial to 1973 FA Cup legend Bob Stokoe outside the Stadium of Light.

The manager, dubbed The Messiah by a generation of Sunderland football fans, died yesterday, sparking hundreds of tributes from fans and former players whose lives he touched.

And goalscoring hero Gary Rowell said it was only right that the club now look at building an appropriate monument to the man who earned an undying place in Wearside folklore.

Rowell said: "He was probably the most iconic and important figure in the club's history since the end of the Second World War.

"People remember heroes like Len Shackleton and Charlie Hurley and rightly so, but Bob was different – they offered the club promise, but Bob actually delivered – he brought home the FA Cup.

"And I think it's vitally important that the club honours his memory and gives the fans some recognition of him in the stadium.

"To me the perfect way of remembering Bob would be by building a permanent statue of him outside the ground."

A FAN'S TRIBUTE: The first Sunderland supporter to arrive with flowers at the stadium was Keith Park, 58, from Horden.

Comment

TODAY Wearside is in mourning for one of its favourite sons.

It was the Sunderland team that Bob shaped, led and inspired which defied the odds and won the FA Cup in 1973.

Bob's dash across the Wembley turf to hug goalkeeper Jim Montgomery is now part of FA Cup folklore.

It was Monty's brilliant double save from Peter Lorimer and Trevor Cherry – the greatest save seen at Wembley – that ensured the 1-0 triumph.

But behind the individual performances from Monty, Ian Porterfield, Bobby Kerr and the others was the inspiration of Bob Stokoe.

He had inherited a team flirting with relegation to the old Division Three. Not only did he win the cup in 1973, Bob propelled the team to sixth place in Division Two.

The cup win in 1973 put the team and the town on the map. The game is still talked about as one of the greatest-ever cup finals, and the match played a massive role in bonding the club and its supporters.

Stokoe's contribution to SAFC was immense.

We believe the club and the city should recognise this. We would like to see a fitting permanent memorial – possibly a statue – to recognise his huge role in the history of the club and Sunderland.

● Tributes to 'The Messiah' – Pages 18, 19 and 20

Junk food die[t] that's making our kids sick

– Pages [1] and 23

SAVE A FORTUN[E] ON A NEARLY NEW C[AR] at Reg Vardy

YOU SAVE £1471 £9[..]

£6999

16.1

REG VAR[DY]

Bob Stokoe was able to transcend the traditional north-east rivalry between the region's footballing giants, Newcastle United and Sunderland, and will forever have a place in their hearts. A statue of him stands outside Sunderland's Stadium of Light, seen below with former Sunderland chairman Bob Murray.

Oldham Athletic for £30,000, and both Tommy Passmoor and Maurice Peddelty moved on.

"The new season didn't start too well and we didn't win any of our opening three games. The new players were still settling in, and I knew that would take time. I am a great believer that you should be judged over an entire season, not just a few opening results. The chairman wasn't at all pleased with our early form and told me in no uncertain terms that things had to improve after the money the club had spent. We were blighted by inconsistency, yet in the League Cup we again showed our potential, knocking out Manchester City 2-1 at Carlisle and then Oxford 3-1, before Aston Villa ended our interest, 1-0 at Villa Park."

By October the team had crept up to sixth in the table and were never to fall below eighth for the rest of the season. The football flowed as the team again began to display real momentum and they looked like potential promotion candidates. However, Bob Stokoe was not to witness the side he had built finish the season in style because that winter brought yet another twist in his football career.

"The first I knew was on the first day of December, when I was told by the Carlisle chairman that Blackpool had asked to speak with me about taking over as their manager. I told him to tell Blackpool I wasn't at all interested, as I wanted to finish the job I had started and take Carlisle up to the First Division. A few days later I got a phone call from Dickenson, the chairman of Blackpool. He was offering me a salary of almost £2,000 a year more than I was getting at Carlisle, plus there was the promise of a substantial transfer kitty. In addition to all of this, Blackpool were already in the First Division. Only just, mind you – they were second from bottom and had amassed just eight points coming up to the halfway mark of the season.

"I told Blackpool to leave it as it was too political and I owed it to myself to succeed with Carlisle. Would they accept that? Not a chance. There followed lots of additions to the basic contract, including win and success bonuses. By success, they meant there was a one-off payment of £1,000 guaranteed if I steered them away from the relegation zone that season. That was never going to happen; even Harry Houdini couldn't have escaped from the situation Blackpool had got themselves into.

"Reluctantly, and with a heavy heart, I asked the Carlisle board what their ambitions were for the football club. My question met with a stony silence and I was reminded that I had already spent £55,000 on transfers that season. I pointed out that I had brought in somewhere in the region of £40,000 from player sales, added to which the previous season we had enjoyed financially rewarding cup runs with additional merchandise sales. Looking back now, it was a petulant disagreement sparked by my attitude at the time. I told the board of directors that I wanted to speak with Blackpool and was told to 'fuck off and do so.' So I did and agreed terms with them on 20 December. My salary was to be a healthy £7,000 per annum. Carlisle couldn't, and wouldn't, even try to match that figure, I knew that.

"Yet when I again approached the board outlining the Blackpool offer and asking to be released from contractual obligations, I was told in no uncertain terms by the chairman: 'Mr Stokoe, you are going nowhere. Now stop this ridiculous attention-seeking and get back to work.' You could imagine how I reacted – badly. There was an immense amount of door-slamming, swearing and wild accusations and threats from all sides. I walked out of the club, talked through what had happened with my wife, Jean, and decided to let the dust settle for a few days before resuming talks with them.

"The next day the whole story was in the public domain, printed in newspapers. I wasn't at all pleased. The leak could only have come from someone at Carlisle who had known of the differences. The directors all denied making any contact with the press. It was damn frustrating, I felt trapped with no way of escape. My relationship with the directors was worsening and falling further apart every minute I remained at the club. Finally I talked to one of the more sensible directors, Andrew Jenkins, and asked his advice. I told him that the club should release me as all of this would affect the players and team performances. He agreed with me and told me that in his opinion I was making a mistake."

The entire matter was dragged through the pages of the national newspapers, with Stokoe at one point stating: "I am bitter and resentful to put it mildly. I am being very shabbily treated – like a little schoolboy – over my request to leave the club." The matter deteriorated when he learned that Carlisle directors had asked for a transfer fee of £8,500 from Blackpool. The Seasiders' board felt that this was excessive, to say the least. "It just shows how far removed the directors were from reality and understanding transfer business. In the end I negotiated a good and fair transfer fee of £5,000 for my services that was acceptable to all parties. I even lined up my replacement, and told Carlisle to go out and offer the manager's job to Ian MacFarlane. It was a sad end to my time at Brunton Park, although before I left on 28 December 1970, I made peace with the directors and the club, apologising for the less than professional manner in which it had all transpired."

Blackpool FC had dangled the carrot and Stokoe took the bait hook, line and sinker. There is very little football clubs can do to prevent approaches like the one Bob Stokoe received during that Christmas period. Money talks and, for Bob Stokoe, the opportunity to manage in the First Division and to be able to command a decent living represented too much to refuse. While some may criticise him for his sudden lack of loyalty to Carlisle, it is fair to say that he felt Blackpool could match his own ambitions. Who would resist such an opportunity in their own professional lives?

"I remember the late Bill Shankly telling me something quite prophetic once. He said: 'Bobby, remember this always. You work to live, not live to work. Don't put yourself in an early grave because of your job. This managing lark is just a job at the end of the day. You are hired and fired on some director's personal whim.'"

So it was that Bob left Carlisle for a life beside the seaside. He had got his wish, that of managing a First Division football team. There is an age-old saying that goes along the lines of: "You should be careful of what you wish for." In this instance, Bob Stokoe was jumping out of the frying pan and into the fire.

8 Oh, I do like to be beside the seaside

I think many of us can recall childhood memories of trips or holidays at the seaside. Bob Stokoe was no different. He enjoyed nothing more than a walk along a sea-front, the brisk sea air filling his lungs. As a child he had spent the occasional family holiday at Whitley Bay on the north east coast. "Blackpool," he recalled "is a place renowned for family entertainment – three piers, the Golden Mile, the Tower, a circus and a zoo. Away from all that it is a nice place with a lot of football-related history, Stanley Matthews and FA Cup finals. In my playing days Blackpool were a decent side; not as good as Newcastle, but a fair side nonetheless. Having the chance of managing them and returning them to former glories was not something to be sneezed at."

All those thoughts and plenty more passed through Bob Stokoe's mind when he finally elected to leave Carlisle and join Blackpool. "The funny thing about the Blackpool move was that when Blackpool originally approached me, I didn't want to come. This was before the 1970 approach, in fact it was before Les Shannon became Blackpool's manager. I had just moved to Carlisle, and at that stage I had no intention of leaving them. I'd done a fair bit of moving around over the previous ten years or so and wanted to set down some roots.

"Eventually, at the end of December 1970, I took over from Jimmy Meadows, who had been caretaker manager since October after Len Shannon had offered to leave the club, an offer the directors didn't at all refuse." Actually Shannon had departed a few days after a woeful performance and another defeat, this time 4-3 at Bloomfield Road by Chelsea. It was to be the start of a seven-game run of consecutive defeats that all but sealed Blackpool's fate for the rest of the season. "The club was in one hell of a state when I first went in. The players had a really shitty attitude. Most were past it and simply going through the motions on a match day, checking their pay slips with a great deal more care than they displayed for being ambassadors for Blackpool Football Club.

"I'll be honest and say that when I first joined Blackpool I couldn't trust anyone. They all seemed to be from the same mould – losers and more concerned about how much money they could eke out of the club than anything else. Within that first week I would remember the wise words of Carlisle director Andrew Jenkins coming back to haunt me, telling me that I was making a huge mistake by leaving Carlisle for Blackpool. He was right, too, it was a mess. No other word for it, a mess.

"I met with players and had a briefing in which I told them that as far as I was concerned they all had a future at the club. However, if they wanted it that way then they had to prove it to me as individual players working within a team ethic. I knew full well that Blackpool had some players who, to be frank, needed kicking out of the club. Fred Pickering and Harry Thomson, for instance, had been suspended by the club. Alan Suddick, a decent enough player, was turning out for the reserves and was apparently quite happy to do so, as long as he got paid. I told all the players, Harry and Fred included, that what had happened before had no relevance as far as I was concerned. At that point I hadn't even bothered to find out what they were suspended for. I told all the playing staff that I would treat them like everyone else, unless they give me cause to do otherwise. Little did they know of my high standards and how tough a disciplinarian I actually could be."

Shortly after the initial meeting with the players Stokoe broke the habit of a lifetime and agreed to meet with the press to answer their questions. "I had decided that I should make a statement to the press to get them off my back. They were being divisive and splitting the club with some of their less well thought out tales concerning my cleansing the club of players I regarded as a waste of space. They were correct in that assumption, yet it was my prerogative to make such a statement and not theirs to put words in my mouth. I knew I had to stay positive and send out the right message to the clubs' supporters. I couldn't tell the truth and tell them I had inherited a pile of crap, and that we needed at least half a dozen new players. They already knew that, but I wasn't going to be the one to confirm it, not yet anyway. Instead I came out with a statement that said nothing yet everything. It read: 'I think we realise we are not going to break any pots this season in the League but we must aim to stay up and then we can start planning further for the future.'

"So came my baptism of fire, my first game in charge of Blackpool, an FA Cup third-round tie against West Ham United at Bloomfield Road. Somehow the team had gone undefeated in three matches, having beaten Coventry City and drawn with West Bromwich Albion and Burnley. I didn't really know what to expect from the team, but to make matters worse, the BBC *Match of the Day* cameras had been attracted to the game as it was one of the few all-First Division ties being played. Added to this, West Ham under Ron Greenwood had earned a reputation for playing entertaining football. It was good seeing Ron again. The last time we had held a serious conversation had been when I was at Charlton Athletic and I had sold him Billy Bonds, who was playing that day. West Ham could offer several big-name players, the likes of Bobby Moore, Jimmy Greaves and Bobby

Ferguson, and I was worried that we wouldn't do ourselves justice. In my team talk before the game I told the players to do the easy thing, play the simple ball and to keep at West Ham from the kick-off."

Orchestrated in virtuoso fashion by midfielder Tony Green, Blackpool put in their best performance of the season. Green's first goal came from nothing; picking up a loose ball in the centre circle, he moved forward, weaving and bobbing his way through a hesitant defence and into the West Ham penalty area before coolly slotting the ball past Ferguson in the Hammers' goal.

"I couldn't believe what I was witnessing, Tony Green was having an incredible game. His thirst and desire to win the ball and distribute sensibly and well excited me." The midfield dynamo didn't just contribute to the game with that one goal, there was more and even better to come from him. After some gritty play from John Craven and Mickey Burns, who were pushing West Ham back deep into their own half and controlling the centre of the pitch, a soft clearance by the Hammers' rearguard fell to Green at the edge of the box. Skilfully, he brought the ball down, dropped his shoulder to avoid a dangerous looking challenge and fired a powerful shot into the top corner of the West Ham net from 20 yards. Bloomfield Road went wild. Few people, and not even the manager, had anticipated such a positive performance. Green turned provider when he released Craven into space and allowed him the opportunity to force home the third goal for the home side. Finally, the rout was complete when full-back Henry Mowbray fired in to make it 4-0 to Blackpool.

"What can you say or do when your players put in a performance like that? Ron Greenwood said afterwards that if the players had given that sort of effort all season they would be riding high among the top-of-the-table teams instead of being relegation certainties. I agreed and couldn't quite understand the Jekyll-and-Hyde character the team possessed, especially as in the next round of the FA Cup we travelled to Hull, where were well beaten 2-0 and outplayed for the entire game. I struggled to get my head round what motivated the team.

"John Craven and Tony Green had proved themselves to be the club's best two players, yet others should have been leading the way. I had few options open to me so I struggled on with the squad for the remainder of the campaign. In the League there was some personal satisfaction for me, in that we held Don Revie's Leeds United to a 1-1 draw at Bloomfield Road. The result meant little at the time; however, in the bigger scheme of things it ensured that the point Leeds had dropped against Blackpool effectively cost them the title, as they lost out by just one point to Arsenal.

"At the Leeds game Don Revie had been at his usual self-righteous, condescending best, talking to the press pack before and after the game, demeaning Blackpool as a struggling club who had raised their game solely because they were facing Leeds United, the team everyone wanted to beat. I wanted to go up to him to tell him that Leeds weren't that important; that the only thing other teams were desperate to avoid when playing Leeds was getting seriously injured, courtesy of the Leeds players' ultra-competitive enthusiasm that involved getting the ball off the opposition by any means. It was a great shame because Leeds had so many talented footballers who, under a different, more confident and positive manager, would have developed into even better players than they already were. As was usual, Revie avoided me before, during and after game. When I did speak to him it was only to remind him that he was a cheat. Sensibly, he chose to ignore my comments, realising that they were deliberately inflammatory. He had crossed me once, and that was sufficient for me.

"Sadly, we won just one more game all season, the penultimate game of the campaign, beating Crystal Palace 2-1. We did go out on something of a high, holding Manchester United to a 1-1 draw in Blackpool, but it was too little, too late. We finished bottom of the pile and were relegated back to Division Two, where I would face Carlisle United and Charlton Athletic."

Now Stokoe got down to wheeling and dealing in the transfer market. The opportunity to rebuild his team was grasped with both hands and out went the likes of Pickering, Thomson, Blacklaw and Rowe, and in came experienced professionals such as John Burridge. The Anglo-Italian Cup competition was part of the pre-season agenda, although Blackpool's first game in the tournament took place towards the end of May, when Verona arrived at Bloomfield Road.

"I enjoy the challenge of overseas football and the Anglo-Italian tournament was great for everyone. It gave clubs like Blackpool the chance to pit their wits against some of the top sides in Europe. In our first game we drew 3-3 with Verona, and in the next game we lost 3-1 to a very good AS Roma side. We then beat Verona 4-1 in Italy and managed to beat Roma 2-1 three days later. The two wins put us into the final against Bologna in Italy.

"It was marvellous. The weather was hot and we had a good few supporters out here with us. I didn't put any pressure on the players to win the competition but told them that if we didn't win it then they would be walking back to Blackpool! Goals from Mickey Burns and John Craven won the game 2-1 after extra time. Success at last, and my first ever trophy as a professional manager. It was European, which made it all the more sweet. I wouldn't have swapped the moment for anything. It was a good achievement and gave everyone at the club the right sort of lift for the coming season."

Blackpool's 1971/72 campaign got off to a flying start with four victories from the opening five games, putting the Seasiders top of the Second Division table, but there followed much inconsistent form that at one stage saw them drop to 19th in the table. Suddenly the critics emerged from the woodwork and began to openly question the manager's ability.

"I always knew that the Blackpool fans could and would turn on not only the manager if things were going badly, but also the players and anyone connected to the football club. Despite everything else that was going on, the team were getting back to winning ways. The turning point for me came in the October when I sold Tony Green to Newcastle United in a deal worth £140,000, getting Keith Dyson to join us at Bloomfield Road as part of the same negotiation. It was excellent business for all concerned, but the fans didn't think so, and nor did Green, who I don't think really wanted to move. As a result of that piece of business I had lard daubed over my car windows in the main car park. Also I was accused of being biased towards Newcastle and of trying to provide them with the best footballers I could lay my hands on. It was absolute rubbish. In Keith Dyson Blackpool got a first-rate footballer with a positive attitude and a desire to achieve."

Certainly Green's subsequent comments about the transfer didn't help Bob Stokoe's argument that he did what was best for the club and the player. Green said: "Leeds were also after me at the time, but the Blackpool manager, Bob Stokoe, wasn't a big fan of Don Revie at Leeds and wanted me to go to Newcastle. In those days, players didn't get any say in transfers, and when Newcastle were the first club to come in with the money, Bob Stokoe was happy to let the deal go ahead."

The Blackpool directors had cause to speak with the manager over his activities away from the football club. A national newspaper had paid Stokoe £15,000 to speak out against corruption in the game. Naturally Bob revealed the intricacies of his issues with Leeds boss Don Revie, whose integrity suffered greatly in the article as other football people also spoke out against him. Blackpool, for their sins, believed all this extra-curricular interest was damaging the reputation of the football club. Stokoe accepted the warning and refrained from further involvement in the matter.

"I have always been asked why, so long after the event, did I sell my story to the national newspapers. The fact is that I didn't go running to them. They approached me and made me an offer so I told them the truth. I wanted to get it off my chest as it had weighed a considerable burden on me for many years, and it greatly concerned me that people like him (and there were others, I am told) could do such things and get away with them. I couldn't believe it when, not long after the revelations, he was put in charge of the England team. What hope was there for our national footballing pride when Don Revie got the job as leader? I could name several more qualified managers who would have been better choices to lead the national side to glory.

"It did make me laugh later when he took off to take that job with the United Arab Emirates. He adopted the role of victim, saying that he felt the whole nation wanted him out of the England job so he pre-empted the sack by resigning to take up this other job. I think that sort of justified my notion as to what type of football man he actually was.

"From a personal perspective that League season had given me much satisfaction. We had beaten my previous employers, Carlisle, at Bloomfield Road, though later in the season it was Carlisle who ended our run of six straight victories as we lost by the same 2-0 scoreline at Brunton Park. Charlton Athletic were put to the sword twice, as we won 3-2 at the Valley, then trounced them 5-0 at Blackpool. I thoroughly enjoyed those Charlton games and made a point of celebrating and showing my utter elation in front of their directors. Quite crudely I received a two-fingered salute from their direction each time I celebrated a goal. No sense of humour, these southern football people!

"There was also a point when I believed we were embarking on a run in the League Cup to match the one I achieved at Carlisle. After getting through to the fifth round, beating Bournemouth, Colchester and Aston Villa on the way, we lost out to Tottenham Hotspur. It did, though, give the fans something to be cheerful about. In the end we finished sixth in the Second Division table, quite respectable I thought, but not so the directors who again told me that if things didn't improve next season then people would be scrutinising my situation at the club very closely. There is nothing like receiving messages of support and loyalty from your employers."

As holders of the Anglo-Italian Cup, Blackpool were automatically entered for the 1972 competition. They were part of a group that included Sampdoria and what is best termed a village team, Lanerossi Vicenza. After two victories away from home over both Italian sides, the home ties would be crucial to Blackpool's chances of progressing. Elsewhere in the competition, Carlisle United were pulling off some stunning results in the toughest group of all, winning twice in Italy and holding Roma to a 3-3 draw at Carlisle. The English club with the best record would go through to the final, and it looked set to go down to goal difference between the two northern clubs. In typical form, Stokoe marshalled his troops and gave them instructions to devastate the Italian opposition, which he considered capable of leaking goals.

"I almost lost count of how many goals we scored; it was a complete mismatch. John Burridge, our goalkeeper, never touched the ball or had a save to make. It's never easy to win a game 10-0, but we did it, therefore negating whatever Carlisle did. We were through to the final fair and square."

The final was a different proposition altogether. Roma were the Italian group winners and they had lost just once, 3-2 to Carlisle in Rome. They were still smarting from that result and took it out on Blackpool in the final. "We were never at the races in that game. Roma looked a different class from when we played them the previous year.

The noise their fans made was deafening, horns and flares were going off all over the place, and there were riot police behind the goals. I'm not blaming the side issues for our defeat, but it didn't help our game one little bit."

Following the competition, it was back to transfer business for the manager. In came players such as Billy Rafferty, Frank Barton, Tommy Hutchison, Dave Lennard, Chris Simpkin and goalkeeper George Wood. It was an altogether new-look Blackpool team that was to seek promotion back to the First Division in 1972/73.

"I had added some real quality to the team. George Wood was as solid a goalkeeper as there was and he marshalled his defence confidently. Up front Billy Rafferty could head a ball farther than many players could kick it. The lad could score goals and was the perfect partner for Keith Dyson and Alan Ainscow. I was quietly confident that we would achieve promotion that season. Few of the other teams looked to have the consistency and strength in depth we could offer."

Apart from a disappointing opening day defeat at Huddersfield, Blackpool made a promising start. In the first home game of the season Brighton and Hove Albion were thrashed 6-2 at Bloomfield Road, then came an away win at Cardiff City. The team fluctuated in the top half of the table, but spent most if its time among the top five sides challenging for pole position. By November, and after a 2-1 victory at Boothferry Park over Hull City, Blackpool climbed into third place in the table. The team had gelled and was clearly making good progress. Then came the news that no Blackpool supporter expected or wanted. Stokoe had agreed terms to join Sunderland as manager.

"When the Sunderland job was offered to me I didn't think twice about accepting it. It was a massive club which had encountered some woeful fortunes in recent times. Furthermore, it was back in the land of the north east, God's country. I was very nearly going home."

The move had been as swift as it had been surprising. The two clubs had allegedly been communicating for a number of days, involving the manager only at the very last moment. The Blackpool board were magnanimous in their praise of what Bob Stokoe had achieved and wished him well, banking the compensation cheque that came from Sunderland. Interestingly, Blackpool asked for more than they had been prepared to offer Carlisle in compensation. They got it, too.

Blackpool fans were enraged that Stokoe would walk away from them to a club that was clearly in trouble near the bottom of the Second Division. Few complained too loudly, though. No doubt many believed that Stokoe had achieved all he could with the team and they wanted a new manager in place as soon as possible. Sunderland fans, meanwhile, were up in arms. Here they were employing an out-and-out Geordie to lead them to salvation. Not only was he an ex-Magpie, but he had never managed a big club before, so immediately questions were asked about his ability.

"I knew the Sunderland fans wouldn't take kindly to a Geordie coming to manage them, especially one who had a history of problems with Sunderland as a player. Supporters have long memories and all sorts of things were being said about me. Some talked about over-the-top tackles I was supposed to have committed on Sunderland players while at Newcastle, others reckoned that I had only taken the job on to make sure they would be relegated. It was all absolute bullshit, but I had only two options available to me – sink or swim.

"I wasn't really sad to be leaving Blackpool. Previously, other than at Charlton, I had felt some sadness when I had moved on to different clubs. But the whole Bloomfield Road experience had affected me. I had become more cynical about directors and club owners. I also saw a side of players that I didn't at all like. I'm talking about avarice and bone idleness. You tend to think that most people will treat you as you treat them, but that was not the case at Blackpool. Certainly, the team I left behind was light years different from the one I inherited, and was full of honest footballers keen to do well for Blackpool. I wished all of those players well. As for the directors, well some of them never talked to me, others treated me like some kind of skivvy, while still others treated me as an equal. There were few who wished me well.

"However, I think the supporters, overall, know I did my best for the club. I have always got on well with supporters wherever I have managed. Supporters tend to be football people, they are much more learned than the people that run clubs and the game itself. At that level it becomes more of an old boys' club and network. In some cases they are so far removed from reality that it is quite disturbing. I didn't ever pretend to have any kind of allegiance to the governance side of things. I managed football teams using every ounce of energy and skill that I could muster to get the best out of my people. Every so often directors and the like would come along and fuck the whole thing up. At Blackpool they were, unwittingly, expert at such matters.

"Blackpool was an experience that's for sure. It gave me my first managerial opportunity in the First Division, and I learned from my time at the club. What Blackpool didn't do for me was to change my way of thinking about the fickle ways of the press and club directors. Piss one off and your card is marked for the duration of your stay. At Blackpool I told one director to stop interfering, to stop being divisive by using players against each other and me. When he asked if I knew who I was talking to, I replied: 'Yes, to you, you arsehole.' He didn't interfere again, but then again he never supported or backed anything I suggested. As for the press, many of them would sell their own granny for a news story. If they spot a flaw, they interrogate people about it and expose it, without once, rightly or wrongly, contemplating the extent of personal damage it can cause.

To sum up my Blackpool experience: a great club, piss-poor hierarchical attitude."

It was clear that Bob's tenure at Blackpool did not rank among his favourite times in football, yet he achieved a modicum of success there, and certainly the relegation from the First Division cannot be laid at his door. When Bob Stokoe spoke of his initial period at the club, he did so without any sense of pride, and without any fond recollections being recounted. Seldom did I see a smile upon his face when he talked of his stay at Blackpool.

9 Sunderland wonderland

*W*hen Bob Stokoe arrived on Wearside he was not greeted with open arms by a certain section of the local populace. He was regarded as a Magpie, a Black 'n' White through and through. There are important differences between the people of the north east, who proudly commit to being from a certain district or area. Just as not all people from London like to be classed as Cockneys, and sometimes refer to people from neighbouring areas in uncomplimentary terms, so derogatory names exist within north east communities relating to the different regions. The people of Newcastle refer to themselves as Geordies. They can't be anything else and wear the term with distinctive pride, whereas people born within sight of the river Wear, or anyone born within the boundaries of the original town of Sunderland, are Wearsiders or Mackems and refuse to relate themselves to Geordies.

The term Mackem is derived from "Mack'em and Tack'em", which dates back to the earlier parts of the 20th century when the ship-building industry was the major employer in the Wearside region. To clarify: the people on Wearside "mak[e] them" and other people such as Geordies "tak[e] them". The use of Mack'em was originally an insult, when Geordies referred to the fact that the Sunderland ship builders were good for nothing else but manual labour and had not the brain for anything else. Of course, the underlying inference was that they, as Geordies, were an altogether superior group and class of people. To this day, the same rivalry exists.

The differences in the social demography of the region are taken one step further when football is incorporated into the equation. Sunderland and Newcastle are bitter rivals with a history of upset and social disengagement. Putting it mildly, there is no love lost between them, though it should be said that as professional football clubs they do act with the utmost decorum and with sensitivity to the issues that are not football related.

One can only imagine how the Sunderland fans felt when someone who was a Geordie and an ex-Newcastle United thorough-bred, such as Bob Stokoe, was recruited by their club to rescue them from likely relegation to the Third Division. Many sections of the Sunderland support still held vivid memories and recounted vastly exaggerated tales of the day (25 August 1956) when Bob Stokoe, then playing for the Black 'n' Whites, had wound up the Roker Park crowd with what they felt was his deliberately ill-timed tackling and foul play against their red-and-white-striped heroes. The on-the-field niggling had started early and had been allowed to continue by the referee.

"Some of the stories circulating from the mouths of Sunderland fans surrounding that game were without any foundation. I gave as good as I got. Sunderland were kicking lumps out of us and some of their players were wound up by their manager, Bill Murray. He was a self-confessed and self-adopted Wearsider (he was, in fact, a Scot, hailing from Aberdeen) and he could be a nasty little man when aroused. He had a distinct disliking for Newcastle and before that game had deliberately been making loud and derogatory remarks about Geordies so that some of us could hear. It was all we could do to keep quiet. I remember thinking: 'We shall let the football do our talking on the pitch.'

"The Sunderland lads were clearly wound up, especially when we played a controlled game and outdid them. That's when the comments started to flow, initially between players of both teams. Then, later, some of the Sunderland team were geeing up their crowd, getting them antagonised and prompting anti-Newcastle songs and chants. I well remember defending a corner in front of the infamous Fulwell End, as loud a section of support as existed anywhere within the game. A few of the Sunderland fans called me a 'shit Geordie bastard' so I winked at them, smiled and blew a kiss to them. The reaction wasn't good as the whole fucking end had seen me do it. I thought they were going to break out on to the pitch and give me a leathering.

"A bit later, I was back there again, defending valiantly and determined not to let Sunderland score. The rain was lashing down in sheets and the Roker pitch was little more than a mud bath. Just the sort of conditions a defender enjoys, ideal for sliding tackles and slowing the opposition wingers right down. I slid in and took the ball from beneath a Sunderland player, putting the ball out for a corner and in doing so I took him down by ploughing through him with the momentum of my slide. 'Bastard' he shouted. 'Penalty referee, the cheating Geordie bastard has just taken me out.' The referee dismissed his claim and laughed off his suggestions, so I made a point of thanking him, right in front of the Sunderland fans. I made a big thing of it and as I walked back to the goal line in readiness for the Sunderland corner I mouthed to myself: 'Cheating bastards, the lot of them.'

"The fans behind the goal had seen what I had mouthed. I'm not saying I did it deliberately, but it certainly got a reaction from the crowd, who by now were all yelling and screaming things at me. Funny thing is, I couldn't hear what they were saying. There were so many yelling for my blood that they drowned one another out. So I gave them another wink and a laugh before leaping high to head the incoming corner clear of our penalty area. What happened in the tunnel and afterwards outside between the players and myself was through emotions running high. It's not true that I head-butted anyone. I might have tried, but I can't remember making contact. Anyhow I think most people would react badly if someone was trying to gouge their eyes out!"

This wasn't the only ill recollection that the Sunderland fans, and in particular those at the Fulwell End, had of Bob Stokoe. Memories of his reaction to the injury that had ended Brian Clough's career filled the pubs, clubs and bars of Wearside. As if having the fans reacting badly against you wasn't sufficient a battle to deal with, Stokoe also had the local press criticising him, calling him a "jobbing" manager who had achieved little or nothing wherever he had been. They also called into question his tactical skill, claiming that he was bereft of success and therefore in no position to take Sunderland forward. The man was effectively the nemesis of the whole of Wearside.

"I recall my first press conference after my appointment. Some of the crap that had been written and said about me really hit a nerve. Sunderland were a huge football club. It was, in fact, a job I had wondered about for some time as I could see that my predecessor, Alan Brown, was struggling with the team and he clearly couldn't progress it to the next stage. At the press conference I had got the devil in me. I had mentally prepared myself for every awkward question that was likely to come my way. In return I had a few things to ask the journalists who had bothered to attend.

"It was like a lamb to the slaughter, or so some of the journalists thought. I was grateful to see a few friendly faces I recognised among the gathering, so that helped calm me down. One reporter asked for my credentials for managing Sunderland, adding: 'Was it not true that the only things I had won as a manager was the sack at Charlton and the impressive Anglo-Italian Trophy.' How I kept my cool I don't know, yet I did and not only that but I humiliated him in front of his peers. 'Anglo-Italian Trophy' I replied. 'Yes, we won that at Blackpool and got to the final the following year, too. At Carlisle we got to the Football League Cup semi-final and were 45 minutes away from Wembley. What exactly have Sunderland been doing in all that time, winning trophies? No, I don't recall them even coming close. This football club isn't in a good position or shape. I intend to sort out the glaring problems and build a team that the people of this area can and will be proud of. If you, the local press, are only bothered about winning trophies then I shall just have to win you over with my style and commitment to the job.' That helped to silence the room and sent out the message that I wasn't to be messed with.

"I formally took over the managerial reins at Sunderland at the back end of November 1972, when the team had amassed just 15 points, won only four of their 14 games and were languishing in 19th place in the Second Division. Certainly relegation looked a far more likely proposition than promotion. I made an immediate impact, telling the directors that I wanted rid of the white shorts and a return of the original Sunderland playing strip that consisted of red-and-white-striped shirts and black shorts. The fans and players appreciated the touch of nostalgia.

"My first game in charge was at home to Burnley, who sat at the top of the table, having lost just once all season. I didn't really fancy our chances, but it was a good opportunity for me to assess the calibre of player I had in the team. I knew that some great talents like Colin Todd had been sold by 'Browny' as he attempted to generate funds to invest in the team. There were a lot of young talented players who lacked experience, the likes of Mick McGiven, Richie Pitt, Dave Watson, little Bobby Kerr, Jim Montgomery keeping goal, Ian Porterfield, Billy Hughes and Denis Tueart. The team lacked motivation and confidence.

"Sunderland fans are no different from those at other clubs, and could be vocally scathing whenever a player looked as though he wasn't trying or was hiding during a game. The chairman, Keith Collings, wasn't the kind of person to talk in riddles. He was a plain straightforward speaker, he wanted a team that was involved in success. He had backed Alan Brown until it became obvious that he had lost the plot, so to speak, then sacked him. That was a career first for Alan. Billy Elliott had acted in a caretaker manager's role since then, keeping things ticking over until I eventually arrived."

In the pre-match talk before his first game at the helm, Stokoe told his players to go out and work for each other. As was the case everywhere he was in charge, he initiated a team ethic, camaraderie and an understanding of each player's desire to succeed.

"It was a queer set-up at Sunderland, I couldn't put my finger on the problem to start with, but it soon became evident that undercurrents were at work. Burnley were expected to wallop us. Instead they met a team full of individuals who wanted to succeed. We were unlucky to lose the game 1-0 through a defensive mistake and afterwards the Burnley chief, Jimmy Adamson, came to see me for a chat and a private drink. He congratulated me on getting the players organised. He had seen them play a couple of times earlier that season and described them as a shambles. 'That's the toughest game we have had all season, Bob. There's something there for you to work on. You will soon get them into winning habits.' Encouraging words. It was too early to consider the strengths and weaknesses of individuals, but a couple of them looked as though they were playing out of position and didn't quite know how to deal with it.

"After the Burnley defeat we went on a five-game unbeaten run that lifted us to 17th place in the table. We were never to find ourselves looking over our shoulders and worrying about relegation again for the remainder of that season. I carried out a bit of restructuring on the playing side of things, bringing in two players from Newcastle United in a £30,000 double deal, full-back Ron Guthrie and central defender David Young. I spent another £30,000 on the signing of big John 'Yogi Bear' Hughes from Crystal Palace. I had always admired the big fella's game and believed he could do a good job up front for us. The sad thing was, he suffered a nasty injury just three minutes into his Sunderland debut against Millwall. Unfortunately it finished his playing career.

"In Dave Watson I had the makings of a fantastic centre-half. The problem was he was being played as a centre-forward, so I moved him back into the centre of our defence. He didn't like it, yet when I explained that the same thing had happened to me in my playing career, he seemed to feel much better about it all. Dave Watson was an excellent centre-half, not quite as good as I was as a player, but he was all right and once I showed him how easy it could be to play the game he was soon enjoying it.

"As a result of the switch I had lost a forward and had already spied a replacement. I had heard through the grapevine that Luton Town boss Harry Haslam was looking to offload a couple of players in his attempt to rebuild his team. He was a real card, a genuinely caring man. Often he would have me in fits with some of his more unprintable stories. I approached him about the availability of striker Vic Halom and he told me I had no chance as a couple of First Division teams were sniffing around. By the end of the phone call I had agreed a fee of £35,000 for the player, who joined us in February 1973. It was absolute peanuts for a striker with a hunger and desire to prove himself. I spoke to Keith Collings and he supported the bid, telling me I could have the player as a reward for steering the team away from relegation. Good of him, don't you think?"

With the press pack now off his back and supporters beginning to witness the fruits of the manager's undoubted ability to motivate and unite his team, the entire atmosphere at the club lifted into a more relaxed state. Relegation was no longer on the agenda and players came to training each day with smiles on their faces. There was an altogether more positive air about the entire club.

"I was in a one-to-one meeting with a journalist a few days after we had thrashed Brighton and Hove Albion 4-0 in a League game at Roker Park in which the entire team had looked confident and workmanlike. I'm not totally sure how the subject came up, but I was asked what my thoughts were on Notts County, who we faced a few days later at Meadow Lane in the third round of the FA Cup. I said that I thought it would be great to embark upon a nice little cup run to give the fans something to shout about and keep the chairman happy."

That third-round tie was not something that attracted a great deal of attention within the football world. County took the lead and had looked likely to score a second as they pushed forward, keeping Sunderland at bay. A terrific flying save by Jim Montgomery was the turning point of the game, as the Rokerites suddenly showed some self-belief. A Dave Watson goal secured a draw and a replay at Roker Park three days later when the home side made no mistakes, duly dumping Third Division Notts County out of the competition, with the two goals coming from Watson and Tueart. Waiting in the fourth round were another Third Division side, Reading, managed by none other than the Roker Park legend, Charlie Hurley.

"We had a tough time against Reading. People were cheering Charlie Hurley and for some reason we just weren't ourselves in the first game, but we managed to earn a replay through a 1-1 draw in front of our own fans, who were not satisfied with our performance and effort. Frankly, neither was I and I told the players so. In the replay we dug deep and managed to ease ourselves into a comfortable lead, winning the tie 3-1. The draw for the fifth round had already been made and we faced First Division Manchester City at Maine Road. Most of the local press saw this as our point of exit from the competition, and in truth it was a huge call to expect us to go there and get anything from the game."

The mental and physical strain of the two cup ties against Reading began to take their toll as the team fell to what was only their second defeat since Bob Stokoe arrived at the club, losing 1-0 at Sheffield Wednesday. Worse still, a local derby clash against Middlesbrough wasn't the best warm-up preparation for the Manchester City tie.

"I worried about the mental strength of some of the players. I had really increased the pressure and pace of training, made greater demands on them collectively and as individuals, and at times had to reprimand them. I know I wasn't popular among the entire group, but I wasn't in the job to be popular. I wanted success for Sunderland, the players knew that and understood the boundaries I drew between acceptable and unacceptable behaviour. A few of them continually sailed close to the wind and when they did so I gave them a short sharp shock. More than once players at Sunderland told me they wanted to leave because of me, only to be told to go away and think very carefully about what they were doing.

"It was about this time that one of the directors approached me and told me about some 'issues' that he had heard about. This involved domestic matters, with players' wives dominating and dictating the way their husbands socialised. I knew that some of them thought they ruled the roost and tended to form cliques, ostracising selected wives from their company and refusing to allow their husbands to socialise with certain players. What a mess. I wanted to try to nip it in the bud before it became too divisive and split the club. The problem was, of course, that you can't make accusations against or demands on players' wives. They aren't contracted to the football club.

"Instead, I opted to speak with selected players individually and explained my dissatisfaction about the attitude they had adopted towards colleagues. I also advised them that I was concerned about certain cliques and associations that had formed. I knew that certain players would go away and speak out to some of their peers about my comments, so some were told that if things didn't improve, then players' wives would be permanently barred from games. For a time this ploy worked. I took the training to new levels and really pushed my players. As we went into the Middlesbrough game I demanded 100 percent commitment. If necessary they would cover every blade of grass in search of victory. It had the desired effect as we thumped four goals past Middlesbrough without reply."

Off the field, matters were progressing enormously as Roker Park attendances escalated from around 11,000 when Stokoe first arrived to the 40,000 mark as renewed enthusiasm spread throughout the region as a result of the resurgence of high-quality, attractive football under the new manager. Within a few months, Bob Stokoe had transformed the negative image many had of him into one which saw him praised as a real leader and ambassador for the club.

"I'm not one to relax when the pressure eases. I had absolute confidence in my ability to turn Sunderland around. Without self-belief I might as well not have bothered trying to manage any team. The team I inherited at Sunderland wasn't a poor one. It just needed a bit of tender loving care, a bit of experienced motivational guidance here and there. After that, suddenly the players believe in themselves. That's what you look for in your team as a manager – aspiration to achieve and a genuine emotion showing that defeat hurts. I hate losing, I am massively competitive and despise losing at anything I physically participate in."

In the FA Cup Manchester City had been installed as one of the competition favourites. City had a pedigree of being a solid cup fighting team and in certain areas of the media Sunderland were written off as a threat to the First Division side. This was a situation that played directly into Bob Stokoe's hands and was used as further motivation for his players to rise to the occasion.

"I always enjoyed going to Maine Road. It was a great ground for atmosphere and I have a good deal of sympathy for the City fans. Having Manchester United as your football neighbour cannot be easy. I knew all too well that if we could close City down and suffocate their strike-force then eventually we would silence the home support. In the end we came away with a 2-2 draw, young Micky Horswill and Billy Hughes getting the goals that earned us a replay. I should say that our travelling support was incredible. There were more than 12,000 of them inside the ground and they were singing throughout the entire 90 minutes, which helped my players. However, despite the euphoria of getting a draw I knew that the job was only half done. We would have to dig deep to overcome them at Roker Park, but we would have a big home crowd behind us, one that would intimidate any opposition team.

"In the replay the players did everything I asked of them. Roker Park was full and the noise generated was deafening. I couldn't hear my own voice as I screamed instructions from the touchline. When Vic Halom hit a fantastic shot to give us the lead you could see the City players' heads drop. It was a goal of real quality and it was fitting that it should be scored in such a fantastic environment. Billy Hughes put us 2-0 up and the crowd were in heaven as we looked head and shoulders better than our First Division opponents. Then Francis Lee struck to pull City back into the game and I could feel myself getting nervous as the minutes ticked by. Billy Hughes slid in our third with about ten minutes remaining and that was it, job done. The crowd were singing my name and calling me their messiah. I didn't like that too much. We had done well getting this far but I didn't want to raise expectations too much because there were still some decent teams in the competition."

Fellow Second Division side Luton Town awaited in the quarter-finals. Luton had comfortably beaten Sunderland at Roker Park earlier in the season, prior to Stokoe's arrival, by a margin of 2-0. They had one of the best away records in the division and Roker Park clearly did not intimidate them. The week before the cup tie, the Hatters seized a psychological advantage over Sunderland by beating them 1-0 in a League encounter at Kenilworth Road.

"You just can't get excited about games against Luton Town. For a start it's in the south and the club just doesn't have that special something to arouse excitement. Again, Roker Park was full and motivated to cheer the team on. Luton came with a game plan. It was to defend at all costs, thwart our front men and try to hit us on the break.

For a good amount of the game I was fearful that we were not going to be able to break them down, then Dave Watson rose for a cross. He towered above their defence and nodded the ball into the Luton goal to give us the lead. The goal really opened the game up as Luton had to come at us. We played a neat passing game and kept the ball off the Luton midfield.

"Once again the final minutes of the game went by agonisingly slowly, until Ron Guthrie hammered a second goal for us. The whistles from the crowd were piercing. They went on for about five minutes and were so loud that when the referee blew the final whistle you couldn't hear it. The place went wild. I admit that I felt a real pride that this set of players had been able to turn in such consistent and magnificent performances that had seen us transformed from relegation strugglers to promotion contenders and now FA Cup semi-finalists. It was fairy-tale stuff and I still have to pinch myself to make sure that it wasn't a dream."

So, the FA Cup competition had just four teams remaining. The numbered balls carrying the names of Leeds United, Arsenal, Wolverhampton Wanderers and the sole representative from outside the First Division, Sunderland, went into the famous black bag at FA headquarters. The draw was unkind to Stokoe's team. They were paired with Arsenal at Hillsborough, a ground where Sunderland had already tasted defeat that season.

"Oh my, when you looked at the Arsenal team you shivered with excitement. They had plenty of class acts. The Sunderland fans had been given the home end of the ground, which was a sea of red-and-white scarves. I simply told my players to go out and enjoy the game as it would quickly become a distant memory. I pulled the Arsenal team to pieces until each and every player sat before me believed that they were better than the southerners. As we came out on to the pitch the roar from our support was unbelievable. Quickly I gave out last-minute instructions and said to the players: 'Do it for them' as I pointed at the huge bank of red-and-white."

The usually reliable Bob Wilson in the Arsenal goal seemed strangely out of sorts with his defenders as the north London side looked uncomfortable all over the pitch. A Horswill drive forced Wilson into action and he turned the effort over the bar. Sunderland appeared to be the more composed of the teams yet for all their endeavour there was no genuine goal-scoring opportunities. The longer it remained like that, the more likely it would be that Arsenal would take control of the game. Then a long clearance dropped to the feet of Arsenal centre-half Jeff Blockley. Looking up he could see Sunderland's Vic Halom racing towards him, and the defender panicked. Bob Wilson, desperate to prevent a calamity, raced out of his goal to help, but Halom was quickest to react to the loose ball that had squirmed away from Blockley. Nipping in, he took the ball beyond both players and stroked it into the net. Sunderland were one up.

In the second half, a throw-in from the player Stokoe was to refer to as his little general, Bobby Kerr, was headed backwards towards the Arsenal goal by Denis Tueart. Wilson ran from his goal to collect the bouncing ball, but before he could reach it up popped Billy Hughes to nod it over him and into the empty Arsenal net.

"At that stage I couldn't believe it. Here we were beating Arsenal 2-0 in an FA Cup semi-final. There wasn't a feeling like it. I was in wonderland but I couldn't let my players see my emotions. Outwardly I had to remain grounded. Then Charlie George got one back for them and once again it was a case of hanging on for our lives. We did it, though, and when the final whistle went I thanked each and every one of the backroom staff who sat in the dugout with me. I looked up towards the directors' box and got the thumbs-up signal from a sea of smiling men in grey suits, the Sunderland directors.

"I don't know why, but I walked away down the tunnel. I didn't know what to do or how to deal with it. Then I heard the famous Roker Roar, and those wonderful fans were singing my name. I was ecstatic and walked over to them. People, grown men, were crying and bowing to me as though I was some kind of god that they were worshipping. It was then that I heard thousands of them calling me the messiah. I think that's when the press picked up on it. Tears rolled down my cheeks. Never in my life had I received such an ovation. I wanted to tell each and every one of them that this wasn't just my doing. It was a collective effort that included them. I walked off the pitch as I could feel myself breaking down with emotional joy."

It wasn't long before Sunderland knew who they were to face in the 1973 FA Cup final. Leeds United had beaten Wolves 1-0 at Maine Road, courtesy of a goal from Billy Bremner. Once again Bob Stokoe was to face Don Revie in a Wembley FA Cup final, something that the media weren't slow in identifying.

"What I didn't know about Leeds in the build-up to that final wasn't worth knowing. I had them watched and went to see some of their games myself, though I wouldn't have accepted Leeds' hospitality – had there been any on offer! They were still in European competition, the European Cup Winners' Cup, and I prayed for a series of niggling injuries that would keep the likes of John Giles, Bremner and their cohorts out of the FA Cup final. They were a tough lot. Physical and ruthless, they played with a win-at-all-costs attitude. If they couldn't match the opposition on a football front, they were cunning enough to play it rough, often looking and playing the victim's role, when in fact they were generally mixing it up.

"I had a lot of respect for players like Giles, Peter Lorimer, Eddie Gray, Terry Cooper and Allan Clarke. They were skilful and strong and they would work throughout a full game, then give more if necessary. But this was one game I was desperate to win, the ultimate challenge of wits and strategy against a man and a manager who, in my opinion, was fortunate to be in charge of any football club.

"In the week of the final, the television went haywire. It was all Leeds, Leeds, Leeds. In comparison, Sunderland Football Club hardly got a mention. Still, my players revelled in the public attention which did come their way, but I didn't like it. The media have a way in which they lull you into a false sense of security, then knock you flat on your face. My preparations for the game were meticulous and disciplined.

"To give an example of how devious television can be, Brian Moore, the football commentator for ITV, invited me to go on air in some kind of FA Cup final special, and they wanted to put a camera on each of the team coaches on their way to the game. I wasn't happy and wouldn't make a decision on it without speaking to others who had physically participated in the modern day cup final experience. I gave my old pal Bertie Mee, the Arsenal manager, a ring and asked him what he thought. He advised me not to go anywhere near Don Revie on television as they would probably try to inflame matters between us. As for a television on the coach, avoid it with a barge pole was his response.

"But I couldn't help but think that a camera on the team coach wouldn't really reveal any trade secrets. In fact, we could use it to the contrary. So I agreed. I made a point of playing us down, informing Moore, who told me that Leeds had individual diets for their players, that my lads had prepared for the final by each eating a big plate of beans on toast!

"As the kick-off approached both teams lined up in the tunnel, and memories of 1955 came flooding back to me. I glanced across at the Leeds players, and one of them mouthed obscenities towards me. I felt my hackles rise but maintained a calm, almost aloof attitude towards our opponents. I had, of course, identified their individual weaknesses to my team in the dressing room before we came out on to the pitch, informing them that Leeds believed we were only there to make up the numbers.

"As we walked out, Don Revie was next to me. He turned to me and said something along the lines of 'Revenge is sweet, Stokoe'. There were a few unnecessary expletives in his statement. I smiled nonchalantly at him and walked on, hands behind my back as though I was out for a walk in a park. I was wearing my tracksuit along with a mackintosh coat, as rain had been forecast and I am a practical man. I stuck my hat on my head, too. I didn't want to get a soaking. After all, this was Wembley."

The game kicked off and for almost half an hour both teams sparred with each other. But then a speculative shot from Bobby Kerr had Harvey in the Leeds goal scrambling to turn it over the crossbar for a corner kick. Billy Hughes swung over the corner, the Leeds defence seemed static and Vic Halom was the first player to react in the penalty area. He got the faintest of touches and the ball fell to Ian Porterfield, who controlled it with his left foot before firing the ball past Harvey and into the roof of the Leeds net with his right. Sunderland were one up.

"It was bloody incredible. Inside I was bursting with emotion but the last thing I wanted to do was to physically release that feeling. I wanted to keep it under control, harnessed to use to motivate my players through the remainder of the game." In the second half, Leeds threw everything at Sunderland but could find no way through. In goal Jimmy Montgomery was in unbeatable form, pulling off the greatest double save Wembley has ever seen, ultimately preventing a Peter Lorimer special from getting past him from very close range and somehow turning it on to the crossbar.

"Everybody in the stadium thought it was in. My heart sank when I saw the ball falling to Lorimer, he just didn't miss from that range. I turned my head toward the Leeds bench in anticipation of seeing them leaping in the air. They very nearly did, but then a look of absolute horror and despair came across their faces. I looked back towards our goal to see the ball go behind and out of play for a goal kick. Everyone around me hugged one another, but I couldn't and wouldn't celebrate yet."

Leeds continued to push forward but by now their spirits were broken as Sunderland gradually began to get more possession of the ball. When the final whistle blew, Wembley erupted into song. "Haway the lads, Haway the lads" came the cries from the Sunderland hordes now going wild in celebration. The players were hugging one another and punching the air with delight when suddenly an overcoated figure, clad also in tracksuit bottoms and a trilby hat, appeared from the side of the pitch. It was Bob Stokoe, his face full of a thousand delights, radiating ecstasy, happiness, joy. His run and his eyes were riveted on one individual, Jimmy Montgomery, the man whose save had won the FA Cup, equally as much as did Ian Porterfield's goal. An entire nation watching the game on television took this Geordie to their hearts. Never before had football seen such an outburst of geuine emotion coming from a manager. The dream had become reality. Bob Stokoe and his Sunderland heroes were FA Cup winners.

"It's difficult to describe how it felt. I wanted to go up to Revie and look him in the eye and say 'Revenge is sweet, Revie; cheats never prosper' but I refrained from doing that and left it until later when it would have more impact, when the FA Cup would be in my hands. I wanted this moment to be for my players. Jim Montgomery had been fantastic all the way through the competition. Micky Horswill was still a kid. How must it have felt for that young man!

"As I reached Jimmy he looked at me and screamed something, I didn't hear what, and we just hugged each other. It was at that point the greatest achievement in my managerial career. I was so proud, I had proved everyone wrong – Charlton, my doubters and the press. Sunderland, my Sunderland team, were again winners. We had made history, too. It was the first time since the war a team from the Second Division had won the FA Cup."

In typical Stokoe fashion he allowed his team and their families an evening of celebration in London, before selecting his team for a fixture at Cardiff City two days later and travelling with the players to Wales on the day after the final success. "We still had two games remaining of our League season. We couldn't win promotion but I wanted us to be as close as we could be. We drew 1-1 at Cardiff, then lost 3-0 at home to Queen's Park Rangers two days later. The players were exhausted both mentally and physically. It mattered little but we finished the season in sixth place in Division Two, and I felt satisfied that we had made suitable progress."

The season that followed saw Sunderland representing England in the European Cup Winners' Cup competition. Continental football represented new territory for the Rokerites but not for Bob Stokoe, who recalled a previous Anglo-Italian success to some local newspaper reporters, who no doubt felt duly humbled by their previous criticisms of such exploits. Sunderland were drawn against Vasas Budapest, with the first leg in Hungary.

"It was all a bit frantic and the fans expectancy had shot through the roof. Overnight we had become the team to beat. The European adventure allowed us a bit of escapism from the rigours of the Football League. We beat Vasas Budapest 2-0 over in Hungary, then won 1-0 at Roker Park. It's difficult trying to keep your players focused when suddenly they are FA Cup-holders, favourites for the Second Division championship and playing in top-class European competition. Every team in the Second Division wants to beat you because of the European association and we really struggled for consistency in our League form.

"In Europe we next met Sporting Lisbon and quite incredibly beat them 2-1 at Roker Park, disappointingly conceding an away goal in the dying stages of the game. In the second leg we never looked like competing with them and we were convincingly beaten 2-0, a result that knocked us out of the competition, 3-2 on aggregate. It was something of a relief for me. The team had become a little arrogant in some of their ways, all down to their recent success, and some believed themselves to be better than Second Division football. These players were advised to prove themselves so, and soon began to knuckle down to my disciplined style.

"In the FA Cup we drew one of my old clubs, Carlisle United, in the third round of the competition. Once again I could have named 100 teams I would rather face than Carlisle. I knew what they were capable of. After all, I had brought in many of the faces who would be opposing our efforts to hold on to the trophy. I was pleasantly surprised by the welcome I received at Carlisle by the home fans. They gave me a big round of applause and congratulated me on my success since leaving them. I admit I very nearly sat in the home dugout as the game was about to kick off. This brought a few cheers from the fans in the paddock, who stand right behind the managers. It was no surprise that Carlisle bombarded us for 90 minutes, but we held strong to earn a draw and a replay at our place, where I was certain it would be a different game. It was. Carlisle were at us from the kick-off. They overran us and scored a decisive goal through Dennis Martin that sent us packing and out of the competition at our first defence.

"I congratulated the Carlisle players afterwards, only to be told that some of my own players had lost belief in me, accusing me of being a one-season wonder. I was hurt by the accusations and shocked that there were still some people within the club who clearly weren't happy with me being manager. Extra training and a few additional miles of running were the order of the day for the Sunderland team after that. The thing is, you can only patch up major differences within what should be a close-knit community such as a football team for a short time. I knew that pretty soon I would have to break up the team, releasing some players who didn't deserve to be subjected to the cynicism of certain other individuals. I was told that despite our success in the FA Cup some of the Sunderland players still held it against me because I was a loyal Magpie. After all we had been through together, animosity reigned in certain areas."

Stokoe was acutely aware of the rift that was beginning to show within the squad. The situation was not helped by emerging cliques among the players' wives. "I wanted to ban the bloody lot of them from the club on match days, but that would have been punishing the innocent ones in the group. Anyway, the chairman would have none of it. No matter what we did, we just couldn't rid ourselves of the clique. It was extremely damaging to team morale and essentially buggered up social events.

"One of the issues facing a manager is that when you build a successful team, bigger clubs begin to take notice of your better players. I had wanted to keep the team together for as long as possible. However, with all the subterfuge taking place I knew I was fire-fighting, running around like a headless chicken trying to heal gaping wounds within the social structure of the team, while striving to maintain managerial control of all the players, together with the requisite respect.

"When Manchester City's Malcolm Allison came calling in March 1973, asking about the availability of Dennis Tueart and Micky Horswill, I went to speak with chairman Keith Collings. City had offered an initial £175,000 for Tueart. I told the chairman to call them back and to inform them that we wanted £250,000 for the player. I wasn't at all keen on losing Horswill. He was still a youngster with a lot to learn and a lot to offer, and I told the chairman to play ignorant on that move. I was shocked when he came back and said that City would meet our valuation of Tueart, with the proviso that Horswill is included in any such deal and that they would pay £100,000 for him.

"The two departures in one fell swoop would have left us short in certain areas, so I asked the chairman to give me a bit of time to contemplate the deal. I made a few telephone calls and was soon hearing some good news. City had been touting around for sale their midfielder Tony Towers. He was just the sort of player who could fit straight into my team. He was still only 21 years old and a raw talent. I carried out a few background checks with people who knew the player and his attitude. The information I received back was encouraging; he was highly regarded and had a good temperament. I left it for a few hours, then went back to our chairman, telling him that we would agree to the deal for Tueart. However, where Horswill was concerned we wanted £100,000 plus Tony Towers. Keith put that to City and, hey presto, they agreed to everything."

It seemed that the easy part of the deal had been sealed. Both clubs wanted to speak to the respective players and agree terms with them. Stokoe was quickly able to sell Sunderland to Towers, who was told how his role was of vital importance to the team. However, news broke quickly of the triple transcation, released from the Manchester City end.

"A significant amount of transfer money was riding on the acceptance of the deal by Tueart and Horswill. Neither player truly wanted to leave and they had to be coerced into doing so." While it was never revealed by the manager, I was told by people who should know that Keith Collings and Bob Stokoe drove the two Sunderland players involved to a hotel at Wetherby and told them in no uncertain terms that they had 12 hours to make up their minds regarding the transfer to Manchester City. I was told that undue pressure was not placed on the pair, though they were told the club had agreed to sell them and that transfer fees were agreed. Thus they learned that, in Sunderland's eyes, they were now surplus to requirements.

"The money had a huge influence in our decision to sell the players. It was too big an amount to turn down and the team did need some weeding out here and there. We couldn't hold on to our best talent forever and you have to consider players' ambitions and do what is best for them. I felt disappointed about releasing both players. However, I believed it would help them both progress in their careers as well as helping Sunderland enormously. Eventually, after some consideration, they agreed to speak with City representatives and the deal was satisfactorily concluded. Tueart went on to play for England and forged a good career for himself whereas, sadly, Micky Horswill never quite fulfilled his potential. I was to later be reunited with Micky when I brought him to Carlisle from Hull City at the start of the 1983/84 season. Unfortunately by that time he was overweight, unfit and didn't fit into the team at all. I released him after just one game."

The 1973/74 season was very much a non-event for Sunderland and Bob Stokoe, even though the team improved on their final League placing, finishing fifth behind two of his previous clubs – Carlisle United, who were promoted to the First Division, and Blackpool, who finished fourth.

"It didn't bother me too much that we finished behind both my previous clubs. Carlisle's situation was unbelievable. First Division football for a club of its size was one of the greatest achievements in the history of the League. Meanwhile Blackpool had developed into a good team (Keith Dyson was banging in the goals) and worthy of fourth place. My job was to make sure that the following season it was Sunderland who was again making the headlines, this time from winning promotion."

It wasn't to be. Despite strengthening the team by acquiring more ex-Newcastle stars, Bobby Moncur and Bryan 'Pop' Robson, the 1974/75 season provided no new silverware or success. The team did start the season like a house on fire, going on an unbeaten run from the first game until the 14th, which they lost 3-1 to Hull City. At this stage they sat comfortably in second place, behind League leaders Manchester United. Most pundits had both the Red Devils and the Rokerites as nailed on promotion winners.

"The 1974/75 season really took a lot out of me. As a football club we had built a formidable reputation since winning the FA Cup in 1973. Some called us a sleeping giant. However, that was wrong, we weren't asleep, we were on the cusp of further success and just not quite able to maintain our challenge for an entire season to win promotion. We sat in second place in the Second Division from November 1974 to April 1975, once again falling at the final hurdle.

Away from football, a serious car crash involving Ian Porterfield had left him seriously injured. I was told by specialists that he would be out for the remainder of the season. His entire playing career was in extreme doubt. The situation didn't help the morale within the club and we genuinely missed the lad's influence on the pitch."

With three games of the season remaining, Sunderland suffered a shock 1-0 defeat at mid-table Oxford that put into serious doubt their promotion aspirations. "After this game, as was usual, I accepted the hospitality of the opposition manager, and shared a chat and a drink with Oxford boss Gerry Summers. As I left the Manor Ground, some Sunderland fans were hanging about outside. I was sharing a joke with Gerry and was laughing when I stepped into the car park. You can imagine what happened next; the Sunderland fans thought that because of my joviality I couldn't care less about losing, and they screamed abuse at me.

I ignored the acidic comments, putting them down to disappointment and emotions running high. It was a long journey back to Wearside that night. I replayed over and over in my mind the missed opportunities we had squandered throughout the season. I was breaking the unwritten management rule that you should never consider the 'if only' situations.

"We made amends in the penultimate game, the last home game of the season, when we thrashed fellow promotion contenders Bristol City 3-0. In the final game we faced Aston Villa, who were already promoted. It was between ourselves and Norwich City as to who got the third promotion place. Norwich had a game in hand on us, and they were to play Aston Villa four days after ourselves. We travelled to Villa Park knowing that we had to win. But we couldn't match the Villa enthusiasm, and willed on by a noisy capacity crowd they beat us 2-0, ending all hope of promotion as Norwich won at Portsmouth on the same day.

"I was truly devastated, shattered and worried about my position. I despised being second best. We were better than the Second Division. We had conceded just eight League goals at Roker Park all season, a record to be proud of and one of the best defensive records the club has ever achieved. But that wasn't enough for some. Now the knives were out and being sharpened by certain elements of the Sunderland press and supporters in anticipation of my enforced departure. How bloody fickle football can be."

The close season saw more transfer activity taking place. Continued failure to gain promotion from the Second Division had allegedly caused some unrest within the squad. When Manchester City came in with an offer of £275,000 to take England centre-half Dave Watson to Maine Road, the club could do little to prevent it. Stokoe's hands were tied. The club wasn't yet in a position to offer its players First Division salaries, not the sort clubs like Manchester City could offer. To exacerbate this problem, the chairman and board had informed the manager that he would have to sell players if he wanted to bring others in.

"I saw this as a forewarning of things to come. In some instances, directors won't give a manager transfer funds because they don't trust his judgement, and ultimately the sack beckons. I wasn't so certain that was the case where I was concerned at Sunderland, yet I did know that some people within the club were keen to see me walk. I wasn't yet ready to walk away and admit defeat, I had become emotionally involved with Sunderland and everything it stood for. Generally speaking, the people of the town were honest and fair and I felt happy there.

Yet it doesn't do to relax and to take your eye off the ball. I knew only too well how opinions and attitudes could change. I needed to get Sunderland back to where they belonged, playing in the First Division. Little did I realise the strain this desire was putting on me personally. Sleepless nights and constant anxiety, I suffered them in the cause of Sunderland AFC."

With a small percentage of the income received from the Dave Watson transfer, Stokoe added to his squad, signing Jeff Clarke from Manchester City as part of the Watson transaction and Mel Holden from Preston North End for a fee of £120,000. Both players settled quickly into the Sunderland way of life and were to prove to be popular figures with supporters. The team accepted the challenge of achieving promotion and duly delivered a level of consistency that can only result in success. Away from the League, the FA Cup offered further excitement, only for the team to fail in the sixth round when Crystal Palace pulled off a shock victory at Roker Park. That encounter is often recalled for the so-called Malcolm Allison incident. Prior to kick-off the gregarious and ultra-confident Crystal Palace manager calmly walked on to the Roker pitch, dressed in an ostentatious fur-collared overcoat, sporting a white fedora hat and puffing away on a giant cigar. The Sunderland fans responded accordingly, singing: "What the fucking hell is that" and pointing towards the grinning Allison.

"A lot of people couldn't handle Malcolm Allison or his arrogance. I always got on okay with him. Mind, he did make a complete fool of himself before and after the 1976 FA Cup tie, although you can't knock the bloke, he got his team wound up and they did knock us out of the competition. I rated him as a coach too. He was tough and, believe it or not, a strict disciplinarian. That is until it came to the finer things in life – champagne, women and cigars. He was a real character who I would always rather have on my side than as an enemy."

The march to promotion was finally achieved with the team winning 19 home games and remaining unbeaten at Roker Park in the League all season. They looked an impressive outfit and one which was capable of holding its own in the top flight of the English game. This was something that Stokoe firmly believed. "We had the makings of a decent team. I wanted to give my players, who had fought so hard and performed so competently and valiantly in getting us promotion, the opportunity to step up to a greater challenge."

It is easy with the benefit of hindsight to criticise this decision, yet it shows once again the amount of respect Stokoe had for his players and team. He believed in them both collectively and as individuals. Wherever he had been as a manager he had been forced to work on a shoestring. It had become second nature to him.

"Clearly now, looking back, this step was beyond the capability of some of the players. I was asking too much of them to compete week-in and week-out against top-class professionals who, by virtue of their First Division experience, were a few seconds quicker and overall more clinical and sharper than some of my lads. It was a tough call. Despite that, I don't actually think we were outplayed or outclassed. Maybe fitness and stamina played a bigger role in our inability to win games, I don't know. What I do know, though, is that I was proud of the lads and all they achieved."

The first three games of the new season were drawn and gave some hope that defensively they were strong enough to withstand the pressure of a higher class of forward line. However, in September Stokoe brought in Manchester United's highly rated centre-half Jim Holton for a fee of £80,000. It was hoped that Holton would add his undoubted experience, as well as grit and determination to the defensive play.

"Jim Holton remains one of the worst signings I ever made in football. He was a smashing and likeable lad but his career never quite reached the level many believed it could. For many years afterwards the Manchester United boss who sold him to me, Tommy Docherty, would joke about conning me into buying the player. I eventually told

Tommy not to carry it on as it's not nice talking about a footballer in derogatory terms, especially as he has now passed away, God rest his soul."

After just nine League games into the new season, Bob Stokoe walked into Roker Park clutching his letter of resignation. During that spell his team had produced no wins, four draws and five losses, a gruesome record and a situation that depressed him greatly. Most recently and significantly for Bob, the team had lost 1-0 at home to Aston Villa during which the crowd had continually called for his dismissal.

"I felt sick before, during and after the game. I had been talking to people like Matt Busby and Jackie Milburn, seeking their advice on how I felt and what I should do. They all said the same thing to me: 'Get out of the game before it completely consumes and harms you.' My own doctor had told me I needed to take a break, unanimously supporting the views of my family, who are more important to me than anything else in life.

"The abuse I had taken from some Sunderland fans since we had won promotion was unbelievable. Internally, within the organisation of the football club itself, I had become a non-person. Directors and senior club staff who should have known better had begun to ignore me. There were private meetings, from which I was omitted, to discuss team affairs. I was stunned and surprised at the way I was being treated by some officials.

"At one time in my life I would have confronted the blighters and told them what I thought of them. Now I couldn't muster the energy or enthusiasm to argue the point. There was an overall feeling of solitude and unhappiness during my latter period at Sunderland Football Club. My health really had began to suffer, and so, with my family's support, I made an executive decision to resign and allow someone else the chance to manage the team. Yes, I was sad, but I was even more excited by the prospect of spending some quality time with my loving wife, Jean, and my family."

Bob Stokoe's overall record at Sunderland is impressive, to say the least. Of 175 senior matches, 82 were won, 45 drawn and 48 lost. In this time he won the FA Cup and the Second Division championship, and provided Sunderland with the opportunity to challenge in first-class European competition.

One Sunderland supporter of the era recalled Stokoe's first spell at the club: "We were a team of prima donnas without the capacity or wherewithal to get ourselves away from the relegation zone of the Second Division. When Bob Stokoe came to the club, he was charged, energised and wholly motivated. He dragged this football club from its knees and led us to places we could only previously dream of. Winning the FA Cup and seeing him belt across that Wembley pitch with a beaming smile on his face represents all that is good about Bob Stokoe and football, a genuine honesty and a belief that good will always overcome evil. He was a man of extreme integrity and at supporters' functions would go round tables interacting with fans and seeking their opinions on the team or certain players. You always got the impression that he listened because he genuinely cared. He could take insults, too, but if you pushed it too far you had to be prepared to take a few from him in return. Always, though, he shook hands and wished everyone well.

"It upset me the way he was treated before he left us when we had just got back into the First Division in 1976. Some of the fans dragged up his Newcastle association and rumours existed that a few of the players, some of who were no longer at the club, were bad-mouthing him to certain football-related individuals. People in the town weren't happy about that stuff and I do know that as a result of their underhanded attitude, certain footballers of the time were not well received here. To be honest, that was a shit attitude to have towards a man who gave Sunderland so much. It was Stokoe, too, who gave some of those players a chance to make a decent living from the game.

"Thankfully, the majority of our support has much more integrity than some of those people and we have nothing but respect for Bob Stokoe. Like we said at the time, he was the messiah, our leader. He made Sunderland what it is today, a highly respected international brand and a respected football club. Mention Sunderland FC anywhere in the world today and people respond with just one thing: Bob Stokoe. No one can or ever will replace him. His legacy will live on for eternity."

10 **Back from the wilderness**

"*I*n theory, the opportunity to spend some time away from the game and with my family, relaxing and doing what I wanted to, was wonderful. The reality was somewhat different. As hard as I tried, I missed the day-to-day involvement of football. It had, after all, been a major part of my life since I was a teenager. Now being out of work didn't sit comfortably with me at all. I spent many days on the golf courses of the north of England, Hexham being my favourite.

"My rehabilitation was a lengthy one and the stress caused primarily by Blackpool, then at Sunderland, had an impact on me. I had always been healthy and saw myself as indestructible. Then something happens and you realise that no matter how well you look after your body, the daily exertions and strains placed upon you do take their toll. There comes a time when you need to take time out, recharge the batteries in preparation for the next challenge, and by the summer of 1977 I was again starting to put myself about, looking for odd bits of work here and there.

"Primarily I looked at scouting jobs. That role always led to introductions with club officials and from there you could openly state your interest in a more taxing position. I wanted to get back into management. I think I had become a bit of a nuisance to Jean, moping around the house, flicking through the football pages and speaking on the phone to ex-colleagues. I found myself acting as an unofficial managerial advisor, and every so often I would take in the odd game here and there."

Rumours abounded during Bob Stokoe's spell out of the game. No one truly expected him to retire, a comeback was certain. At various club grounds when he was seen casting his expert eye over the 22 players competing before him, it would often cause something of a sensation. Supporters and journalists spread spurious gossip that he was taking over at several clubs: Carlisle United, Hartlepool United, even Wolverhampton Wanderers. The fact of the matter was that Bob was on scouting missions, helping out a number of clubs and managerial friends.

"As the new football season kicked off I hadn't got myself fixed up with any particular club. I had received good offers but I now had a strict criterion. Any club I managed would have to be in the north. I spoke with Lincoln City after Graham Taylor left them in the summer, but something didn't feel right about the job. Lovely place, but I had a sixth sense that caused me not to pursue any interest. As it turned out, George Kerr got the job and left after just six months, so my gut feeling was right. I went to take a look at Halifax Town. Alan Ball senior was there as manager, his second stint at The Shay. Again it wasn't right for me. I actually had my eye on one position that genuinely ticked all the right boxes, but the club was in complete turmoil and I wasn't certain that it would be right for me health-wise, even if it was offered to me."

Newcastle United was, in October and November 1977, a club seemingly spiralling out of control. Manager Richard Dinnis had always seemed to be struggling in the position, not because he was incompetent or out of his depth, but because of the constant interfering in team affairs by senior club officials at boardroom level. The season had begun on a high note, beating Leeds United 3-2 in front of a St James' Park crowd of more than 36,000. The result masked many problems and there followed an absolutely miserable run of ten straight defeats, finally halted late in October with a 1-0 victory against Chelsea.

Two weeks later and the club were once again making the headlines. Lord Westwood, then the most powerful man at Newcastle United, launched a broadside attack on ex-manager Gordon Lee, claiming that Lee had ignored many talented players because they were black. As if that wasn't sufficient he then went public with his condemnation of Richard Dinnis for not moving home to Newcastle. It made the manager's position more or less untenable. Two days later he was sacked and this statement was issued: "The directors thank Mr Dinnis for the success which he achieved after the defection of Gordon Lee to Everton, but in view of the disappointing per-formances of the team it was decided that change was unavoidable."

Bob Stokoe was torn: "I knew the Newcastle job was going to be coming available and there was a huge part of me that wanted it. Yet when I think back to how I had been treated at some clubs, how damning and condemning the supporters and directors of Newcastle United were and historically always had been towards managers or players they took exception to, or had grown tired of, then I realise that I was right not to talk to them.

"I was very informally approached, well sounded out about whether I knew anyone who may be interested in the position. However, I think my lack of enthusiasm and passion expressed itself clearly and I heard no more. The strange thing was, it was reported within 24 hours that the job had been offered to both Frank O'Farrell and Bill McGarry. Both had turned it down, although McGarry soon reconsidered his decision and accepted the job.

"It's not something I regret because I was never formally offered the job, so it was never there for me to make a decision upon. That said, I knew that clubs like Newcastle were far too political, and lacked the realism of football at a lower level. That was not the sort of working environment I needed."

His absence from the day-to-day rigours of running a football team were soon to come to an end. Unknown to anyone outside the boardroom at Gigg Lane, Bury were about to sack their long-serving manager Bobby Smith and they had already pencilled in the name of a suitable replacement.

"Bobby Smith was a canny lad. He had been with Bury for a few seasons and won them promotion out of the Fourth Division. He was having a rough time of it at the beginning of the 1977/78 season, with the side struggling and without a win in eight games. He was sacked after Bradford City beat them 2-1 at Valley Parade, which dropped them down into a mid-table position. I knew that there was a belief within the club that the team should be challenging for promotion.

"When I got the call asking me if I would be interested, I jumped at it. I had fond memories of Bury, not only as a football club but as a town, so much so that some of my family settled there. I saw it as a chance to help the club. They say you should never go back to a club where you have managed or played, but I wanted to work at Bury and wanted to build a team worthy of promotion back into the Second Division."

It came as some surprise to the new manager that the enthusiasm and motivation he had once known at the club had disappeared. His arrival spawned suggestions that he was a spent force simply using the club to get back into the management game.

"I was shocked by what I found at Bury. There was an underlying cynicism about the place. This bloody awful attitude ran right through the club and on to the terraces. I soon realised that my return to the club hadn't been greeted with wide acceptance. To the contrary, I was made to feel like a leper. There was little I could do about making people like me – that's never really bothered me too much anyway –

but you do need, as manager of a football team, to have the fans on your side."

Concentrating solely on team and football matters, Stokoe soon had the Bury players pulling in the same direction and performances began to pick up. In the League Cup, prior to his arrival, Crewe Alexandra, Oxford United and Millwall had been beaten, all after replays. Awaiting Bury in the fourth round was a bigger tougher potential scalp, First Division West Bromwich Albion.

"I had history with West Bromwich Albion in this competition. I had not forgotten how they had caused me some hurt by knocking my Carlisle team out of the semi-finals in 1970. Now I had the chance to avenge that defeat. It was a horrible evening for football, cold and damp, ideal for cup-tie surprises. The players were really geed up for the game and needed little motivation from me. My instructions were simple: close them down and give them no room, hassle and intimidate them until you hear the final whistle blow. Ian Robbins got the goal that sent us through. It was a fine performance and won over some of the support. We followed up that game with two League wins, beating Plymouth Argyle and Oxford United, and those results pushed us back among the teams challenging for promotion."

A local newspaper made comment about the impact the new Bury manager was having on his team: "That the Shakers' players have responded to new manager Bob Stokoe there is no doubt and that in itself has made an impression on the amicable Geordie. 'I want a positive approach from them and I am getting it' said Stokoe. 'It's a good starting point and we can build from there.'"

Going into the all-important Christmas period, an air of hope was prevalent, though this was quickly dashed by Preston at Deepdale, who blasted four goals without return on Boxing Day. Two points were picked up from home draws against Colchester and Carlisle United. Then, typifying the inconsistent form of the team, the opening two games of 1978 saw them score eight times, winning 3-0 at Rotherham and then 5-2 at home to Cambridge United. By now, everyone at the club had one eye on the League Cup competition, with Nottingham Forest the fifth-round visitors to Gigg Lane. As if to spice up the tie, Forest were managed by none other than Brian Clough.

"What can you do? Once again the fates had conspired to throw up a cup-tie with some bitter associations. Not that I held any grudges, but Cloughie certainly did. I rang him prior to the game to try to calm any potential flashpoints and to wish him luck on the night. Our conversation, if that's what you could call it, was one-sided. He never gave me the chance to offer the olive branch. 'Stokoe, you are a bastard of a man, why are you calling me? I don't want to converse with you, are you listening? I have nothing to say to you. Haven't you done well for yourself, back at Bury in the Third Division? You, man, will not stand in my way, so fuck off, okay?'

"That was it, that was my moment with the great Brian Clough. He was right, though, we could do little to prevent his team from winning the game. Forest were clearly a team with an abundance of purchased talent."

That match provided Bury with a gate of 21,268, their biggest home attendance since 1966. The following game saw the Shakers put in what was arguably their best performance of the season, thrashing Exeter City 5-0 and in doing so climbing up to sixth place in the Third Division. Despite this and the decent run in the League Cup, Bob Stokoe was still denied much in the way of plaudits by many associated with the club.

"It was hard for me. I felt that whatever I did at Bury would never be good enough. As it happens, I didn't actually have a good deal of success. The team lacked an inventive play-maker and some of the players were continually making excuses in the dressing room as to why they had played so poorly, none of which were admissions that they were at fault. It got to the stage where I flew off the handle at some of them, putting them on the spot and trying to strengthen their resolve. When you get footballers who continue to refer to the weaknesses and inadequacies of the previous manager, it gets infuriating after a time. I had seen at first hand the devious intentions of some of the insecure players at Sunderland. Now, here I was seeing the same thing at Bury, with everything being blamed on poor old Bobby Smith."

There can be no other way of describing Bob Stokoe's second term at Bury but as a disastrous six months. It hurt him a lot that this once-proud club had fallen prey to indifferent attitudes in the dressing room. His philosophy of building a united body of players who were equals, and without any delusions of grandeur, seemed archaic at Bury, where much more than excellent motivation skills were necessary to kick-start a positive attitude.

"The rest of the season at Bury was dreadful. In fact, the only decent performance we put in, where I could say genuinely that we looked like a cohesive unit, was at Carlisle United, when we beat them 3-0 on their own Cumberland turf. It was pleasing to see them play with such freedom, although I'm not so certain whether it was a good performance by us or a piss-poor one from Carlisle, who looked to be in a worse state than we were. It was very satisfying to be afforded a great reception once again by the Carlisle supporters. As I made my way down the Brunton Park tunnel after the game I heard them shouting to me: 'Come back here Bob, we need you.' I would have jumped at the chance had the opportunity been there."

Five of the remaining seven League games were drawn and the other two were lost, leaving Bury in the fairly healthy position of 14th in the Third Division. It wasn't enough to placate the angst clearly evident in many pockets of the club's support.

"We were booed off so many times that I lost count, and in the end it stopped having any impact on me or the players. I was glad the season was over and was contemplating how to hand in my resignation when I was told that Blackpool had come on with a request to talk to me about the vacancy there. It helped both Bury and myself out of an embarrassing situation. I agreed to become manager of Blackpool for the second time, hoping it would not be anything like as bad an experience as it was the first time. On 20 May 1978 I joined Blackpool, who had been relegated into the Third Division for the first time in the club's history. It was a challenge to say the least."

11 **Going back to Blackpool**

*T*he motives behind Bob Stokoe joining a Blackpool club in dire straits were not of a mercenary nature. Much was suggested at the time and subsequently that he had simply used Bury as a stepping stone to getting back into management, only to callously discard them when a bigger, more high-profile opportunity came along. Nothing was further from the truth. The reason he left Bury was simple. He had ambition. Bury were clearly going through a period of change. The team, and indeed the club, needed to be stripped back down to its basic infrastructure and rebuilt. This would take time and patience. It was clear from the way Stokoe was greeted – or not as the case may be – by some of the Bury directors and committee that he wasn't going to be granted the luxury of either time or patience.

"Of course I wanted to do well for Bury when I returned there, bearing in mind much was expected of me. The majority of the directors expected me to wave a magic wand and produce instant success. It was asking a lot of me or any manager. I told them early on that some of the players I had inherited were not up to the task I had charged them with. Asking me to transform them into a promotion-winning side at that level of the game was like asking to me make a silk purse from a sow's ear.

"I got the impression they saw me as some kind of trouble-shooter, a hatchet man of sorts, cleansing the club of all its problems.

I simply wanted to be allowed to manage and build a football side capable of doing its supporters and the people of the town proud. Instead, I could see them making me into some kind of scapegoat for their own failure to invest in the playing side of things. The Bury team needed an injection of fresh and positive faces and that clearly wasn't going to happen while I was there. I have nothing but fond memories of my time at the club, particularly my first spell there."

Blackpool offered a far greater challenge. Relegated and clearly in an ailing state, they turned to Bob Stokoe in the hope that he could live up to his messiah reputation and help revive the fortunes of the team and the club. History was repeating itself in more ways than one. It wasn't just that he was returning to Blackpool for a second spell in charge. More curious was the fact that he was once again picking up on the misfortunes of a previous manager, Allan Brown, a man for whom Stokoe had a healthy respect and whom he had followed into Bury, albeit after a four-year gap. One can hardly suggest that Brown – not to be confused with the Alan Brown who had bossed Sunderland before Bob had taken over in 1972 – had failed in what he had achieved at Bloomfield Road. In fact, he was part way through a rebuilding process, with the nucleus of a good, solid team taking shape under his guidance.

Brown had joined Blackpool in the summer of 1976 and immediately set about bringing in some extra quality to the squad he inherited from his predecessor, Harry Potts. In came striker Bob Hatton, who developed a lethal goal-scoring partnership with Mickey Walsh. Together the duo scored 36 goals during 1976/77, then a season later Hatton fired 24 goals in all competitions for Brown's side. For 1977/78 Blackpool had been installed as pre-season promotion favourites, though some questions were asked when George Wood was sold for £140,000 to Everton and replaced with apprentice goalkeeper Iain Hesford, who had been Wood's understudy for a season. It was a bold, yet confident move. Brown also introduced another apprentice, talented winger Jeff Chandler, who had joined the club in 1976, having been snatched from beneath the noses of a number of big London sides.

The team teetered on the edge of the promotion-chasing pack and at one stage in November sat in third place. The open style of football was encouraging fans back to Bloomfield in numbers as promotion looked a very distinct possibility. Brown was pleased with how his players were attacking and scoring goals. Sadly, they had a propensity to concede them, too, and up to the beginning of the New Year they had kept just three clean sheets. Consecutive home victories when the team scored five goals, against Charlton Athletic and Blackburn Rovers respectively, in January and February seemed the ideal foundation from which they could launch the final push for promotion. Everything was looking good.

But in typical football style, drama was not far away. Blackpool conspired to undermine their own success. After what was described as an acrimonious meeting with the board of directors, Allan Brown was instantly dismissed, though some say he resigned. Whatever the situation, it was clear that sharp words had been exchanged and it was well known that Brown had become increasingly disillusioned by the board's interference with first-team affairs. Blackpool moved swiftly to replace Brown, giving temporary charge of first-team affairs to Jimmy Meadows. The new man at the helm struggled and, from being promotion candidates and still among the favourites, they plummeted in such dramatic style that the seemingly impossible occurred. They were relegated to the Third Division along with Mansfield Town and Hull City.

"I wasn't too concerned by the alleged politics that had taken place at the club. I had suffered previously but a lot of things had moved on since then. I regarded Blackpool as a club with big potential. It was a compliment to be asked to return. There was a new chairman and vice-chairman at the helm, and a new secretary, too. You get to rely on a good club secretary a great deal. He is pivotal to communications within the club and if he is any good he will give you lots of information. The chairman and the vice-chair both did a great public relations and marketing job on me. They put it to me in such a way that the manager's position at the club was purpose-built for Bob Stokoe. It was another challenge. Naturally I asked what the level of their ambition was and was told that the immediate goal was to get out of the Third Division. The down-side was that no funds were available for me to work with. 'Ah well', I thought, 'been here before. It's the fine art of negotiation.'

"I moved quickly to bring in a new coach, making an approach to Dick Young at Carlisle. The money wasn't great, but more than he would ever have been on at Brunton Park. Dick was honest with me. The money didn't matter; he just didn't fancy the travelling up and down the M6. That aside, he was in the throes of permanently retiring from the game and reminded me that his club would always be Carlisle United. His achievements there were what he wanted to be remembered for. He did point me in the direction of another up-and-coming coach and right-hand man I could rely upon. It was someone I knew very well. He had played for me at two clubs and he was devoutly loyal and hardened to the cruel ways of football." So it was that Stan Ternent took his first managerial steps in the game. He couldn't have wished for a more knowledgeable mentor.

The build-up to the new season wasn't the most inspiring for supporters, with player sales being the headline-grabbing news. The most notable departures were Mickey Walsh and Bob Hatton, although some incoming transfer activity did take place, a striker with the splendid-sounding name of Victor Salvatore Ferla Davidson being one of the few highlights. The name may have had a cosmopolitan ring to it, but Vic Davidson was actually a Glasgow lad who arrived from Motherwell. Blackpool had entered the Anglo-Scottish Cup and were joined in the group stages by local rivals Preston North End, Blackburn Rovers and Burnley. They lost every game, Preston giving them a real lesson in finishing in the 4-2 defeat at Deepdale. This was followed by a 1-0 defeat at home to Blackburn Rovers, then a woeful performance at Turf Moor against a lacklustre Burnley side that still managed to win 3-1.

"Publicly I had to put a brave face on the situation. I told the *Blackpool Gazette* that performances in pre-season competition didn't matter. It was all about a learning curve, a matter of improving fitness and looking at the various strengths we had in the team. Privately, I was seething at how we had laid down and allowed our opponents to walk all over us. Quite incredibly, at the home game with Blackburn some of the fans behind me were yelling for me to get the sack. One of the local constabulary just happened to be walking past when the comment was shouted. He looked at me and, with a wry grin on his face, he said: 'Welcome back, Bob, they have missed you!'"

The week before the League season commenced, Stokoe and Ternent were back at Brunton Park for the first leg of a League Cup game between Carlisle and Blackpool.

"Stan wondered whether the Paddock fans would be on their best behaviour at Carlisle. On their day they can be the most humorous and supportive in the game; the problem is they had a tendency to be a miserable lot and vocal in their criticism of players and team performances. You can't fail to hear them when you are either sat in the dugout or stood by the pitch. I reassured Stan that we would get a good welcome and we did, better than ever.

"Andrew Jenkins, one of the directors, greeted us with a big smile and friendly handshake in club reception, an encounter that had not gone unnoticed by the Blackpool directors, who looked on in clear disdain. Before we got to the dressing room we were ushered outside by another club official, where a group of supporters wanted our autographs and a friendly chat. Stan couldn't believe it: 'Fuck me, Bob, this lot worship you don't they. I expected a lynch mob as we are now working for a different club.'

"I laughed and refreshed Stan's memory that honesty pays. If you are open and genuine with supporters, no matter what decisions you make and where your career takes you, the supporters will always remember such attributes. We managed a 2-2 draw at Carlisle, not a bad result in a two-legged cup tie. It gave me some confidence that we could do okay in the League season. Four days later we beat them 2-1 in the second leg at our place, earning ourselves a second-round home tie against Ipswich Town. That was very pleasing."

The winning form continued into the League season, which started on a really positive note as Vic Davidson netted his first Third Division goal in front of 6,215 spectators, in a 1-0 victory over Oxford United. However, that was essentially the only positive of a bleak month of August. In the following game, at Watford, Blackpool were on the wrong end of an absolute hiding, losing 5-1 to the Hornets. Four days later they were beaten again, this time 2-1 at Rotherham United. Then, on the last day of the month, the team put in what was arguably their best performance of the season, beating Ipswich Town 2-0 in the League Cup, thus earning a lucrative tie against Manchester City in the third round. Three consecutive League wins in September provided aspirations of promotion as they moved up to sixth place in the table. This was followed by a lengthy and damaging period of inconsistency that at one stage saw the team drop to 16th position, angering fans.

In a desperate attempt to halt the slide, Stokoe looked to some of his ex-players. Sunderland stalwarts Dick Malone and Bobby Kerr joined, but sadly they were not the players they had once been, and lacked pace. Kerr, in particular, never made any impact in his seven appearances. It was cup competition that offered the best route to success for Bob Stokoe and his players, and the tie against Manchester City looked extremely winnable. A season's best Bloomfield Road crowd of 18,868 turned out see their team put in a battling performance and earn a 1-1 draw with City, a Derek Spence goal being wildly celebrated by supporters and the management team accordingly. Unfortunately in the Maine Road replay City comfortably eased through to the next round, scoring three times without any Blackpool response. Disappointment and disillusionment was etched all over the face of the Seasiders' manager as he departed Maine Road.

"I expected so much more from the players in that tie. They seemed to freeze on the night, overawed by the surroundings and the encounter. City were just more clinical in everything they did. Once you fall a goal behind you have to defend like your life depends upon it, weather the storm, then regroup and come back fighting. City never gave us that privilege. It was a hard defeat to take as I genuinely believed after the first leg that we had a chance."

Just over a month later, Stokoe's team had another opportunity of a cup run to get the fans excited and to help build team confidence. The FA Cup threw up a first-round Bloomfield Road encounter with Lincoln City, a club which had previously shown an interest in the services of the Blackpool boss.

"Somehow we managed to struggle through against Lincoln, but only by the skin of our teeth. It was a typical cup tie, everything to lose and little to gain. We had already met and beaten Lincoln in the League at Blackpool. Lincoln were a strong physical side and I had told my team to give as good as they got, to put themselves about and get involved in everything. There was no room for shirkers of responsibility. Despite this, some players hid. It was a relief when Jeff

Chandler fired the second goal for us. It gave us some breathing space in the game."

The fans were not impressed by the quality of football, or lack of it, on offer and made their feelings known, once again yelling for Stokoe's dismissal. "There was a point in that game when I thought to myself: 'Bob, there has to be an easier way to earn a living than this.' The bloody supporters were really going for it and I could understand why; some of our play was, at best, rubbish. As team manager I took full responsibility for that kind of performance. We had motivated and psyched them up and got them into good physical shape for the game, but all that disappeared as the confidence drained out of them.

"Sure, it would be easy for me to say that I could do nothing about it once the players went out on the pitch, but that would be a cop-out. I knew that I had done everything right, maintained positivity and provided individual support for each player, raising confidence and team spirit. But all that counts for nothing once you get a few hundred irate and incensed fans – and that's all it was – hurling abuse at you. It can work one of two ways. It can sap the players' confidence and they get worse, or it can push a player to try and work harder, to confront his demons. That's when you get an idea, as manager, who has the appetite to do well."

Lincoln City were beaten, then next on the FA Cup agenda for Blackpool was a return to Gigg Lane and Bury. "You couldn't write such a script could you, who would have believed it, a return to Bury for a cup tie? It was my first return since leaving them the previous summer and I wasn't relishing it, either as a contest or as a visiting manager."

He was right to feel such trepidation as the major part of the Bury support was hostile towards him. The needle his return had aroused would undoubtedly have benefited Bury more than Blackpool. "It was the first time I could remember I didn't look forward to going to a football game. The Bury people are the salt of the earth and most of them welcomed me and greeted me with genuine kindness. Unfortunately, there was a rogue element that viewed me as some sort of anti-Christ. These people seemed bent on making my afternoon a hellish one. They didn't have to work too hard at it, as my own players were doing a bloody good job for them. We were dreadful, Bury overran us. They did precisely what I predicted, the very things I warned my players about in the pre-match team talk. It had seemingly fallen on deaf ears and we were well beaten at 3-1.

"That was one of the lowest points of my career in the game. I can understand and deal with one set of supporters (the opposition) having a go at you, but when they join forces with your own support and both attack you, then it's hard to take. I didn't blame the Blackpool support for being upset and offered my genuine apologies to some of them outside the ground. They understood and were reaffirming what I already knew, that the board needed to invest wisely in the first team.

Then out of nowhere came this middle-aged man, obviously a local. He came right up to me, his face flushed red and twisted due to the torment he felt inside, with white spittle coming from the corners of his mouth. He called me 'a traitor, useless and despised.' What do you say or how do you deal with a situation like that? It does frighten you and cause you to contemplate your position and personal safety, and internalise why he felt such anguish, especially after his team had beaten yours 3-1. It was over now, what was done was done. My return to Bury had been a baptism of fire, showing just how emotive a sport football is. If only I could generate half as much passion in some of my players as that Bury fan had shown so aggressively towards me!"

Behind the scenes, Blackpool FC was in some confusion, too. Stan Ternent was to say later: "The chairman appeared to change every time we won a throw-in." It was a difficult time for the football club and not the ideal time to be employed as first-team manager.

"I'm never one to quit or to admit defeat, but it seemed to me that the team were never likely to win promotion that season. Everything I had tried had made some difference, but collectively the bunch was not prepared to do battle. I used a total of 28 different players during that season, which obviously didn't equate to stability in the team. The day it dawned on me that I was losing an uphill battle was actually after we had beaten Shrewsbury Town 5-0 in mid-March. In the dressing room after the win I immediately got them focused on the next game, Watford at home. It was Watford who had thrashed us earlier in the season and I told the players it was a chance to exact revenge. I looked into their eyes, wanting to see determination and passion, but there was nothing looking back out at me. We drew with a very good Watford team, who were to win promotion behind Shrewsbury Town, the very side we had humbled the week previously. Those two results said it all for me and they spoke of inconsistency."

Another of the teams to win promotion that season was Swansea City. In a blaze of attacking football they stunned the Blackpool home crowd into silence as they breezed past Stokoe's team, winning 3-1 and showing how vast the gulf between being promotion contenders and settling for mid-table obscurity really was.

"That game (against Swansea) sent our supporters over the top. I accept a certain level of criticism, but when it comes to physical violence, that's something altogether different. Someone in the Blackpool support threw a brick at our dugout. It struck Stan Ternent on the head and drew blood. Shocked, he turned to me and said: 'Fucking hell, Bob. I've just been hit by a brick. Let's get out of here. I need to get the police over here now and get this reported so the bastard who threw it can be arrested.' I told him he couldn't do it, just to get the injury treated as the brick had come from one of our own supporters. How bad would that look for Stan and what kind of message would it send out from us, getting our own supporters locked up? Thankfully Stan understood the principle behind what I said.

"That wasn't the only time we had things thrown at us at Blackpool. A bottle of yellow piss narrowly missed my head one day. Then there were six-inch nails, broken glass, coins and bits of metal. Also I was regularly spat at – and all this was by so-called fans of Blackpool. Like everywhere, there is always that rogue element that will cross the line between acceptable and unacceptable behaviour. I did often reply, always with a smile on my face, to some of the more insulting comments and incidents. The problem was that you can't show any area of weakness to these people, otherwise they will seize upon it and use it further. The vast majority of football fans at Blackpool were decent and many is the time I have shared a drink with them at club social events.

"We finished our home League campaign with a great display of attacking football, beating Swindon Town 5-2 with five different goal-scorers. But it was too little, too late, to sway my opinion that some of the players weren't good enough. I had been contemplating my position at the club for some time. Being honest, I opted to see through an entire season and to make a firm decision about my future at the club during the summer. Resigning from a job, any job, is not something that should be taken lightly.

"Our last game at Sheffield Wednesday provided hardly the fondest parting memory for me. Yet another defeat, this time 2-0, meant that we had finished the season in 12th place, higher than I thought we would manage or deserved to be. I was acutely aware that my reputation was in tatters, having achieved little or nothing at Bury or Blackpool the second time around. I didn't worry too much about that. Maybe the old adage that it's never good to return to your former club was right after all.

"All that summer I pondered over the decision that I knew had to be made. I left it late. With just a week to go before the new season started, I decided to quit. My hand had been forced, I had had enough of director interference. They had bought a player behind my back, Brian Smith from Bolton, spending £52,000 on him into the bargain. I was livid and handed in my resignation, informing the board later that day, 17 August 1979. I told them in no uncertain terms how I felt. To my surprise they seemed genuinely stunned by my decision. It was a tense situation but the decision is not one that I regret. I told them that they were the most unprofessional group of buffoons I had ever worked for. There was an awkward silence as no one quite knew what to say to me. There was a kind of apology, a shake of the hands and that was it done. Before I left I told them not to bullshit about why I had walked away part way through a challenge. I also informed them that I had introduced to them one of the finest young prospects in League management and to give the vacant manager's job to Stan Ternent. They agreed and thanked me for all I had tried to achieve. Cheeky bastards."

12 **Spot of bother at Spotland**

*B*ob Stokoe wasn't out of the game for long. A long-time friend and associate, Bobby Moncur, then manager of Carlisle United, was soon on the telephone to offer him a northern scouting position. It was a popular choice at Brunton Park and allowed Bob the opportunity to renew old acquaintances and to offer the odd word of wisdom to Moncur.

"At that point I confess to feeling more than a little disillusioned with the people who ran football clubs. They seemed to lack the spine and courage to tackle things head on. Dealing with problems face to face is very much better than going behind someone's back and usurping or undermining their credibility. I never ask for anything but honesty. If people cannot commit to that then there is something seriously wrong. The other problem with directors and many people in the media is that they all believe that they are better managers and coaches than those who are paid to do the job. They need to concentrate on doing their own jobs properly before having a go at the manager. I can laugh about it now, but when you are working day to day in that environment, it's not good, not healthy. Some football clubs are built on a foundation of mistrust and starve the supporters of information. In some cases, the manager is frozen out, too.

"When Bobby Moncur asked me if I fancied helping the club as a scout, with mileage expenses being paid, I couldn't resist. My old pal

Jack Watson helped me out, too. He was one of the best scouts in the north east and what he didn't know about up-and-coming talent in the northern game wasn't worth knowing. He was well known and well respected, too. He travelled into Scotland to seek out the best young playing talent, and he used to tell me that he was special. He would say to me: 'Bob, some know me as special agent double-oh-six-and-a-half. I am Sheffield Wednesday's man in Scotland!'

"I decided that if I was to help Carlisle, who, like so many clubs at that time, were struggling financially and restricted in the transfer market, then I needed good young talent that could be nurtured. I had to recruit my own team of contacts as I couldn't possibly take in every game. I needed experienced people and Jack Watson headed that list. The bugger would send me off all over the place to see players and everywhere I went I was treated like royalty. Returning to the grass roots of the game really grounded me. I remembered when I was a youth and how I believed the game to be honest and full of genuine people.

"I never thought that improper practices would take place in a game so simple. That naivety was kicked out of me over the years as I saw many things that created my cynicism.

"There was a club I visited as a scout who played their football in the Second Division, a big club who shall remain nameless. The junior team had been playing an evening local cup match in the stadium. There were two men and a dog in attendance. Afterwards I thought it would be good to go and have a drink in the social club. Shortly before closing time I saw this chap come in, and empty the contents of the pool table and gaming machines into his pockets, dozens of silver tenpenny pieces. I thought to myself: 'He must be desperate for cash.' When he turned around, I recognised him. It was the club chairman. He trusted no one but himself and was so bloody messed up and mistrusting that he emptied the machines himself every night.

"Another director I knew of used to turn up at games in a big mustard-coloured Rolls-Royce and he would park it prominently in the official club car park. It was all part of his image, yet he couldn't afford to tax the bloody thing. Someone reported him and he was prosecuted for it. As if that wasn't bad enough, the owner of the same club was arrested after a game for technically stealing a car, a Volkswagen Golf! So you can see why I became cynical and took with a pinch of salt anything certain football club owners or directors ever told me."

Bob put his heart and soul into scouting for Carlisle, and his appearance at certain grounds ensured that he remained on the football radar, so it wasn't long before a managerial position beckoned. Once again it was one of his former clubs who sought out his experience. Rochdale were going through a metamorphosis and were in something of a transient state. For the first time in 27 years there had been a change in chairman. Fred Ratcliffe, a loyal and generous servant to the club, had stood down, though he retained some control within the bureaucratic powers that ran the football club when he became club president.

Replacing him as chairman was Andrew Hindle, a man who so wanted to succeed and wasn't afraid to make decisions in order to get the right people in place to deliver for him. That spelled the end for Rochdale boss Doug Collins, whose final game in charge was a 1-1 draw at Hereford United. Collins had failed miserably to change the team's fortunes. It was almost 20 years since Rochdale had finished above the halfway point in Division Four and among that lot were several bottom-place finishes.

Not that Collins could be blamed for that. However, he had been given money to spend during his tenure, and there had been no visible improvement in performances or results. He had broken the club's transfer record by signing Alan Weir for £12,000, then splashed out a

further £8,000 on Darlington midfielder Dennis Wann and later spent
£5,000 on striker Jimmy Seal. Performances remained poor and led to
derogatory descriptions of the team, such as: "They are like a circus –
ten clowns and a performing Seal!"

Collins was sacked in the week leading up to a first-round FA Cup
tie with Scunthorpe. Arguably there is no good time to sack a manager
and, in some instances, the quicker it is done, the better it is for the
team and the club. Little was made of the dismissal in the national
media but locally there were many who felt that Collins should have
played himself, while others believed he had signed too many
individuals and not enough team players. Certainly, the capture of
Colin Waldron – who had been playing his football in America for
Atlanta Chiefs – and Eddie Cliff from his old club, Burnley, smacked
of desperation on the manager's behalf. Presumably he hoped their
influence and experience could transform the team. Within 24 hours
of Collins' departure, a new manager had been appointed. His name
... Bob Stokoe.

"It was nice to be asked back to Rochdale and I wouldn't have
accepted the position had I not believed that I could positively change
things for the club. Andrew Hindle was a fair man. He asked me to go
in for a season and to see how I felt. He told me that I would need to
be ruthless but whatever decisions I made he would back, just as long
as I kept him informed.

"I knew the enormity of the situation. It was a grim task at best,
and I had been told there were quite a few players who just were not
good enough for that level of football. Doug Collins had bought
unwisely, in my opinion. Even on paper I couldn't understand some
of the purchases he made. I looked at the playing list and saw people
like Colin Waldron. Don't get me wrong, Waldron was a decent player
while he was at Burnley many years previously, but a lot of things had
moved on since then. For a start he had moved away from the

Football League, and it doesn't take long for you to lose your sharpness and skills. As always I decided to give everyone a chance; thereafter it was up to them if they seized that opportunity."

It wasn't only the team that was in the doldrums. Everything to do with Rochdale FC was in a state of disrepair. Finances were nil and the club was losing money on a weekly basis. The ground was literally falling apart everywhere you looked.

"I could have cried. The Rochdale I knew so well from my previous time at the club was gone. It didn't look as though anyone cared about it. The ground needed more than a lick of paint to make it respectable, the supporters' toilets were unclean and stunk to high heaven, and there were gaping cracks in some of the concrete ter-racing, not with just the odd weed growing out them, but complete weed gardens. Rubbish was strewn about and building up behind the pitch perimeter fence. The place had been unloved for too long and I decided to set about changing all that."

First the training was stepped up in an attempt to raise fitness levels and during five-a-side games Stokoe's involvement often added needle to some exchanges as he would leave his leg or his foot out just sufficiently to trip or block his opponent. "I was called a few names but I was thoroughly enjoying myself again. The odd display of emotion from a player doesn't harm anyone as long as it is channelled correctly. I could see that some of the players were beginning to respond to my ways. I told them early on that I wasn't going to fuck about, I wanted to help them if I could, develop their quality of play and instil in them a bit of pride about playing for a club like Rochdale."

The local press were an enthusiastic bunch and were keen to get a few words from the new manager. In a hastily thrown-together press conference with no more than half a dozen people present, the Rochdale boss put a brave face on the situation he had inherited and tried to put a positive spin on matters: "I think there are prospects for

Rochdale. Obviously we are not the best footballing team in the world as our League position shows, and I am not kidding myself about the quality of our football. But as long as I get commitment from the players I will be happy."

Stokoe handed the team captaincy to defender Paul Hallows as he set about making his mark on the players and performances. Sadly, Hallows sustained an injury in the next game that kept him out for the remainder of the season and ultimately ended his playing career. The new manager's first game in charge saw progress made in the FA Cup competition as Scunthorpe United were beaten 2-1 at Spotland. A week later, the same team defeated the Dale at Glanford Park. This was followed by a victory over Aldershot in early November, only the team's third League success of the season. However, more significantly, it was their second win in three games under the new manager.

"I couldn't quite believe what I was watching. Having beaten Aldershot, then knocked Tranmere Rovers out of the FA Cup, we travelled to Huddersfield Town, who were top of the League. It was always going to be a tough game, but we had won three out of four games since my arrival and I expected to see us put up a decent fight. It never happened, it was like turning on a tap and nothing coming out. We never challenged them and they absolutely destroyed us. We conceded five goals but it could easily have been ten. Watching from the sideline it was painful. I couldn't even say that my players' heads dropped. They seemed apathetic about whether they won or not and that to me is unforgivable. I laced into them, not one of them deserved any credit. The goalkeeper wasn't marshalling his defence properly, the defence wasn't providing cover for the goalkeeper, our midfield was running around like a group of headless chickens, while our forwards had high and long balls pumped in their general direction and they were forced to chase after them time and again. It was like watching football at primary school level. Wherever the ball went, all our team chased after it. I swore that if they ever put in a performance like that again then they would really see me angry."

There was instant improvement with a 1-1 draw at Hartlepool and a 2-1 win at Bradford City. Next up was Bury. "Whether it is fate or just plain old luck, I don't know, and at the time I didn't care. I just didn't want to see my players lose. I had sensed that, in certain areas, the players were resisting my discipline. I knocked that out of them with extra running and fitness work. The older players hated that very much and one of them cast the odd dirty look my way but never dared speak out against me. If he had, I would have dropped him like a brick, team-wise and in the physical sense.

"Bury weren't in the best of form, either, and were struggling in the lower reaches of the Third Division. I felt we could beat them, a feeling that was enhanced by the presence of Billy Rudd at Spotland. Previously Billy had been on the coaching staff at Bury before joining our camp to look after our reserves. I had known him for many years as I had first arrived at Rochdale back in 1968 when he was a tenacious midfield player. So, using every piece of information we had, I set about priming the players in anticipation of the Bury cup tie."

Once again the press seized upon the connections between the two clubs and provoked an anticipated big crowd into instant rivalry over Bob Stokoe's revived allegiance to Rochdale. Not that the Bury fans cared too much about that, although they did want to win to prove once again to their old manager that they were a far superior football club and team.

"On the day of the game the town was electric. Fans were down at the ground first thing and there was a good air of positive enthusiasm generated. The Bury fans joined in to make the atmosphere much more competitive. When they arrived it actually felt like a good old-fashioned local derby."

A crowd of 10,739 was in the ground for the tie, the first time since 1971 that such an attendance figure had been attained. The supporters weren't to be disappointed by a contest played out with real grit and determination by both sides and which finished at one-apiece. In the replay a few days later, Rochdale did their damnedest to cause a cup upset, twice taking the lead but finally succumbing 3-2 with both sets of players receiving a meaningful round of applause from both sets of supporters at the end.

Post-match news interviews with managers can sometimes be clouded by emotions and, for the enterprising journalist, they can be fruitful as occasionally he might pick up a few quotes that prove to be financially rewarding and newsworthy. Cue Kevin Keegan during his first term in office at Newcastle. After a victory against Leeds he allowed his emotions to get the better of him on live television, making him look a little less than composed and professional.

Bob Stokoe was acutely aware of how the press could manipulate things. It depended on whether you were flavour of the month with them as to how you would be portrayed in the interview. In the hostile-to-Stokoe environment that was Gigg Lane, the Rochdale boss displayed a calm, controlled manner as he told the waiting press corps: "I was proud of the way the lads battled and pleased with the performance in many ways. We now have 21 vital battles left to be fought and we need at least 21 points from them to stand any chance of finishing outside the bottom four. All I ask from the players is commitment and I will be happy if they are prepared to battle."

Fair and valid comment. It was clear that he wasn't asking for the world from his players, simply effort. Four days later, he was not so amused when Rochdale crashed to a 5-1 defeat against Tranmere Rovers at Prenton Park. It was, in essence, the beginning of the end for the manager and many of the players, too. After the shambolic performance on Merseyside, he said to various reporters and gathered souls: "This was one of the most embarrassing performances I have ever had to watch and I've seen a lot of football in my time. This was the worst of all. There are times when performances should be talked about publicly and times when it is best not to do it, because whatever I say I have still got to rely on the same players for future games. However, I feel the performance at Tranmere deserves some sort of public criticism. I care about things, and I care about people, especially those from Rochdale who paid good money to watch the game and had to suffer that sort of stuff. I felt badly let down by that kind of lacklustre attitude. I am not criticising the defeat. We are not good enough to think we can go away from home and expect to win. It was the way we lost. I have never been the best of losers but this display left me very angry."

Looking back years later, Bob said: "I admit I was angry, upset, pissed off, all the things you should be after you have been so badly let down. I was on the phone to the chairman for much of the week. Thankfully we didn't have a game because of the freezing weather. I offered to resign and told him that I wanted to sack all the players who had turned out in Rochdale colours that day. They were a disgrace to the club, to football and most of all to themselves.

"The chairman calmed me down but I wasn't about to forget it and let the dust settle on proceedings. No, I wanted to punish the players, to make them understand that you cannot react like they did and get away with it. People from Rochdale had travelled to Tranmere, using their hard-earned cash to go and watch and support their side. Did those players respond to that? No, they did not, they claimed their salaries under false pretences. I reminded the chairman that he told me I had to be ruthless. Here I was being just that. I told him I wanted to fine all of them for lack of effort and wanted his backing. He agreed and told me to go ahead.

"When I told the players some of them reacted like spoiled brats. I told them if they showed as much passion in their play as they did about money then none of us would be having the conversation we were. There was various cries about getting the union involved. I told them to get whoever they wanted involved, but it was my decision and my decision stood. I wanted the matter kept in-house, but one of the players spoke out to the press, no doubt earning himself a nice little backhander in doing so."

The Professional Footballers Association were quick to react to the fine, with their chairman, Gordon Taylor, further exacerbating matters, going public to say: "If Stokoe is allowed to get away with this it would set a dangerous precedent. There could be terrible consequences for our members. If managers did this every time a team lost it would be chaotic." The entire matter was being bandied about in the public domain, doing no one any good, least of all Rochdale FC. As the manager of the team, Bob Stokoe should have been entitled to some integrity from his playing staff and from the PFA, yet clearly neither had shown any. Various threats were made by the players union, which seemed more than keen on taking the matter to tribunal.

In a show of public morality, many Rochdale supporters spoke out against the players and gave their backing to the manager. The press must have been rubbing their hands gleefully. They had got hold of something that would sell papers and some hacks actively encouraged players to speak out (anonymously) against the manager and his subsequent actions. Meanwhile Bob Stokoe knew that he still had a football team to manage, although any mutual respect that had existed had now seemingly flown out of the window. He was deeply annoyed by the public response of Gordon Taylor and reacted accordingly: "Some managers might have swept the issue under the carpet, but I am not prepared to do that. We have a hell of a fight on our hands to get clear of the bottom four and we will only do it with commitment and discipline from the players. I am not going to stand for performances like that. I could shout at the players and kick their backsides. But this time more positive action is needed. I had no intention of making it publicly known that I had fined the players and myself. I spoke to the players collectively and individually. I told them the fines were not because we lost, but because of the way we had approached the game. I fined myself because I could not be divorced from the situation. I feel my decision was right. If a tribunal says I was wrong I will hold my hands up. But I will stand by my actions even if it costs me my job."

The players threatened to take strike action. However, this time the intervention of Gordon Taylor calmed matters: "If this happened in private industry there would be a massive walkout. But we have told the Rochdale players not to walk out and not to refuse to play," he told reporters. A Football League commission was hastily assembled and heard all the evidence, finding in favour of the manager and stating that he was within his rights to fine players. The union would have none of it and refused to let the matter rest. They appealed and some players spoke out privately. One claimed that it had become a personal battle by the players against Stokoe, and that they would put him in his rightful place, the dole queue! It should be said that throughout all this turmoil, the board of directors stood by the manager, as did the majority of the club support, many of whom turned on some of the more experienced players because of the despicable manner in which they were treating the football club for their own ends.

The matter was set to be aired at an appeal, but just before the hearing took place Bob Stokoe, encouraged by the club directors, lifted his threat of fines, so preventing a full strike by the so-called professional footballers of Rochdale FC. In various interviews after the event, Stokoe said: "If the issue had gone on and the committee had come down on my side I understand the PFA were prepared to go all the way, and that would have meant the possibility of a strike. The PFA felt it would have been preferable to terminate players' contracts rather than fine them. Rochdale's union representative, the midfielder Bob Scaife, told the committee the players had given 100 per cent at Tranmere and that was it as far as I was concerned. How can I fight that?"

Once more looking back from a distance, Stokoe said: "It was a tough time for me and the supporters of the club. I had exposed clear inadequacies in some of the footballers who expected to be paid a decent wage for playing for Rochdale. It proved that certain players felt no pride in doing so. They were jobbing footballers with no ambition and no self-respect, utter mercenaries.

"I never wanted or expected it to blow up like it did. That was the players' fault. Well, a certain player really. I knew who it was, who was doing the mixing and feeding journalists with tittle-tattle. I had no option but to keep going. For me, the main thing was trying to keep Rochdale above the bottom position. But with some of the players I had at my disposal it was always going to be difficult."

He could never have imagined how difficult the players were going to make it, as their own dignity appeared to matter little to some of them. Rochdale went through a period where they failed to score in nine consecutive games, a staggering total of 810 minutes, although Dale player Ian Bannon did manage to put the ball in the net, exquisitely lobbing his own 'keeper to score an own goal. During this run of awful results, Rochdale dropped into bottom place in the Football League, leaving the manager helpless to resolve matters. At various points he told reporters: "I would like to drop five or six players. But I can't drop anyone because I have no one else to bring in. There isn't any money to buy. To buy we would need to sell and I haven't had any inquiries about players. On the game as a whole against Crewe, the lucky people were those who missed it."

As the season progressed, supporters gradually turned against the manager, blaming him for the team's demise and failure to move up the table. "I had taken enough, but not sufficient to force me to walk away. I felt as though I had been done like a kipper. What I had taken on was an impossible task. I spoke to some of the press and told them how I felt: 'I am having to take the stick for someone else. I inherited a situation that was none of my making. Doug Collins said the manager who followed him into the job had it made. He must have been joking. If the players haven't got it, I can't put it there. In fact, some of them couldn't care less about Rochdale FC. I have tried to be nice to them. I have shouted at them time after time, and I have tried to put it over to them that some could be without a job if we have to apply for re-election and don't get back into the League. But it doesn't seem to have any effect on them . . . I can't buy because of the financial situation. I feel absolutely helpless and on a hiding to nothing. I like to think I am as good a manager as anyone else. But I cannot do any more to try and motivate the players than what I have done. It is the saddest period of my career as a manager.'" After a 3-0 defeat at Aldershot he added: "Some of the players have been consistent, consistently bad. But they know I cannot leave them out. I have tried to get things through to some of them, but in some cases I have been met with blank stares."

As the season petered out Stokoe revealed that he had given free transfers to 11 players and placed another four on the transfer list, all this before the team had played their last game. Of the entire first-team squad he had inherited from Collins, he had said the club should keep just six players: Mark Hilditch, Denis Wann, Brian Taylor, Eric Snookes, David Esser and Bobby Hoy. In almost spiteful manner Esser quickly announced that he wanted away.

"I spoke to each player individually to break the news. It wasn't something I enjoyed or ever envisaged, but when you see jokers, like some of them clearly were, claiming a wage for doing absolutely nothing, under false pretences, then you have to do what is correct. I admit there were a couple who I exchanged a few words of negativity with, but I wished them all well with the rest of their careers, whatever that may have been. In some cases it certainly would not be as a professional footballer. Very few wished me good fortune in my future. Hopefully it will have been a good life lesson learned for each of them.

"Now we had the perilous situation as bottom club to try to win re-election into the Football League. Of all the seasons to finish bottom we picked that one, just as Altrincham were emerging as real candidates for a Football League place. The voting is never an easy affair, but I called in a few favours and spoke to every club personally, in an effort to keep us in the League. I tried to sell the positives of Rochdale, using ease of travel, accessibility, how loyal and committed its support is and how we were trying to build a club that could compete and wanted to improve."

Curiously, two directors who had openly promised Stokoe that they would vote in Altrincham's favour never got to place their vote. One of them had been directed into the wrong room and told to wait in there until someone went to fetch him, and by the time he surfaced voting was over. The second director, meanwhile, had been waylaid chasing around after a mysterious telephone call and completely missed the voting process. Was Bob Stokoe behind any of this? "That's a trade secret, I'm afraid, that not even I will divulge. What was certain was that Rochdale won the voting by the skin of their teeth, remaining in the Football League by just one vote.

"At least I achieved one thing at Rochdale, keeping them in the Football League. It would have been devastating to that town had I failed. Whole generations of people have followed Dale through good and bad times, and let me tell you, it's mostly bad for those fans. They deserved much more success than they have received, yet still they get behind the club and despite all the odds being stacked against them they have survived time and again. I knew it was time to go. I felt the challenge at Rochdale was too great for me. I would have liked to have had a crack the following season but under the circumstances I don't think I could have enjoyed it and it wouldn't have been right for me or the club."

13 Home is where the heart is

*I*f you dared even suggest to Bob Stokoe that by the time he had left Rochdale for the second time he should have been ready to quit the game because of the ill-treatment he had received, you would get the response I did to such a comment. "You must be codding, old lad. Football and me part company? Never! When I left Rochdale I resolved to never put myself in the position where I was putting my health at risk again. The Rochdale experience was one of those things that I really wanted to put behind me. The club was a good one, the supporters were spot on, the footballers – well, let's just say some of them needed to take a good long look at themselves in the honesty stakes and ask if they genuinely believed they had done their best for the club. I doubt few could say yes. When I left, I closed the door on Rochdale and locked it, never to be opened again. In the meantime it was back to the golf courses of Hexham and Bishop Auckland for me."

At the time one of Stokoe's former clubs, Carlisle United, were experiencing one of the worst starts to a football season in their entire history. Under the leadership of Martin Harvey the team had under-achieved enormously, although Harvey should be not be totally blamed for the inadequacy of the side which lacked a certain cohesiveness. As a coach-cum-trainer, Harvey was a great asset. As a leader, he simply couldn't cut it. By coincidence, Carlisle's first competitive fixtures were against Rochdale, the side that finished bottom of the entire Football League in the previous season. A 2-0 win at Brunton Park was followed by a 1-1 draw at Spotland, putting Harvey's team into the second round of the League Cup.

In the League, Sheffield United were the first opponents in a game at Brunton Park. It provided the perfect opportunity for Carlisle to shine as in the corresponding fixture the previous season Carlisle had beaten the Blades 1-0. This time round there was just one team in it, Sheffield. Carlisle looked like a side destined to struggle. They lacked confidence and the kind of innovative attitude that belongs to winners. It was dire stuff as the visitors ran out comfortable 3-0 victors. A draw at Huddersfield briefly raised expectancy, but five straight defeats soon showed deficiencies that were not going to be easy to resolve. Consecutive League reverses at Chester (1-0), at home to Newport County (1-4) and at Plymouth Argyle (4-1) sealed Martin Harvey's fate. Added to this were two 2-1 defeats against Charlton Athletic, both home and away in the League Cup. Attractive it was not and the Brunton Park faithful expressed their concerns by demanding Harvey's dismissal. Their calls were not unheeded and Harvey was asked to stand down with immediate effect, with an offer to revert back to a coaching role, presumably to satisfy contractual legalities.

"I was a bit surprised when Carlisle rang and offered me the job without any advance negotiation. The call basically said: 'We are desperate and we need your help to steady a sinking ship.' After the Bury, Blackpool and Rochdale debacles I was a bit hesitant about once again returning to the scene of former triumphs. The reality was that Carlisle United, in many ways, had been my best friend in football. They supported me when others doubted or questioned my ability. When I returned to Brunton Park as part of the opposition I always received a warm welcome from the club and its support. If there was one club in England that I would not have wanted to see struggle, that club was Carlisle United.

"I promised the club I would get back to them as soon as I could. I needed to make a few phone calls to find out what issues there were within the club. The directors may not have realised just what was going on in the dressing room, and my old mate Dick Young was a fine advisor. He let me know that Martin Harvey had lost the trust of the players by continually bollocking them and putting them under pressure the whole time. Players like little Gordon Staniforth were finding it tough, their talent being suffocated by the defensive style of play and lack of confidence throughout the team. Dick was honest. He told me that I would be daft not to come back. He knew the club wasn't in as bad a state as any of those I had gone to since leaving Sunderland. I told him I would be back.

"The following day I rang the club and spoke to the board, telling them how I would change things around a bit without spending a fortune for the rest of the season. To be honest, I think my statement about not spending any money struck a chord with them and the job was mine."

It was one of football's worst kept secrets. News that Bob Stokoe had been seen at Brunton Park and was seemingly in talks with the club swept through the city. It was the sort of news that aroused a good feeling that once again the team was going to be in safe hands. Not that there was anything wrong with likes of Bobby Moncur or Martin Harvey, but they were not people who understood what the support wanted or expected. The fans of Carlisle United, perhaps more than anyone, know what it is like to be betrayed. The prime example was after the highlights of 1974/75, when First Division status was achieved, only for the manager, heralded as a king by the fans, to run away and join Workington Reds as soon as the going got tough after relegation.

Since then the club had been blindly seeking an alternative, looking for well known northern names to arrest the slide and turn it back towards good fortune. Dick Young was the only genuine leader who had displayed that knowledge and understanding since the days of Ashman's petulant departure.

The slump in form was immediately arrested, at least on a temporary basis. A 0-0 draw at home to Gillingham doubled the points tally to two; it also saw the team slip down from second bottom to bottom place in the League. Hardly the best position to be in for a new manager.

"It's never easy trying to pick up a team who are struggling at the foot of the table, leaking goals like a sieve and sinking faster than the Titanic. Carlisle as a club were fine, the basis of the support was there, but once again it was the playing side of things that had turned supporters away. The reduced revenue from fewer people coming through the turnstiles impacted upon the directors, who in turn put pressure on the manager to quickly get things right. The manager panicked and couldn't cope, taking his angst out on the players in the dressing room. The players, in turn, didn't quite understand tactics or know what was expected of them. Now it was for me to start putting things right.

"I make no bones about it. There were a few footballers who I didn't fancy at Carlisle and a few who clearly didn't fit in. I really liked what I saw in young Peter Beardsley, a fantastic little footballer with a great attitude on and off the pitch. Peter would have run through brick walls if I'd asked him to; he was the model professional back then. Poor old George McVitie was past his best and there was a hell of a lot being asked of him. Defensively, we looked suspect. Trevor Swinburne was a solid and reliable goalkeeper, but in front him we had some unreliable defenders who lacked confidence and weren't the greatest readers of the game. Big Ian MacDonald was holding it all together with Bobby Parker trying to disguise the defensive frailties and marshal the midfield. We needed a complete cleansing. More importantly I needed to instil confidence into the team before we found ourselves stranded and adrift at the bottom of the table.

"I met with the board of directors and went through my aims and immediate goals and objectives. They told me that I had to keep the club in the Third Division as relegation would spell catastrophe. I was told that a little bit of money would be released if I could get players who would prove to be financial assets. Also it would be essential to buy cheap and sell on at a big profit. I assured them I would find players that would enhance the team and stave off relegation.

"Next I called a meeting with the players. They were really down in the dumps, and had every right to be, having conceded six goals at home to Chesterfield, three more at Millwall and four at Walsall. I wasn't shy in expressing my feelings on the matter. It was shite and I laid the blame firmly at their door. I was forced into having to shuffle the team round to try to fill deficiencies and skill gaps. To add to my woes, players were feigning injury as a result of the loss of confidence. So a little tender loving care was needed to keep things together. The last thing I needed was the continuation of my reputation as a manager who ripped teams apart and destroyed morale, which was basically what some of the folk at Rochdale had tried to imply."

Results improved only slightly, yet by November 1980 the team had pulled themselves up to 22nd in the League standings. Third from bottom was progress and better than being bottom. More significantly, heavy defeats were no longer occurring and a 3-1 loss at high-flying Barnsley was taken very badly by the manager.

He said after that game: "We put Barnsley under a lot of pressure but didn't take our chances. Defensively we look weak. I need to make them courageous and treat every match as being important. Certain players in my team hid today. I won't have that."

The team was strengthened with the £100,000 purchase of England under-21 defender Paul Haigh from Hull City. Haigh was to be an excellent servant to the club. The signing effectively ended the Carlisle career of Gary Watson, who made a few fleeting cameo appearances before being released. Also joining at around the same time was Alan Campbell, a player Stokoe had worked with and nurtured in his days at Charlton Athletic, and the hugely inspirational Russell Coughlin, a midfielder from Blackburn Rovers. Three back-to-back draws in the League set the team nicely for a first-round FA Cup tie against West Cumbrian rivals, non-League Workington.

"Workington still had a point to prove at that time. They had only dropped out of the Football League a couple of seasons earlier and desperately wanted to show the football fans of Cumbria who was the top local team. I told my players to fight and commit to every challenge. If any success was to be achieved, we would have to silence the Borough Park crowd who, from personal experience, could be intimidating. We held on for a 0-0 draw and a replay at our place. I was pleased with the way the team seemed to be bonding. There was lots of leg-pulling and an understanding beginning to develop. For the first time since my Sunderland days, I saw footballers enjoying being part of a very special and select unit. As one player summed it up as we left the dressing room to take to the pitch that day: 'Come on boys, we are in this together.' That genuinely made me smile."

In the lead-up to the Brunton Park replay, United lost a League game 2-0 at Exeter City. It was a result that dropped them down to second from bottom and resurrected fans' concerns that the team was about to drop into the Fourth Division for the first time in almost 20 years. The manager would have no such talk mentioned inside the walls of Brunton Park.

"The local press were always going on about relegation, defeats, injuries, all doom and gloom and pessimism. I told them to focus on the good stuff, how the team were beginning to gel, how we had been unfortunate to lose in some games and had never stopped believing that we could win. I explained the Exeter result away by mentioning the travelling distance between the two cities, and how it genuinely took it out of the players. I knew we needed a good result against Workington to get people believing again."

That is just what happened. In a 4-1 trouncing of the neighbours, Peter Beardsley produced some scintillating skills and finishing as the players brought in by Stokoe really stood out. A few days later and Colchester United were hammered 4-0 at Carlisle. Once again Beardsley did much of the damage, though it must be said that the passing skills and overall influence of Coughlin in the United midfield complemented Peter's style perfectly. Results for the rest of that season displayed the inconsistency Bob Stokoe knew existed. The loan signing of veteran striker Bryan Robson helped on the goal front, with 'Pop' netting six times in nine appearances. At one stage during Robson's time at the club, the team climbed to 14th place in the table, eventually avoiding relegation by finishing the season in 19th place.

"What a relief it was to get through that season. I had a lot of options open to me during the summer. I could wheel and deal in the transfer market and get rid of some of the dead wood the club had inherited. I knew the players I wanted to bring in and the board of directors backed me to the hilt. For the first time in my career I was given the freedom to create and build my very own team, a challenge I relished."

Accordingly several players were moved on, namely Ian MacDonald, Steve Hoolickin, Jimmy Hamilton and George McVitie, who retired. In on permanent moves came Jackie Ashurst, Dave Rushbury, Bob Lee, John Crabbe, Tony Larkin and 'Pop' Robson.

"The signing of Bryan Robson was of major significance to the club. He was a goal-scoring legend at Newcastle and West Ham, and he proved in his loan spell that he still had the hunger to score goals and the desire to do well. He told me before he left that he wanted to come back to us, so I wasted no time in the summer in getting him signed up. At the back, the loss of Ian MacDonald was a blow. I would have liked Ian to stay but I think he had had enough of being part of a struggling team and he fancied a new challenge. We sold him to Dundee. In his place I brought in Jackie Ashurst, who I had known and watched over the years. He was a tough, sensible footballer who could lead by example. Dave Rushbury was another good lad I brought in. He liked nothing more than to push forward from defence with the ball at his feet; he was a defender who desperately wanted to be a centre-forward, another lad with a great attitude."

During the pre-season build-up United took part in the Football League Trophy. After losing 4-2 at Burnley, they responded with two home victories over Blackpool and Preston, winning 1-0 and 3-0 respectively. In the League, after a somewhat nervous start, the team suddenly clicked and between November and February went on a nine-game unbeaten run, winning eight of those games. There were six consecutive wins at one stage and they climbed to the top of the table. Sadly, the weather that winter was dreadful, resulting in countless match cancellations. While many other clubs were able to continue to play, the games in hand were mounting up for Carlisle.

"I remember one game, an FA Cup tie against Bishop Auckland, which was postponed eight or nine times before we actually got it played at Workington and won 1-0. Our pitch had flooded under two feet of water because the River Eden, that runs behind the stadium, had broken its banks. Added to that problem, there were the heavy frosts. The flood water froze into a solid block. It was more akin to an ice-skating rink than a football pitch. Our groundstaff worked wonders in getting it all thawed and sorted out, and there was a constant stream of volunteers to help out whenever necessary."

United were forced to play catch-up with their opponents, and played five games in the space of two weeks. The toll of such efforts began to show as four of the five games were drawn and the other lost as the team slipped down to fifth place. A midweek home win over Reading put them back on top of the pile in March as the race for promotion really began to hot up. Fulham were the team in form, and maintained a consistency that would ordinarily have seen them finish as champions. However, that season there were two other clubs of equal quality competing alongside them, Burnley and Carlisle United. The press were keen to play on the incredible transformation of the Brunton Park outfit, from relegation fodder the previous season into what some people described as the best footballing team in the division and promotion challengers. It reflected well on the club and on the manager.

"I was in my element. When I arrived at the club everyone seemed lost and had no focus. Now everyone had smiles on their faces and were focusing on the following season in the Second Division. I have never been one to count my chickens before they hatch so I never mentioned promotion to the team. That could have led to complacency and I certainly wasn't going to have that in my dressing room."

Five wins out of six League games in April seemed to have assured promotion. The team had been top of the table during all that time. A 2-1 home victory over Wimbledon at the beginning of May should have been the point when United kicked on to win the championship. Instead it caused the team some uncertainty.

"It was the Wimbledon game that set us back a bit. Before the game some of the players believed we would get a few goals past them. Wimbledon being what they are, fighters, had us on the run and could so easily have beaten us. We managed to get the win but the manner of the victory was not what some of the players expected. Defensively we had the wobbles and the team over-analysed it. I tried to talk the fear out of them and hoped that we wouldn't carry it into our next game at Burnley, who were chasing promotion with ourselves. We lost the game and that seemed to knock the stuffing out of some of the players. Burnley were fast closing the gap on us. We needed two wins and a draw from our last four games to go up as champions."

A point at Reading provided some leeway with three games remaining, one of which was at home and the other two away at relegation-threatened Wimbledon and then bottom club Chester. There was every chance that United could go up as champions. Then, as so often happens in football, disaster struck. Wimbledon put in their best performance of the season to beat Carlisle 3-1 at Plough Lane. In the penultimate game, at Brunton Park against Bristol Rovers, United knew they had to win because the night before Burnley had beaten Southend United 4-1. The team again froze, losing 2-1 to a Bristol side that looked far superior and wanted the win more.

"We were flat as pancakes after the home defeat by Bristol Rovers. I could sense the nerves in the dressing room before the game, and told them to go out and enjoy what they were good at, playing football and winning. Bristol were all over us like a rash, closing us down and keeping Russell Coughlin quiet in midfield. Gordon Staniforth was forced wide and couldn't get inside their defenders and Bob Lee was out-muscled up front by their two big central defenders. No matter what we tried we couldn't get back into the game once we fell behind. It was dreadful. The fans had turned out in their numbers expecting a day of celebration. Instead we offered up nothing. We now needed to go to Chester and win to assure promotion."

That's just what the team did. In a nervous encounter, it was 'Pop' Robson who scored the all-important goal that gave United the victory and sent them up into the Second Division. The final whistle signalled a mass pitch invasion by the Carlisle support. Clearly they outnumbered the Chester fans and proclaimed Bob Stokoe as the King of Brunton Park.

"It was marvellous. After the season the club had suffered before, here we were 12 months later celebrating promotion to the Second Division. I was proud, very proud. The team I had started to build had looked good but I knew the hard part was still to come. A couple of those players would not be able to cut it in the Second Division, which contained the likes of Newcastle, Chelsea, Derby and Leeds. Those are big clubs with massive resources. If we were to compete with that sort of company I would again need to change things round. How would the directors take to that, could we afford it? Asking for more money to bring in additional players and increasing the wage bill in doing so wasn't going to be the easiest of tasks. I knew I could offset that by explaining that generated income would be guaranteed with the likes of Newcastle and Middlesbrough offering us bigger home gates. I knew that would please at least one of the club directors as it meant he would sell more of his pies!

"There was a formal celebration for the team as we set off in an open-top bus through the streets and down to the tallest building (Dixons' Chimney excluded) in Carlisle, the Civic Centre, to meet the mayor and other civic dignitaries. Thousands of fans had gathered outside and were chanting my name. Once again I felt my emotions taking over and I wept tears of joy. I felt content with my lot and as we went out on to the balcony to face the cheering crowd I saw a few of the players with tears in their eyes also. I recall being asked by a television crew if this was the proudest moment of my career. What a stupid bloody question. Of course it was. That and winning the FA Cup with Sunderland are achievements that will never be forgotten because they were achieved in the face of adversity, struggling teams battling against the odds to come through and win. Carlisle meant so much to me. What we had achieved in the space of a season was incredible."

True to his word, Stokoe shuffled his pack during the summer months. Bryan Robson moved on to be replaced by former Watford striker Malcolm Poskett. Also joining was Newcastle United's Alan Shoulder, a player who originally made his name in Blyth Spartans' epic FA Cup run of a few years earlier. Shoulder was a class act and from the north east to boot, as were many of the team – Swinburne, Ashurst, Houghton and Poskett to name but a few.

"That set of players really hit it off. I was concerned about losing 'Pop' but did wonder whether he would have had the pace for regular Second Division football. I had signed Tommy Craig the previous season. What a footballer he was. Despite his maturity he was still top-notch and had a lot to offer. A player who reaped the benefit of some of the experienced guys I had brought in was Paul Bannon. He learned a lot from the likes of Bob Lee, Tommy Craig and Mally Poskett. Such was his improvement that he got a regular place in the first team."

The season opened in dramatic style with a 3-0 win at Derby County, with new signings Poskett and Shoulder (two) grabbing the goals. Expectancy was high; few anticipated such a result in the first game at the higher level. The goals continued to flow; a 3-3 draw at home to Bolton in the League Cup, where Staniforth, Ashurst and Coughlin were on the scoresheet, was followed by a 2-3 defeat at home to much-fancied Grimsby Town. That set the cynics off on their march to doom and gloom, stating that Carlisle were out of their depth and Stokoe finished as a manager at that level.

"You do hear and read some of those cruel remarks, and there was a time early on in that season that I was concerned. We lost heavily (4-0) to Bolton in the League Cup and after that came a dreadful scoreline but not a dreadful performance when we were savaged 6-0 by Leicester at Filbert Street. We didn't play badly, it was just that Leicester really hit form that day. Their forward line included Gary Lineker, Steve Lynex and Alan Smith. I told the lads not to get too down about it, there was still a lot of football to play that season, and I put it into their minds that the reverse fixture against Leicester at Carlisle would be one we could all look forward to!

"I could not have asked for a better, more instant response than the one I got. Our next opponents were Crystal Palace. They were one of the promotion favourites that year. What I and every other person at the game saw that day was one of the best individual performances from a Carlisle player in several decades. Malcolm Poskett was devastating and pulverised the Palace goal at every opportunity. It was great to watch. One of his goals involved the most perfect finish you are likely to see, a flick with the back of his heel, tremendous stuff. The team performance was exceptional and showed that we were not destined for a relegation dogfight as some pundits had suggested."

The team achieved some highs and lows throughout the season, the highs being the defeats of Newcastle (2-0 at Brunton Park) and the 5-0 drubbing of Bolton Wanderers that included a wonder strike by Tommy Craig, who had fast become a fans' favourite. A final and respectable League position of 14th was achieved, higher than clubs like Chelsea and Middlesbrough.

The following season, 1983/84, is one that will live long in the memories of every Carlisle fan who witnessed it. Without doubt, apart from the 1973/74 First Division promotion-winning team, this Carlisle United side was the greatest ever seen. Clubs like Chelsea, Newcastle, Manchester City, Sheffield Wednesday and Leeds had spent big. Newcastle for example, could boast Keegan, Waddle and Gascoigne within their ranks. Carlisle, meanwhile, had topped up their squad with the astute signings of defender Don O'Riordan and an unheard-of goalkeeper by the name of Dave McKellar, who was to prove to be one of the best 'keepers the club would ever have. Other fringe players such as striker Kevin Dixon, midfielder Graham Bell and defender David Moore joined and were to play bit-part roles during the early stages of the season. Mick Horswill joined, looking greatly overweight and out of sorts, nothing like the player he once had been, and he departed after just one game. Mick Buckley was another to join three months into the season. Buckley, though, made an impact on the side, as did lanky striker Andy Hill, a recruit from Derby County. Curiously, the season got off to a poor start, as three defeats from the opening four League games caused some concern among the Brunton Park faithful.

"I always believed in the boys. They were strong, they were fighters and, like me, they hated defeat. The season didn't really kick in until the first game in October when we travelled to the Baseball Ground, Derby. The County people were baying for our blood and keen on revenge after we had achieved a 3-0 double over them the previous season. It was the Malcolm Poskett show. When Malcolm was on top form he was among the best finishers in the country, unflappable and devastatingly accurate. Few people realised it, but he had a ferocious shot on him, too. Derby had no answer to him that game and we humiliated them 4-1 in front of their own fans, all our goals coming through Malcolm.

"I can remember Southampton, then top of the First Division, visiting us in the League Cup. They were unbeaten up to that point, but Malcolm scored two crackers past Peter Shilton, making him look almost pedestrian in doing so. We won 2-0 but it could so easily have been four or five in our favour. Afterwards Lawrie McMenemy, the Southampton manager, told me we had the look of a team going places, and that we could easily compete in the First Division with performances like that. I had to take it as a compliment but I wasn't about to get carried away. We lost the return leg 3-0 at The Dell after extra time. As the season wore on we just seemed to get stronger and stronger. I let David Moore go because he was unsettled with the travelling from Grimsby and he could twine a bit so it wasn't a huge loss. Kevin Dixon was clearly out of his depth, having joined us straight from Tow Law Town, but he did okay for himself back in the north east. In Jack Ashurst and Don O'Riordan I reckon I had the best defensive pairing in the division, likewise up front with Poskett and Shoulder. I would tell the players how good I thought and knew they were. It was as though we were all on some kind of mission. There was a real belief that we could do well, better than anyone expected."

A 2-0 home win against Manchester City in November moved the team up into ninth place in the table. It was a much more comprehensive victory than the scoreline suggests, as Carlisle pinned the big-city slickers back into their own penalty area for most of the 90 minutes. Craig and Buckley bossed the game, making City look second-class citizens. Goals from Poskett and Shoulder sealed the win. The December of 1983 saw what many claim to be the most incredible sequence of results in Carlisle United's entire history, five straight wins. It wasn't simply the wins that remain so astounding, it was the nature of the opposition.

On 3 December, big-spending Leeds were put to the sword at Brunton Park, a Malcolm Poskett goal settling an affair that frankly should have been finished by half-time. Such was Carlisle's dominance that goalkeeper Dave McKellar did not have to make a real save throughout the game. This was a Leeds team that included £1 million pound signing Peter Barnes, Frank Gray, David Harvey, George McCluskey, Andy Ritchie and European Cup winner Kenny Burns. It was a performance that said it all about this Carlisle side. They were winners. Next came a 2-1 win at Crystal Palace, followed by a 4-2 home win against Barnsley. Boxing Day saw a local derby at Middlesbrough, a Jack Ashurst header settling the matter and giving Carlisle maximum points. The following day a very costly and exciting Newcastle team arrived at Brunton Park and were well beaten 3-1 by the Cumbrians as Carlisle moved up into fifth place. It was an astonishing run of results and one that had the entire football world again talking about the magic of Bob Stokoe.

"To say that the run of results in December 1983 was my greatest ever as a manager would be an understatement. It was quite incredible. The teams we were beating had greater resources, and had spent them, yet we just wouldn't accept that we were second best to any of them. The players just kept going and going. I was thrilled by the way we were playing. Right after games you wanted the next team to come along straight away. Border Television sent Eric Wallace along to see me. He asked how good I thought the team was and what it could achieve. I told him that there was nothing that this set of players couldn't achieve in the game. They were the best and the most talented group I had ever managed."

The dream continued as the team lost just once in 22 games, and after a 3-0 home win over Charlton in mid-March, Carlisle United sat in third place in the table, a guaranteed promotion spot. It seemed that the impossible was possible. The media couldn't get enough of Bob Stokoe, but it was unwanted attention. He wanted the football and his players' attitude and skill to do the talking.

"I was actually getting a bit concerned. I could see that players were exhausted. It had been a long, hard season with the toughest bit yet to come. The final push for promotion would need a couple of extra players brought in to boost the squad size and to allow us to rest some players in anticipation of the final few games. I asked for a meeting with the directors. I needed their backing in the transfer market, though not for big-money signings. I explained to them that the squad was really too small and we needed to strengthen it to get us promotion. I was stunned by their response. 'There will be no further transfer activity this season, Bob. We are running a tight ship and can't afford to bring extra players in. If the players who have got us this far cannot take us up into the First Division then we or they don't deserve it. That should be sufficient motivation for them to see the job through.'

"It was perfectly obvious to the directors that the players were mentally and physically exhausted. I went to my assistant, Tommy Craig, and told him to get the players together. I wanted to give them a pep talk. I think Tommy expected me to say that we could bring in a few players. I wasn't going to lie. In the end I couldn't bring myself to explain to the players that the directors weren't prepared to give any further backing to the promotion push. It seemed fairly obvious to me that they didn't want promotion. Not all of them, but some of them were certainly worried by the prospect of putting their hands in their pockets to subsidise First Division football."

In what can only be described as a dramatic capitulation, Carlisle failed to win any of the remaining nine League games, losing five and drawing four. The physical exertions of the season had tired them out at the most crucial stage. There are those who say that the players deliberately threw it away on the advice of the directors. That is not the case. The players and Bob Stokoe were desperate to succeed. The directors must surely have been aware of the implications of not getting more bodies into the squad at a vital point of the season. Oddly enough, a similar set of circumstances arose at Carlisle United more recently, when promotion was easier to win than lose, yet was seemingly thrown away by a dramatic loss of form in selective games, causing the memory of the 1983/84 season to resurface.

"It was a disappointing end to a memorable season. They were fantastic times and the players really treasured them, as I'm certain the supporters still do. If we had won promotion, I am not so certain that we would have come back down straight away. Those players were special. I think they would have given many First Division teams a good kick up the backside and beaten them. But that's speculating, and I don't speculate."

The following season saw one or two additions to the playing squad as players like Ian Bishop, John Cooke, John Halpin and Mick Halsall joined the club as it began a further transition. The season failed to live up to its predecessor, as it became clear that the players could not find it within themselves to replicate previous successes.

"It was a bit sad, to be truthful. The previous season had taken a lot out of me, too. I could see some of the players just weren't as hungry. Through no fault of their own they had been put on, abused if you like. At a time when they needed support, the football club had let them down. That's not something peculiar to Carlisle, it happens right across the board in football. It's one-sided from the top down. The shit never goes up, but it certainly comes down in bucketloads.

"Some of the boys I brought into the club that year were super footballers. Johnny Halpin, for example, had served his time at Glasgow Celtic. What a player. I believe he could have been better than Kenny Dalglish had he got the right breaks"

As it was John Halpin got the wrong breaks, injuries to his leg and his cheekbone damaging his progression into one of the most skilful players in the British game. "Few players excited as much as John Halpin did. He was a smashing lad, always listened and did what was asked of him. Ian Bishop was another lad with an abundance of skill. He was struggling to make a breakthrough at Everton, but when he joined us he seemed to come on in leaps and bounds. Ian and John Cooke forged a great midfield partnership. With the players struggling and with me unable to field a consistent first XI, we toiled for most of that season and finished in the bottom half of the division, our best performance coming on television when we beat Manchester City 3-1 at Maine Road.

"By now my health was beginning to suffer again. Those sleepless night were returning and I was becoming a bit crabby at home. I decided to finally retire from the game. It wasn't a step I took lightly, but my health and my home life were my priorities. I informed the board at the end of the season that I would go away for a few weeks and think about everything. I did just that and told them to make Bryan Robson first-team manager. I made the latter judgement on impulse. I thought 'Pop' would be a better manager than anyone else. Tommy Craig had been with me at crucial times but Bryan seemed to have the edge on him. It was a decision that greatly upset Tommy Craig and many supporters of Carlisle United. Hindsight is a great thing. With the benefit of it I would not have put Robson forward. Craig was clearly the better choice. I seriously erred as I now believe Tommy to be by far the better coach of the two."

Putting it bluntly, 'Pop' Robson was useless as manager of Carlisle United. He couldn't stand the pressure and literally ran away from the club without caring about the effect that would have on the team and performances.

"The first I knew of it was when I was out on the golf course. I was just about to putt when a golf cart come whizzing over. It was one of the boys from the club house. He was all excited and out of breath. I asked him what was up, thinking it must be something mighty important. It was. He told me that Carlisle United had been on the phone and I had to ring them directly. They needed my help.

"As quick as a flash I was on to them. They told me what had happened with 'Pop' so I agreed to come back for the remainder of the season only and during that time I would identify and bring in a new manager who could shadow me for a few games before I retired for the second time.

"It was a bloody dreadful season. 'Pop' had really made a balls-up of the signings, upset players and had lost the dressing room from day one. The heart had been ripped out of the team. In goal we had an ex-Newcastle man, an overweight-looking Kevin Carr; Wayne Entwistle was up front; Mark Gavin, a speedy winger, joined from Leeds. All were useful players who, if treated properly and given the correct guidance, would do well at any club at our level. The rot had already set in by the time I came back. The confidence was shot in many players and the whole thing had a feeling of a club going down about it. I made a few adjustments over the season, bringing in Scott Endersby in goal; Scott McGarvey, an orange-coloured striker – I'm talking about his suntan – from Portsmouth; Rob Wakenshaw, whose sole claim to fame was scoring on his Everton debut against Manchester United; and, vital to the season's plans, there was central defender Wes Saunders.

"It was an awful time, results were poor. We rallied a bit in March with four straight wins, but it was too little, too late, once again. By the time we faced Charlton Athletic at Brunton Park in our second-last game of the season, we needed to win to avoid relegation. Charlton had to win to gain promotion. I so desperately wanted to shove it up them. They had tried to ruin the early days of my managerial career; now here was a chance for me to return the favour as I closed in on my retirement from the game.

"From the moment they arrived at the ground, they let everyone know they were there. Loud, noisy and brash, they had a swagger about them that made me want to knock them out of their rhythm. During the game we raced into a 2-0 lead and there was hope. Then occurred the most foolish and unforgivable thing any footballer has ever done to me.

"One of my midfield players, loan signing Jim Tolmie, turned from the halfway line and launched the ball back towards our goal.

Our 'keeper wasn't expecting it and was out at the front edge of his penalty area. Suddenly a gust of wind carried the overhit ball from Tolmie beyond the outstretched arm of Scott Endersby and into the net, putting Charlton right back in the game. In the second half they scored two more to win the game and relegate us. I had a bit of a bust-up with some of their players afterwards as they congratulated Tolmie for helping them relegate us. In one altercation one player said to me: 'Once a loser, always a loser, Bobby.' He was too young to remember my time at Charlton but had clearly been told to wind me up about it. There was no love lost between me and anyone connected with Charlton Athletic. As a result of their abhorrent behaviour that day, they are a club I have never truly held any affection for.

"Before I left Carlisle for the last time I introduced Harry Gregg to the club. He was willing to invest a bit behind the scenes and fancied being the manager. Harry was a good man. I left Brunton Park for the last time one summer's evening in May 1986, having attended a club forum, mixed with fans, and formally handed over the reins to Harry Gregg. I was leaving behind a major part of my life and didn't know what to expect next. My love affair with Carlisle United was over in the physical sense, but no one can erase the memories of some great years at a fine club."

14 A Roker choker and after

"*I*t was strange being out of the game after Carlisle, but my health did improve no end. I had lots of offers to work in sports shops or to become a publican, but football is the only thing that matters to me. Once you have been in the game and savoured football in the north as much I have then you can't just drop it and move on. It stays with you. I was doing the odd bit of scouting and consultancy work here and there, when I got the final managerial call of career. It come from an unlikely source: Sunderland.

"The club had fallen on really hard times. Lawrie McMenemy had led them to the brink of relegation, spent a sackful of money in doing so, earned another sackful for himself and buggered off. Now, I know Lawrie. He's a genuine kind of guy, not the sort to make a cock-up of things deliberately. But I suspect the Sunderland challenge was just too big for him. The club had a poor season in 1986/87 and Lawrie had been unable to get them motivated. He left with just seven games remaining. There was no one else who would look at the job – taking on a team all-but relegated does not look good on your managerial CV. So they turned to me and, like the bloody fool I was, I agreed to do my best to keep them in the Second Division."

The return of the messiah – Bob never liked that description – wasn't exactly how anyone would have wanted or envisaged it to be. Games were running out. In the first one at Valley Parade, Bradford

City took full points off Sunderland, who dropped into 21st position and edged closer to relegation.

"It was difficult us being such a huge scalp that everyone wanted to knock us down. Every goal conceded and every point dropped was shoving us closer to the drop. I could see that the writing was on the wall. The players were responding to my ways but didn't have the fire in their bellies to battle for a full 90 minutes. Sensing that they had already accepted relegation, I moved to reassure the directors of the club that I would do all I could to save them, but confirmed that the Third Division wasn't the worst position they could find themselves in. It would give them the chance to rebuild and come back a stronger, more formidable outfit."

A 1-1 draw with Leeds at Roker Park wasn't the best result the club could have wanted, but hope sprung eternal when Shrewsbury were beaten 1-0 at Gay Meadow, moving the Rokerites up to 18th position. However, when Bradford City took maximum points from another 3-2 encounter, with just three games remaining, there looked to be little hope of any kind of resurrection.

"We beat Palace at Roker Park and then won another point at Millwall, leaving us with a final League game of the season at home to Barnsley. It was a game that we could win and I had everyone focused before the kick-off. The fans were magnificent in their vocal support of the team and we took the lead. Later, Mark Proctor missed a penalty, which was to prove one of Sunderland's most costly misses ever. Once Barnsley scored we fell apart and at full time had conceded three goals, losing 3-2. The dressing room was like a morgue.

"We had finished third from bottom, and in those days that meant there was still a lifeline via the play-offs. I told the players that they had two chances to get the club out of the mess they had put it in. I blamed them and not Lawrie McMenemy. It was them who crossed the white line and played the football, it was only them. Who, if they were completely honest, could say they had given 100 percent in every game. It was them who made silly mistakes that cost goals and ultimately games. Now, it was up to them to put that right. Two games against Gillingham would decide whether they were heroes or zeroes."

In the first leg of the play-off at Gillingham, Sunderland stuttered and misfired, losing the game 3-2. Still, it was only half-time in the broad scheme of things. With two away goals in the bag, everyone knew that Sunderland would go into the second leg as favourites to avoid the drop.

"Gillingham came to Roker Park and completely took us by surprise. They took the lead and when we fought back with two goals from Eric Gates and regained the lead on the night they came at us again. Tony Cascarino got them level, only for Gary Bennett to head us back in front. At full time it was 3-2 to us, the tie finishing at 5-5.

"We moved into extra time and I looked into the eyes of some of those players on the pitch. My stomach sank as every so often I saw nothing looking back at me. There was little I could do but hope. That diminished when Tony Cascarino sent another flying header into our net. It was game over, both for me and for Sunderland.

"Few of the players realised how much the defeat meant to the masses outside on the terraces. I was ashamed that the club, the team, could find itself in such a situation. I was interviewed on the radio and on television. What can you say? I know what I wanted to say: 'I did my best but you have been let down by a set of players who don't deserve to represent Sunderland.'

"That maybe wouldn't be fair on some of them, yet on others it was as accurate as could be. Afterwards I went out and shook the hand of every Sunderland supporter I bumped into. Each one thanked me for my brave efforts and apologised for the rather cruel end to my previous time at the club. It was harrowing to see the sadness and dejection etched upon their faces. It was also pleasingly sentimental for me to know that I was still respected for what I achieved at Sunderland and would not be remembered for the ill fortune that befell them. I walked away from Roker Park, as I had done at Carlisle a year earlier, sad but content in the knowledge that I had achieved some success and created many fond memories for myself and for the supporters."

After years on the golf course and doing the odd bit of scouting here and there, Bob Stokoe was back in the public spotlight when he was revealed in 1991 as Chelsea's chief scout in northern England. It was a shrewd move by Chelsea boss and Sunderland old-boy Ian Porterfield, who realised that Stokoe knew northern football inside out and would point out the talent Chelsea should be snapping up. It was also a fine and respectful appointment that displayed the high regard in which Stokoe was still held in the modern game. Sadly, the relationship between manager and scout didn't run smoothly, with reports of various disagreements. Porterfield described Stokoe as difficult and inflexible whereas Stokoe, somewhat more sensitively, simply said that he didn't agree with some of the decisions made by the Chelsea manager. There was a parting of the ways.

"I often think back to the Ian Porterfield I had as a player and later as the manager I worked for. He was under a lot of pressure at Chelsea, a big club with big ambitions. I'm not too sure that it was his idea to bring me into the Chelsea fold. I fancy that came from Colin Hutchinson, a man who I had known well at Carlisle, where he was managing director. Later he moved to a similar position with Chelsea and was a close business friend of Ken Bates. My take on it all is that Porterfield was in trouble, he had a team of under-achievers and he wasn't the most diplomatic of managers. Maybe Colin thought my experience would rub off on him or he would turn to me for advice. Both Ian and I knew that the latter was never going to happen, simply because of our history, a history that Colin Hutchinson or anyone else involved would be aware of. Let's just say that Ian never found me empathetic to his circumstances and so decided that he was always right and knew better than I did.

"After Chelsea I was given a brief at Newcastle United, helping with the reserves and the youth. To be honest I never really knew what I was supposed to be. As with everything else I had done in my professional career, I put my heart and soul into it, but things weren't right. I saw some poor and unprofessional treatment of the youth team and club apprentices. I spoke my mind to the so-called trainers concerned and on one occasion was called a silly old bastard and to shut the fuck up. I just so happened to bump into one of the directors shortly after that and when he asked me how I was and how things were going, I told him straight. That was the end of me with Newcastle United. I did go back a couple of times for public relations functions. I can tell you that was all a front, I wasn't really welcome there. I had spoken my mind, been honest, told the truth. Sometimes the truth hurts."

So it was that Bob Stokoe's football career came to an end. He will be remembered with great fondness throughout the game as a man of great integrity and honesty. That's just the way he wanted it. I can only hope that this volume has provided an insight into what a real football manager is about. There will never be another like the great Bob Stokoe, a Messiah, a King, a Leader, a Cult Hero, a Gentleman. He was the finest manager in the history of northern football. Gone but never forgotten.

15 **And did those feet ...**

I was present at Bob Stokoe's funeral, which was attended by hundreds of people at the West Road Crematorium's East Chapel in Newcastle at 11.45am on Tuesday 10 February 2004. I found it very hard to control my emotions, as the man who had for so long been my idol, then my friend, was now gone. It was wonderful to see football fans of all the clubs Bob represented in attendance as all rivalry was momentarily cast aside in honour and respect of one of the game's greatest players and managers.

Among the mourners were some familiar faces, each asked by a respectful press for their own personal eulogy of Bob. Sir Bobby Robson of Newcastle United spoke of "a lovely fella and one of the greats". Carlisle United's Hugh McIlmoyle recalled: "Bob Stokoe gave me my career. He made me club captain from 1967 to 1970 and we won promotion. I had been doing all right but he gave me such great confidence in myself, it made me as a player. He could instil such fantastic self-belief. He was a good man and a fabulous manager."

One by one, some of the game's greats paid tribute to the man who was described by all as a winner on the pitch and on the manager's bench, yet always a true gent away from the football arena. The Reverend Neil Cockling, Methodist minister at Prudhoe, near Bob's home village of Mickley, Northumberland, conducted the service and recalled the modest man who enjoyed relaxing with his beloved wife, Jean, at their caravan at Silloth on the Cumbrian coast, walking his dogs and playing golf.

"He will be remembered by all as a real gentleman. Such was Bob's standing that we can see Sunderland and Newcastle here together today to celebrate his life."

The service lasted around 45 minutes and began with the hymn *Abide With Me* and ended with a recording of Frank Sinatra singing his classic *My Way*.

A few days later I was at Sunderland for the FA Cup fifth round tie against Birmingham City. The revered old trophy was brought along to the game and stood pitch-side as many members of the famous 1973 winning team led a two-minute silence. A version of *Nessun Dorma* was sung. A civic memorial service also took place in Sunderland.

My own personal memories of Bob, who I knew for almost 30 years, are of a man passionate about many things. However, his family took priority over everything he did. I found it remarkable that he could pick up conversations where we had left off, despite the fact that perhaps we had not communicated for a week or so. Wherever he was, whoever he was with, he would always make time for others. He cared about people. He touched upon many lives. To all those who remember him with great fondness, he truly was very special.

Paul Harrison
July 2008

The things he said:

"There are few things in life that remain the same. The one that does so for people of the north east is: 'Once a Geordie, always a Geordie.'"

"If pushed I would have to say that memories of High Spen still put a smile on my face. Great times and great people. The naivety of youth."

"It was the proudest day of my life when I pulled on a Newcastle United shirt and looked around the dressing room at the wonderful players that surrounded me. That is until I married my wife, Jean; nothing can surpass the happiness that brings to me."

"My wife, Jean, and I have had a canny living out of football and the game doesn't owe me anything. We have lived in 14 different houses and never once has she complained."

"St James' Park was once regarded as the Wembley of the North. Everyone wanted to play there, it's a remarkable stadium."

"I have countless people I can say influenced my football career, none more so than me. I am my own man where football is concerned."

"Football journalists are experts at one thing – being completely ignorant about the game."

"Sunderland are a great club, always have been. Ask Don Revie."

"I've played against some tough players in my time, but our own Frank Brennan during training matches tops the lot."

"Of course I was disappointed by not being selected for England. Winterbottom was a southerner and didn't appreciate my honesty or opinions. it didn't matter that I was the best centre-half in the country at the time, he didn't like me."

"Carlisle United is a smashing club. The supporters are among the best, the club directors are three leagues below them."

"I don't regret going back to Rochdale. I was good for the club, though I think the majority of the players who were there during that time will disagree with me on that."

"At Sunderland I didn't fall out with Roy Greenwood through football reasons, it was his beard that I didn't like. Anyone who can let that amount of hair grow on their face and then tell me that they aren't hiding behind it is clearly deluded."

"My job is in the dressing room, not upstairs. I always hated boardrooms when I was a manager. That isn't my style."

"I once tried to buy a player for Carlisle and was told there was no money in the transfer pot, so I tried to negotiate a deal with the player and his club, involving them taking our club tractor in exchange. Our groundsman wasn't best happy and threatened me with his fork, so I didn't pursue the player."

"The best manager I knew in the game was Bill Shankly. He was passionate and honest and successful. He gave me much advice in my early days in management. Thanks Bill."

"Leaving Newcastle as a player was a blow to my pride, but it was to hurt them more than me."

"Blackpool is a nice club. It's what went on upstairs that let them down when I was there. If a director cannot look you straight in the face then he's hiding something. No one at Blackpool looked me straight in the face."

"I was so proud to stay at the Savoy after winning the FA Cup with Newcastle, I lay in bed that night and admired myself living it up in such posh surroundings."

"The club I disliked the most as a player was Sunderland. They made it tough for you at Roker Park and you were covered in bruises and cuts at the end of the game."

"The club I disliked most as a manager was Charlton Athletic. I couldn't find anything good to say about them then, and still can't now."

"My favourite ground has to be St James' Park, followed by Roker Park and Brunton Park. Great fans at all of them."

"I have never been able to understand people who aren't motivated by the Roker Park crowd. The fans here are very special and I'm convinced that as long as they keep turning up, then Sunderland will never slide into oblivion."

"I don't think there is any football club I wouldn't manage, though Leeds would be stretching the imagination too far."

"I should have given myself a little longer the first time at Roker and I would have liked a crack at the Black'n'Whites if it had been formally offered."

"Many years ago I vowed not to return to Wembley unless I was involved with a team. The memory of 1973 will always be special for me and that is the way I would like it to stay."

"I can live with players making mistakes. But I can't live with players who don't give total commitment."

"Jim Tolmie destroyed the work of an entire season at Carlisle. He effectively and singlehandedly brought to an end my managerial career at Carlisle. I can never forget what he did, the greatest own goal of all time, the effect of which relegated us."

"The greatest footballer I have seen in all my time in the game, Jackie Milburn, by a country mile."

"Bury was good to me, the people of the town are wonderful and patient with the football club, except when it comes to matchdays."

"I couldn't believe it when I walked into Charlton Athletic as manager. They had contractors painting the crush barriers. I had never seen that before. Anywhere else I had been it was a players' job. How affluent, I thought."

"I once went to see a game at Romford FC after a tip-off that they had several talented players. We left after 15 minutes and went to watch the dogs instead."

"There is a real difference between football clubs north and south, and it's not flat caps and Woodbines."

"I visited Gravesend FC to take in a game while I was at Charlton. Grave? It was bloody dire. What a soul-destroying place."

"I have always enjoyed a game of golf, it helps me to relax. I take it very badly when I lose."

"The day at Roker Park when Brian Clough clouted our keeper, Chris Harker, was difficult. I still think he went in way too hard."

"The greatest team I personally built was at Carlisle in the 1980s. What a set of players they were. If the directors had invested in two new players when I asked them to, we would have won promotion to the First Division. They didn't want promotion, they couldn't afford it. That still rankles with me. The players I wanted to bring in would have cost £15,000 for the pair."

"At Carlisle I would regularly get invited to visit Carrs biscuit works in Caldewgate. I loved visiting there as I generally came away with tin after tin of broken biscuits. Great for having with a cup of tea."

"I have scored a few own goals in my time, the greatest of all was taking the Charlton Athletic manager's job."

"There wasn't a bad player in the Newcastle teams I played in, except maybe Jimmy Scoular, and that was simply down to his arrogant attitude."

"I once met at a civic function with the Mayor of Carlisle, who referred to me as Mr Ashman. I kept reminding him who I was and he kept introducing me as Mr Ashman. I told him to stick to politics as the simple task of remembering folks' names was clearly too much of a challenge for him."

"I think Bobby Robson would be in the top three all-time greatest managers this country has ever had. He is a very special man."

"I had words with Stan Bowles when he was at QPR and I was manager of Sunderland. We had just won the FA Cup and had it on display during the pre-match warm-up. He deliberately kicked the ball at it and knocked it over. I called him a clown and a disgrace. Whenever I saw him thereafter he would apologise to me for being a disgrace."

"I once told professional footballer Chris Balderstone that he should stick to playing football as he was crap at cricket. Chris went on to represent the England national team as a cricketer and became a first-class umpire."

"Billy Bremner isn't really that tough a footballer, judging by the amount of crying he does to the referee during a game."

"Jack Charlton is one of the nicest men you could wish to meet and an honest and good manager, too. He is a Geordie."

"Paul Gascoigne will make a name for himself inside and outside the game. He's a character and loves the attention."

"After a defeat as a manager, I was once asked by a journalist why my team lost. I told him that it was down to us being second best at everything on the day. He then asked me if their was any positives I could take away from the day? Yes, I told him, the tea was lovely."

"I don't believe in holding back my feelings of angst from players. After all, it's their fault if they don't listen to what I have to say and we lose."

"People say I'm competitive. I just like to win, that's all."

"It's important to give of your best in all you do or aspire to. That way you are being honest with yourself."

"Football has been great to me, it owes me nothing. I am proud to have been associated and earned a living from it."

"It's important for a manager to have a bond with the fans, to understand and listen to them. Their judgement is far more reliable and honest than any sort of feedback you will get from some of the sycophants within clubs."

"Rochdale deserve better."

"Blackpool, there is more to Blackpool than the Golden Mile and the Tower. Hidden deep among the back streets that are lined with guest houses and cheap hotels there are memories of Stanley Matthews, Alan Ball and football floating around. It's up to me as manager to find those and to reinvigorate the interest in the football club, making it every bit as much an attraction as that damn laughing clown is on the pleasure beach."

"I enjoy a game of snooker and find it relaxing. It is good to get away from the pressures of football and do something you derive great satisfaction from. There is a strategy to the game, as well as skill. It's great to win."

"I just ran on to the pitch, I had no idea where I was going, I wanted to say thank-you to Jim Montgomery, our goalkeeper, so I made for him. I seemed to be running for a fair while. I had no idea whether I was going to cry, laugh or scream. It was a marvellous feeling. When I got to Jim, I was out of breath. It was fantastic, all I could hear was our fans celebrating."

"After the FA Cup final win a couple of the Leeds lads congratulated me on the win, others were a bit more blunt and told me to fuck off. Nothing like dignity in defeat, I say."

"We fell at the first hurdle in our defence of the FA Cup, to Carlisle United. They were better than us over both games. They work as a team and have no prima donnas in their side, whereas we have half a dozen at Sunderland."

"My relationship with the local press I would describe as manageable. My relationship with the national press I would describe as defunct."

"The best thing about life is the coming home to my family after a long day in football and knowing that I am loved and respected unconditionally. My family really matters to me."

"Some day I will look back on my life in the game and think to myself: 'Ouch, that hurt.'"

"Footballers today are spoilt. The riches and the subsequent avarice within the game have damaged it beyond repair. I genuinely fear for clubs like Halifax and York, as the basic economics of the game seem to be forcing smaller clubs further down and out. Those places need a Football League club to support. Something has to change sooner rather than later."

"I enjoyed spending time at a place called Silloth on the Cumbrian west coast. It was the fault of Carlisle trainer, Dick Young, who would take the players running and exercising along the sand dunes at Skinburness. There is no finer place in all the world to gather one's thoughts than on the 'bracing' sea-front at Silloth."

"I met and played against many of the top names in football. I wasn't impressed."

Career records

PLAYER	League Games	FA Cup	League Cup	Goals	Honours
Newcastle United	261	26	0	4	FA Cup Winner 1955
Bury	81	0	0	0	Third Division Champions 1961
MANAGER	**Games**	**Won**	**Drawn**	**Lost**	
Bury	166	60	38	68	
Charlton Athletic	87	25	25	38	
Rochdale	47	13	18	16	
Carlisle	98	39	30	29	
Blackpool	81	29	28	24	Anglo-Italian Cup Winners 1971
Sunderland	175	82	48	45	FA Cup Winner 1973 and Second Division Champions 1976
Bury	32	8	13	11	
Blackpool	46	18	9	19	
Rochdale	27	5	7	15	
Carlisle United	218	79	59	80	Promotion to Division Two 1982
Carlisle United	33	13	5	15	
Sunderland	9	3	2	4	
Total	**1019**	**374**	**282**	**364**	

Notes

Two limited edition beers brewed in his memory in the North East (2004):

Stokoe's Trophy – 2,500 pints brewed

Bob Stokoe's Best – 60,000 bottles

Voted in the top 100 North Easterners of all time

Select bibliography

*T*here has been no definitive work covering the football life and career of Bob Stokoe until now, and the majority of the material between these covers has been documented by the author in countless interviews carried out intermittently over almost three decades. However, some works do provide an insight into the clubs Bob played for or managed, although few throw meaningful light on his personal story. I would like to mention the following:

Carlisle's Cult Heroes: (Know the Score Books 2007) – Paul Harrison

Carlisle United – The Complete Record: (Breedon Books 2008) – Paul Harrison

The Lads in Blue: Carlisle United History 1995 – Paul Harrison

The Footballer Magazine, November 1994: A Real Manager – Paul Harrison

My Dear Watson: (Arthur Barker 1981) – Penny Watson

Blackpool – A Complete Record: (Breedon Books 1992) – Roy Calley

Sunderland AFC, the Official History 2000: (Sunderland AFC Press 2000)

Bury AFC, Brochure 1985 – Peter Cullen

The Survivors – Rochdale AFC: (Sporting and Leisure Press 1990) – Steven Phillipps

Story of Charlton Athletic: (Breedon Books 1990) – Richard Redden

Newcastle United Story: (Pelham Books 1969) – John Gibson

Newcastle United – The First 100 Years: (ACL & Polar 1992) – Paul
    Joannou
St James' Park Encyclopedia: (Mainstream 1995) – Paul Harrison
The Book of Football Obituaries: (Know the Score Books 2008) – Ivan
    Ponting

Newspapers and other media forms consulted: Blackpool Citizen,
Blackpool Gazette and Herald, Bury Times and Journal, Carlisle
Evening News and Star, Cumberland News, Daily Mail, Daily Mirror,
Evening Chronicle (Newcastle-based), Goal magazine (April/May
1973), Guardian, Independent, Hartlepool Mail, Hexham Courant,
Lancashire Evening Post, Lancashire Telegraph, Manchester Evening
News, Newcastle Evening Chronicle, Newcastle Journal, Northern
Echo, Rochdale Express, Rochdale Observer, Sunderland Echo, Daily
and Sunday Telegraph.